Pra

"*Loose Cannons* is an unforgettable memoir, a remarkable and astonishing story which will leave you laughing, crying and cringing until the last page."

— Warren Driggs, author of *Mormon Boy, A Tortoise in the Road* and *Swimming in Deep Water*

"An unflinching account of mental illness, abuse, and neglect hiding in plain sight. The memoir is courageous, agonizing and demonstrates the resilience of the human spirit."

— Carrie Gaykowski, CSW

LOOSE CANNONS

A Memoir of Mania and Mayhem in a Mormon Family

Diana Cannon Ragsdale

LEGACY
launch pad
PUBLISHING

Contents

Part Three
Loose Cannons

To my strong, beautiful and courageous children, Stephanie, Scott and Haley.

"Three things cannot be long hidden: the sun, the moon and the truth."

— Buddha

Excerpt from Joyce Cannon's Journals

FAMILY PORTRAIT
Grandma Dot's House 1966

Just look at them. Don't they look like an ordinary, all-American, Sunday-dinner-at-Grandma's House sort of family? Those bright smiles almost convince you these are happy, well-loved children without a problem in the world.

Perhaps a shadow in the mother's eyes and the 30 extra

pounds she carries hint at the depression and despair she struggles with, so the house they left and will return to is in a state of chaotic disarray with dishes growing mold in the sink and baskets full of clean laundry dumped in a corner of the living room where the ironing board has taken up permanent residence. Before anyone can leave the house, it's necessary for the mother to iron shirts and dresses, find clean socks and underwear while the children take baths upstairs. Then she curls whatever hair needs curling. It's imperative they all look normal.

Part One
Little Blue Suitcase

Painted by Diana 2018

Chapter One
January 1962

My baby sister Messer and I sat on the kitchen floor playing near my brother Tip's feet as he leaned over the stove cooking our family dinner, not a parent in sight. Messer (our nickname for Melissa) was only wearing her underwear as she sang to her pink bunny. With one eye on her, I picked at the peeling, gray linoleum floor, getting hungrier by the minute.

Tip was so small that he had to stand on his tippy toes to stir his pot of boiling water.

Even though he was 10 and older than me, at six I was almost as tall as him. Tip pulled a spaghetti noodle out of the water and threw it onto the wall in front of him so it stuck. We all watched it slither down until it was close enough for him to grab again. Right before it came completely unstuck, he popped it in his mouth and kissed his fingers like a chef.

"Perfection!" he announced with a grin, flicking off the burner and turning to the sauce. Tuesdays were Tip's night to cook, which meant we could all count on his favorite dish, overcooked spaghetti drenched in canned meat sauce.

My eight-year-old sister Beth, dressed in a faded floral sun-suit, hustled into the kitchen to check on all the noise we were making, while her twin Anna kept playing outside. As Tip rinsed the noodles, she dragged our wobbly yellow metal stool across the floor, clattering the whole way. Nothing glided in our house.

Beth climbed over the stove and grabbed the spoon from Tip, flipping her long brown hair out of her eyes. From below, I saw her belly nearly touch the flame as she stirred the sauce.

"Get away from that," Tip yelled, his face red with anger. At three years old, Messer was small and scrawny, so she dove into my lap like a scared baby bird surrounded by hungry cats. We were the only two oddballs with blonde hair in the whole family, so we were two of a kind. I licked my thumb and wiped the crusted milk from Messer's upper lip as she tucked my ratty hair behind my ear. We looked at each other instead of watching the argument above us.

"You don't know how to do it right!" Tip snarled at Beth. "Only I know how to cook spaghetti." He snatched the spoon out of her clenched hand and puffed his chest up.

"You're a brat," Beth said.

Tip raised the spoon above his head like he was going to hit her so Beth jumped off the chair, startling Messer and me as she thudded on the floor.

"Go back outside!" Tip barked. We were being so loud that Anna finally snuck into the kitchen as well. She was eight years old and a dedicated thumb sucker like Messer, only she was a lot more skittish. Still, she was concerned for her twin sister after hearing Tip's yelling—she was always worried about Beth.

Though not identical, they almost always wore matching clothes. They had even invented their own secret language, which only they understood. Anna twirled her curly red hair and watched Tip shout as her large brown eyes filled with tears.

"Boo!" Tip hissed at her as she stumbled backward. Anna was the biggest 'fraidy cat of all of us, and Tip liked to remind her. Anna muttered a few secret words to Beth, who nodded.

Finally, our oldest brother Linc, cool and cocky at 12 years old, strutted in sporting a stained white T-shirt that was way too small and cutoff jeans. He was whistling his favorite song by Herman's Hermits, "I'm Henry VIII, I Am." When Tip joined in, Linc swatted him on the back of the head.

"I own that song. And you're ruining it," Linc said, pointing his finger menacingly in Tip's face and then grabbing him by the shoulders. "Don't ever sing it again."

Linc turned his attention to the rest of us. "Nobody sings that song but me, you hear?"

I started humming Linc's tune under my breath so the others would barely hear it, but Linc glared at me until I stopped. Then he poked his finger into Tip's chest to drive his point home.

"Keep your hands off me," Tip shot back at him, swatting his finger away. "You're not the boss."

Linc's green eyes narrowed as if he was a snake preparing to strike. My brothers locked eyes like they were about to start punching each other like they always did before Beth jumped in.

"Be quiet or you're gonna wake Mom up," she warned.

Anna took the opportunity to slide behind Beth, trying to disappear. She was always attempting to be invisible, which was a good skill to have in our house.

Linc shoved Tip, knocking him into the stove and almost spilling the hot spaghetti sauce.

"You're gonna ruin dinner!" Tip shouted. "Get out of my kitchen!" Tip sure had a mean temper, especially when it came to his spaghetti.

I looked up at the stove, my stomach growling. The pot was boiling over, and clumps of sauce were splotching all over the floor like lava from a volcano. When a hot blob hit Messer on the forehead, she started screaming. Not knowing what to do, I dragged her into the dining room where we hid under the dinner table. I started kissing the red spots that had popped up on her skin, but she wouldn't stop crying.

"Mommy, Mommy, Mommy!" she sobbed. I cradled her closer, bringing my lips close to her ear.

"Shhhh," I whispered, hoping my voice didn't sound scared. "Mommy's in her room sleeping. Please don't wake her up." It was fine if Linc and Tip fought or Anna and Beth got caught up in it, but nobody could wake up Mom.

From under the table, I watched Linc and Tip crash into the wall with a loud *bang* as they wrestled each other in a tangle. Behind them, Anna clung to Beth as they both inched toward the back door.

A moment later, I smelled exhaust through the window and felt the rumble of our old '55 Chevy pulling into the driveway. The engine cut off and the driver's door opened with a high-pitched creak.

Just like that, everyone else in the kitchen scattered—it reminded me of when Dad's sister Aunt Mary Ann switched on the dim red light in our filthy basement and cockroaches ran to hide in every direction.

Anna and Beth jack-rabbited out back and hid under our grungy patio furniture. My brothers raced into the TV room and propped their feet up on the coffee table, as if they'd been sitting there quietly all afternoon watching *The Three Stooges*. I stayed under the dining room table with Messer, who immediately stopped crying.

Dad barreled into the kitchen, the screen door slamming behind him, and we watched his long skinny legs shuffle past the dining room table. He wore the same clothes to work every day: a pair of tan trousers that didn't quite reach his shoes (and that showed a thin line of black sock around each of his ankles) and an old white-collared shirt with a skinny black tie. He rattled his keys like a guard in a jail.

The house got quiet except for the laugh track on TV. Messer and I were silent, frozen in our hiding spot.

Dad went straight into the TV room, and I shuffled around under the table to get a better view. Ignoring Linc and Tip, he turned off the box and put on his favorite record by Herb Alpert & the Tijuana Brass. Tinny trumpet notes filled the household and he started tapping his scuffed penny loafers along to the beat. He made his way to his worn easy chair, which was a sorry shade of beige.

"Joyce, where's my drink?" He barked over the music. Dad was tall at six-foot-two, and when he sat in his chair, all you could see were spindly legs.

Snatching the newspaper from the coffee table, he pulled his trusty red pen from his pocket and uncapped it, all while chewing on a wooden matchstick resting on his lower lip. He pushed his thick black-framed glasses down to the point of his nose and disappeared behind the paper. Mom still hadn't answered.

Dad crumpled the newsprint into his lap and flung the pen across the room, startling Linc and Tip as he stormed to the base of the stairs with a face like a tomato.

"Joyce!" he boomed, his voice echoing through the house.

He took another step but changed his mind and walked back into the TV room, grumbling to himself and saying cuss words. Linc picked at a scab on his ankle as Tip quietly made his way back into the kitchen to check on whatever was left of his precious sauce.

"Where'd my pen go?" Dad snapped.

Linc dropped to his knees to look for the pen under our decrepit couch as I heard Mom finally coming downstairs. I could smell her before I saw her: she had an overpowering scent of cheap Tigress cologne—strong enough to hide the odor of burnt spaghetti sauce. I peered out from under the table to see that Mom was still wearing her faded housecoat and dirty slippers from the morning, but she had taken the time to put on bright pink lipstick (even if it looked clumpy on her thin lips). I tried to see how she was feeling from her face—she wasn't mad or happy. She just looked empty.

Messer and I stayed where we were, eating morsels off the floor, when I heard a sound I knew well: three ice cubes clinking against the bottom of Dad's favorite glass before she twisted open a bottle of liquor.

Mom's slippered feet shuffled by, and the smell of scotch burned my nose, making me gag. I turned to watch her trudge into the TV room.

"These idiot writers at *The Tribune*," Dad muttered, busy marking up the paper with his red pen that Linc must've found (*What a miracle*, I thought). She quietly handed the drink to Dad without a word, before turning and marching upstairs again.

"You worthless bitch!" he shouted at her as she kept walking. "Come back down here and take care of these half-wits. They're going to burn the house down!" She didn't change what she was doing and was upstairs again, but Dad kept hollering from his throne.

"Get dressed and bring that fat ass down here, or I'll come up and *drag* you down those stairs!" I covered Messer's ears with my hands and made silly faces at her so she would laugh, but all of the hollering made her pee and suddenly we were sitting in a warm pool of urine, and we couldn't move without coming out of our hiding place. My stomach growled louder but I ignored it, just hoping it wasn't loud enough to make anyone look under the table.

Tip knew to wait until Dad finished his first drink to ring the bell hanging from a chain on our closed-in porch and announce that dinner was finally ready. Dad had told us before that the bell was from the Cannon family farm by the Jordan River in South Salt Lake. He was proud that it was old and came from the 1800s, but we didn't see why that was such a big deal—it was just a giant piece of cast iron some-body spray painted silver a long time ago.

Anna and Beth raced into the kitchen to take their seats, and from under the table, Messer and I watched their feet line up side by side. Linc sat in his place at one end of the table as Dad sat at the opposite end, his restless feet nearly kicking Messer in the head. When Mom's slippers finally reappeared, I knew it was finally safe to come out. I pulled Messer out from under the table who was wearing nothing but urine-soaked underwear. With all my strength, I lifted her into her sticky wooden high chair—nobody helped me or cared that her underwear had left a big wet spot on my faded blue tank top. After she was in her seat, I sat down and peeked over at Mom, her eyes looking red and puffy.

Messer started climbing out of her high chair toward the comfort of Mom's soft lap.

"Put her back!" Dad yelled. Mom's face went blank as she put Messer back, staring straight ahead and saying nothing. Tip ignored the fighting and went around the table serving his spaghetti with pride (even though there was no salad or bread along with it).

As we ate dinner, Dad was in the middle of telling Linc about all the suspicious cars passing in front of our house. Nobody was feeding Messer, so I was doing it until Dad noticed that I hadn't touched my food.

"Diana!" he snarled loud enough to make me drop my knife. "Let Joyce feed that baby and you eat your damn dinner." Mom didn't react. Instead, she kept putting food on her fork and lifting it to her mouth.

"I'm telling you, Linc, I've been battling with divine manifestations," Dad said between mouthfuls. "I call it The Game. All those cars driving by the house at timed intervals are spies. They're watching me and sending messages about how I'm supposed to feel and act. A white car means I'm to feel pure; red means anger. I think they're after me. You're going to have to help me run this household, you know."

No one knew what to say to Dad's ranting so we all kept eating—except for me. I just kept twirling my noodles. Suddenly, Dad whipped his head to the left toward Tip.

"Non-chompus!" he shouted, his teeth and jaw looking tight. It was what he always said to people who chewed loudly around him—no crunchy things were allowed around him, especially chips and carrots. "Non-chompus" was his warning before a backhand.

I watched as Messer snuck food to Ginger, our deaf cocker spaniel who had taken our hiding spot under the table. When the morsels stopped coming, Ginger started humping Dad's leg.

"Somebody put this goddamn dog outside," he roared as he kicked her, making her yelp. Mom slumped her shoulders and sobbed. Her tears caused a ripple effect: Mom started crying, then we four girls started crying, too. Linc and Tip's faces looked hard, and they both drummed their fingers on the table. With tears streaming down my cheeks, I realized Mom never looked pretty anymore—she didn't comb her hair or wear makeup like she used to. She was only 33, but she looked like a sad old grandma.

"I can't do this anymore," she mumbled. She was standing up to leave when Dad reached out to stop her and ripped the pocket off her housecoat. Mom twisted around until she got out of Dad's grasp and ran off blubbering up the stairs.

"I have valuable information that they need," Dad said to Linc as if nothing had happened. We could all still hear Mom crying upstairs as Dad twirled his spaghetti. "They're after me for sure." I had no idea what he was talking about. From everyone's faces, nobody else did either.

Dad turned and glared at me to make sure I was eating, so I shoved a huge bite of noodles in my mouth and tried to swallow. The noodles got stuck because I swallowed too fast, and it felt like my throat was closing—and then it actually *was* closing and I was choking. I couldn't breathe and thought I was going to die but no one moved to help me. Everyone was looking at their plates, away from Dad.

Just then, we heard a loud crash above us, and Dad jumped up from the table and into the hallway, skipping up two or three stairs at a time on his way to the second floor. I jumped up from the table too and over to the kitchen sink to spit out the spaghetti, coughing up what was still stuck in my throat. I started walking away when I felt sick again, so I ran back to the sink to barf up the rest of my stomach, leaving noodles everywhere.

I could still hear scuffling and arguing upstairs, plus lots of swearing and heavy thumps as furniture fell over. Then my dad shouted, "What the hell are you doing?"

Without cleaning up my mess, I went back to my place at the table. Everyone sat quietly, poking at their food and each other and ignoring the racket upstairs. I wondered if my parents had tipped over the vial of mercury that Dad kept hidden in the study, which was off limits to us kids. When Dad wasn't home though, we'd sneak into the room and play with the liquid metal, squishing it with our index fingers and watching it turn into tiny silver beads that bounced across the floor. We were always in awe that it could keep coming back together like a little miracle, like it was a magical living creature.

Linc and Tip's whispers caught my attention.

"I think maybe he's right. Maybe somebody is spying on us and tapping our phones," Tip said quietly.

"Don't be an idiot," Linc shot back. "Dad works at the newspaper. What could they possibly want from him?"

Since I threw everything up, I was suddenly hungry again. I wondered if any cookies had fallen behind the food drawer, which was my secret stash. While Linc and Tip argued, I snuck off into the kitchen, pulled out the heavy wooden drawer and stuck my whole arm in to feel around for anything bigger than a quarter. Finally, jackpot! There was a whole chunk of bread back there, and it was only a little stale! Without letting anybody see me, I snuck out to the back porch and climbed onto the squeaky swing, humming Linc's forbidden "Henry VIII, I Am" song and enjoying my little feast.

I rocked and sang until a flood of flashing red and blue lights swept across the screened windows. Carefully stashing the last of my bread under the cushion, I raced back inside where two police officers stood in the hallway, speaking to Dad.

"She was just discharged last week," Dad exclaimed, gritting his teeth and walking around in circles. He looked nervous and sweaty. "I swear I'm gonna take her back to that looney bin and leave her there for good!"

The younger of the two cops with a baby face tried to calm my father down. "You're not taking her anywhere," he said. "You're in no condition to drive."

The other officer was older and had a big scary nose. A moment later, he saw me peering from around the corner.

"Are you okay, honey?" he asked. "Where's your

mommy?" I pointed to the top of the stairs, and big nose ran up there to find her. After that, I heard him calling for an ambulance on his radio.

"I knew those bastards were after me," Dad said, throwing his arms in the air. "Fucking FBI!"

"Please calm down, sir," the baby face said. Dad pointed to the door.

"Shut that—they can't know what's going on," he said. "They're trying to use this against me!"

"Who is, Mr. Cannon?"

"The house is bugged," Dad said quietly. He started reaching into his pocket when the baby face pulled out a gun and pointed it at him.

"Drop to your knees!" The cop yelled. Dad got down and the cop grabbed his arms and cuffed them behind his back. As the officer pulled Dad to his feet and moved him toward the front door, a stick of Wrigley's spearmint gum fell out of Dad's pocket.

At the top of the stairs, I saw the older cop half carrying Mom down the stairs because her legs were as limp as wet rags. He tried asking her questions, but she wouldn't respond. All my brothers and sisters were standing right behind me scared silent as they carried her out the door. Once the door closed, everyone raced to the front window to watch except me—instead, I snatched the stick of gum off the floor and hid it in my pocket before joining them on the couch.

Linc and Beth pulled back our lace curtains so we could see better. Mom was being strapped into a bed with white sheets in the back of an ambulance. I felt a little jealous—she was going to get to sleep on clean linens! I imagined they smelled like violets, or like our Grandma Dot. My own bed upstairs had no sheets and smelled like pee. Mom almost never did laundry anymore.

Mom disappeared into the ambulance as the doors closed, but I could still see Dad's shadow in the back of the police car, his head slumped forward. It was getting dark on Second Avenue and a few of our neighbors poked their heads and noses out their doors to see what was happening. Linc pulled Messer in close and none of us made a sound as the flashing lights swept over our faces.

As soon as the cars pulled away and the lights and noises stopped, we were all alone. After a while, when nobody was watching me, I crawled into Dad's armchair in the corner and shoved the piece of gum in my mouth, chomping as loud as I wanted.

Chapter Two
March 1962

Mom finally came home two months after the night Tip made spaghetti and the cops showed up. Dad pulled up in his Chevy with a cigarette dangling from his mouth and got out of the car. He tried hard to pull Mom's wheelchair out of the trunk and finally got it free just in time because I thought he couldn't get any more frustrated without something bad happening. He unfolded it and helped Mom in without losing his cigarette the whole time.

Mom looked weird—she was old and shrunken like Mrs. Love, our 80-year-old neighbor. Her little blue suitcase rested on her lap as Dad wheeled her toward us. I was really worried.

"What's wrong with Mom?" I asked Linc. He was the oldest and smartest so I thought he would have a good answer, but he didn't say anything. All he did was stand there, silent.

After Mom's discharge, she locked herself away in her

bedroom, living like a hermit, unable to cope—and we were lucky if Grandma Dot showed up on Saturdays to help out.

Linc took charge and made a cooking schedule so we wouldn't starve. Everyone except Messer had a weekly dinner assignment. Anna and Beth shared Wednesday, which meant frozen Morrison Meat Pies, which I hated unless it was doused in ketchup. Linc heated up canned corn and chili on Thursday, and Dad served TV dinners on Fridays. Grandma Dot brought us 25-cent Dee Burgers on Saturday afternoons, so that meant cold cereal with powdered milk at night. On Sunday, we ate soggy tuna sandwiches. I was in charge of frozen fish sticks and tater tots on Monday nights. I hated those, too, but not as much as the meat pies. Everybody (except for me, 'cause I still choked on the noodles) looked forward to Tuesday when Tip made his special spaghetti, our only real cooked meal that didn't come out of a box.

One afternoon, Messer and I were swinging in the backyard on our rusty play set, making up songs and listening to the birds. With our parents continuously "checked out," we were easy prey. It was my job to watch Messer as usual, and I couldn't help but admire her white, wispy blonde hair blowing in her face. She was pretty—prettier than the rest of us, with her big blue eyes and a round face. She looked like a little angel.

Mom mustered up the energy to call for Messer from the second-floor bedroom window. Messer jumped up and ran inside, leaving me alone on the creaky swing. I felt like I was going to cry, but I blinked the tears away and pulled an old Oreo out of my jumper pocket. I kept swinging, staring at my dirty bare feet. I could hear Mom softly singing a lullaby upstairs and pictured my baby sister curled up in her arms. *She always chooses Messer,* I thought. *She's the only one invited into Mom's weird world.*

I heard something behind me, and when I turned around to look, I saw Nasty Jim crouched in the bushes behind the fence. My family called him Nasty Jim, but I guess his real name was just Jim.

"Psst! Come over here," he said. His hands were moving around in the pockets of his dirty overalls. "I've got puppies in my house. Do you want to see them?"

I jumped off the swing too fast and my cookie fell in the dirt. Everyone had warned me to stay away from him because there were a few times that Nasty Jim asked my sisters and me to pull our dresses up and our underwear down, and then he would show his ugly nasty parts to us. My stomach felt all twisted because I knew I shouldn't be going anywhere near him, but there was nothing to do because my cookie was gone and Messer left me alone outside. And I wanted to see the puppies.

I climbed over the rusty fence and looked back at our house, secretly hoping my mother and sister might rescue me. All I saw was my half-eaten cookie in the dirt and the empty swing still swinging. The second-story window was empty, too. I kept walking toward the brown brick building in our backyard where Nasty Jim lived in the basement. I still just wanted to be curled up in bed with Mom and Messer.

When I got down there, Nasty Jim pulled a brown-and-white puppy with a wet nose out of a box and handed him to me to play with. I was glad it wasn't a trick and that there was a cute puppy, but I had only just started petting him when to my shock I heard my mom outside.

"Let me in! Let me in now!" she yelled. She was pounding on Nasty Jim's door. "I know you're in there you sick son of a bitch! If you have my daughter in there I'll kill you!" She kept banging and then pushed the door open until she was right next to us. I looked at Nasty Jim and he seemed confused about why she was so angry.

"You fucking pervert! I'll call the police!" She screamed. My mom grabbed my hand and dragged me out of the house, tugging my arm so hard it hurt.

"Ouch," I cried, but she didn't seem to hear me as she was ranting and mumbling to herself. I could only make out the cuss words.

Once we were inside again, Mom shut and locked the door behind us and told me to go watch TV. Instead, I followed her upstairs quietly thinking maybe she would let me in bed with her and Messer now, but Mom shut the door and clicked the lock before I could get in. I fell down on the hardwood floor and waited. After a few moments, I crawled into a dirty laundry pile next to me and wrapped as many clothes as I could around myself. I put my fingers in my mouth like I still did sometimes from when I was really little and lay there, still as stone. I could only hear the television blasting her favorite soap opera like normal and I cried and cried until I fell asleep.

Chapter Three
June 1964

We were always hungry because Mom and Dad rarely cooked or stocked the pantry for us, or because they were gone somewhere. If we wanted to eat, we had to find food for ourselves. There was a dumpster by the fence between our house and the old apartments that my parents called The Roach Motel. One day, Messer and I were looking out the window and saw an older man throwing garbage in the dumpster. We waited until he went away to come up with a plan. We tied our sheets and blankets into a rope, just like I had seen on TV a few times. I tied one side of the rope inside the room to the leg of our bed and threw the other part out of the window so I could climb down from the second-story window against the brick wall. When my bare feet hit the fence, I balanced one foot on it and put the other on the edge of the dumpster, being careful not to fall in.

I held onto the rope with my left hand and dug in the trash—and found an unopened package of Oscar Mayer bologna! I climbed back up the rope into our bedroom (it was a lot harder on the way back up) while Messer kept watch and held tight to the sheets, struggling to hold my weight.

We were so excited to open the package, even though the meat smelled kind of funny. Still, it was good enough. We dug in Messer's closet for the light blue Easy Bake Oven she got for Christmas one year and turned it on so we could cook the bologna. Through the tiny window of the toy oven, we watched the meat curl up into little bowls—and when it came out, it tasted so good that we ate the whole package in one sitting.

A friendly Hispanic family with a lot of kids lived across the street from our house, and one of the daughters named Eva was my friend. She was the same age as me and I was jealous of her long beautiful black hair, so I pretended not to notice that she smelled kind of funny (since I usually smelled funny, too). The kids in our class were always teasing her about the open sores on her skin, but I didn't care about them. Eva was also really good at stealing snacks and other things we needed from stores, so I watched her every move so I could learn how to do it, too.

On some Sunday afternoons, Anna, Beth, Messer and I walked up the hill to Smith's Food King with Eva and her sister. Once we were inside, we went up and down the aisles grabbing things like beef jerky, candy and cookies, plus other things we needed like binkies, seasoning packets and pencils. One time, Beth and I were shoving malted milk balls in our pockets when our luck ran out. We were about to leave when a security guard came up behind us and put his hands on the backs of our necks.

"That's stealing," he said. "You're going to have to come with me."

He led us into his small office toward the front of the store and told us to sit down on his folding metal chairs. His nametag said Security Officer Bob Billings and he explained to us that we were in trouble—big time.

"I'm going to have to call your parents. What are your names and phone numbers?" he asked and reached for a pen.

Just then, Beth burst into tears and I mumbled that our parents would murder us if they found out. We just sat there shaking and crying for a while and I think Security Officer Bob felt bad for us. After what seemed like forever, he decided to let us go.

"If you promise never to come into the store again for the rest of your lives, I won't call them," he said, pointing a finger at us.

Wiping the snot off our faces with our sleeves, we both nodded to the security officer. We were happy to accept the offer. After that, we headed home.

I knew if I ever got caught for something big like stealing, Dad might lose control and beat me black and blue. He had gotten angrier and more violent, and it seemed like he only took it out on me and my older brothers. He rarely laid a hand on the twins unless they came home late from school or a friend's house. I wondered if it was because I wasn't as smart or cute as they were. Maybe if I followed the rules more, things would be different.

Chapter Four
February–October 1966

Dad sat at the table with his face in his hands. When he looked up at me, I saw tears dripping down his cheeks, which shocked me. I had never seen him cry before. Grandpa Ted had suddenly passed away, and Dad was crumbling. I tried to cry, too, and managed to shed a couple of tears, but I really didn't feel sad like everyone else seemed to. I just felt disappointed and angry that our cousins Sammie and Linda got to go see Grandpa's open casket while Messer and I were stuck at home alone because we were too young.

After Grandpa's death, Dad started saying strange things to us once again. He thought the FBI had planted bugs in our ears, so he rarely spoke to us. Most of the time while Mom was "vacationing" at the psych ward or having coffee with the neighbor ladies for hours, all four of us girls were locked in mine and Messer's bedroom to keep us safe. Sometimes she was gone all day and we couldn't get out to go to the bathroom, so we just went on the floor like we were monkeys. Our room was always a mess with toys and clothes everywhere, so it would get all over everything.

One time, I was in the living room looking into the mirror when Dad snuck up on me with a can of Schlitz beer in one hand and a lit cigarette in the other.

"Just what in the hell are you doing?" he barked. "Where did you get those glasses?"

I backed away from the mirror startled and sat on the couch. My knees went weak, and I didn't trust my legs to hold me up. I looked down and took the glasses off.

"They're my friend's," I said. "She let me borrow them. I think I need glasses." I kept talking quietly, but Dad interrupted me.

"What?" he shouted. "Speak up, imbecile, I can't understand your mumbling."

I lost my words after that because I was so scared by his voice.

"Don't *ever* wear someone else's glasses, you hear me? You want to be a cross-eyed freak forever?" I heard my shinbone crack before I felt the stabbing pain and his foamy beer spilling all over me and the floor.

"Goddammit," he spat as he lost his shoe and limped away. "I think you broke my toe!"

As he was leaving, a huge goose egg started growing on my shin and turned deep purple with blood coming out, running down my leg toward my dirty sock. My hand was clenched hard, and when I finally opened it, I realized I had bent my friend's glasses. I panicked and tried to straighten them, but I was crying so much that I couldn't see what I was doing, and then I got nervous I was crying too loud. I took a couple deep breaths and sniffed in my snot so Dad wouldn't come back in the room. I couldn't believe he kicked me so hard just because I borrowed Jenny's glasses—I just thought they might make me look smarter. My whole leg still hurt really bad, but now all I could think about was that I hoped Jenny would forgive me.

A little later that night, Linc helped me put ice and a bandage around my leg. After hugging him, I went downstairs quietly and saw everyone gathered around our dog Ginger. While Dad was kicking me, she had had a litter of puppies. All the kids were smiling but not Mom—I don't think she wanted to care for them any more than she wanted to care for us.

I hid my leg from Mom that night, but the next day, I climbed up to get in her lap and she noticed the giant purple bump. She set her romance novel down next to her bowl of chips and pulled my leg closer to inspect it. She was about to ask what happened, but luckily for me she got distracted by the new puppies. I was afraid of tattling on Dad because he would be even angrier at me. A pair of the pups got under Mom's bare feet and she kicked at them, bumping me out of her lap.

"Who the hell brought these puppies up from the basement?" she yelled.

In the middle of everything, there was a loud knock on the door, and Grandma Dot walked inside.

"Tug, are you here?" she called out in a broken voice. Tug was a name she called Dad sometimes. Grandma Dot hadn't been the same since Grandpa Ted's passing. Her shoulders were always falling forward and her pale blue eyes didn't sparkle much anymore.

I was still excited to see her, so I jumped up to say hello, but just as I was about to hug her, a shower of dirty laundry fell from above and landed at Grandma's feet with a loud thud. Then, a countdown echoed in the hallway.

"Three, two, one!" As Grandma looked up, Anna and Messer were holding hands and giggling as they launched off the second-story banister and crash-landed in the pile of dirty clothes.

"Oh, good night," said Grandma, shaking as she backed away and clutched her chest with both hands. Anna and Messer popped up out of the pile and ran into the kitchen, laughing hysterically. I finally hugged Grandma, taking a big whiff of her violet perfume. To me, it smelled like angels.

"Where are your parents, Diana?" she asked. I took her hand and led her down the hall to the living room, where Mom was still kicking the yelping puppies while Beth and Tip were fighting in the background. As we came in, Tip got on top of Beth and pinned her down, punching her in the chest over and over again.

"Get off me!" Beth cried. In the background, the TV was blaring the song from a commercial that I recognized. There was laundry hanging from the lamps and furniture everywhere. The phone rang and Mom ran out of the room without even saying hello to Grandma Dot, who gasped at what she was seeing.

"Where is your father?" Grandma Dot asked, turning to me with huge eyes. I shrugged as I scooped up a tiny pup, giggling as it licked my chin. A second later, there was a shriek from the kitchen and we turned to see water spraying everywhere from the portable dishwasher hose. Anna, Messer and Linc were soaking wet, and my brother Linc was fuming.

"You ruined a whole loaf of bread!" he screamed. "I bought that with my own money!" It was Sunday, tuna sandwich day, but now lunch had been ruined and the kitchen was flooded. The puppies were drenched, too, and they ran off leaving a trail of water across the hall floor behind them. I held my favorite one up to my face and hid my mouth in his fur, trying not to laugh. Everyone looked so funny with sopping wet hair and clothes. Linc finally reached over and yanked the hose off the faucet, realizing that there was a hole causing the spray.

"Where is your father?!" Grandma Dot shouted, emphasizing each word.

"Upstairs, sleeping," answered Linc. "He worked graveyard, so he'll sleep all day." Linc grabbed a dish towel, wiped his face and then swatted Anna with it. Messer swished her pink little feet in the water like she was playing in a puddle.

Grandma Dot headed upstairs while the four of us kids started cleaning up the mess. Anna mopped up the floor with rags while Linc tossed away the soggy bread and cleared the counter. I ran into the hallway and gathered up the piles of clothes as Mom kept gabbing away on the phone. A minute later, Dad appeared at the top of the stairs, shirtless with messy hair, staring at the disaster below.

"You can't believe what I walked into, Tug," chortled Grandma Dot while fingering her pearls. Half asleep, Dad trudged down the stairs with Grandma close behind. "It's a nightmare down here," Grandma Dot continued, tilting her head toward Mom. "The kids are completely out of control and Joyce is doing nothing about it."

"Welcome to my world," Dad said sarcastically. Walking down the hall, he saw Anna trying to sop up the remaining water on the kitchen floor. "What did you do?" he yelled accusingly to Linc.

"What did *I* do? I was trying to make everyone lunch while you were sleeping."

Dad didn't like the way it sounded so he smacked Linc across the face with a backhand and stormed off to find Mom on the phone. He turned purple with rage and Grandma Dot stood in the corner watching, her arms folded tightly across her chest.

"Diana! Messer! Get those goddamn puppies downstairs. Tip and Beth, clean up those clothes. Joyce, get off the fucking phone!" he shouted over the noise of the television. Dad gripped his head as his face flushed with anger. "This has got to stop!"

Messer and I swooped up three puppies each and scurried downstairs. As we gently set them all back on their blankets and kissed their noses, Messer saw a tiny tail sticking out between the box and the plaster wall. As we pulled it away, we saw that the seventh puppy wasn't moving. The poor thing had been smashed into the wall. I picked up the little body and ran upstairs. Dad was still yelling at everyone, but it got quiet when they saw the lifeless puppy in my hands.

"Is it dead?" Anna asked. Everyone gathered around me and the puppy except for Mom, who quietly slipped out of the room.

"I'll take care of this," said Linc, taking the pup from my hands.

"Let's go bury it in the pet cemetery," Beth suggested. Everyone thought it was a good idea, so they all followed Linc out the back door, except me. Holding that dead puppy made me feel sick. And besides, I wanted more time with Grandma.

Dad helped walk Grandma Dot toward the front door, who seemed like she was shaking pretty bad. As I came up to follow them, he put his hand out like a stop sign.

"Stay inside the house, Diana," he said, shutting the door in my face. I ran upstairs with tears streaming down my face. All I could think of was that poor little puppy. Wanting to see what Mom was up, I snuck up to her bedroom door and peeked through the crack to see her rushing around and pulling clothes out of her drawers, her bedroom in shambles. *Why did she need to clean her room at a time like this?* I thought. Her little blue suitcase was out, but then she put it away under the bed. My stomach fluttered a little. *At least she doesn't have her little blue suitcase out again*, I thought.

Later that fall, the day after another visit to the psych ward, Mom came floating down the stairs, dressed in a light pink, neatly ironed sleeveless blouse and white pedal-pushers, her bright pink, shiny lipstick perfectly applied. She looked like one of those famous models I'd seen in a magazine. Her black hair framed her face perfectly with a pin curl on each side. She smelled differently, too—like a bouquet of summer flowers, which was way better than the cheap perfume Dad always gave her for Christmas.

From the bottom of the stairs, I took a long look at her.

"Mommy, you look beautiful!" I said. She smiled, dabbing me on the nose gently with her index finger.

"Thank you, honey," she said. "Today is a good day!" Though I immediately felt warm inside, the next thing was that I grew immediately suspicious. Grandma Dot had told us that Mom had been given happy pills in the hospital and now I wondered what was in them. Mom glided into the kitchen, poured herself an iced tea and squeezed a lemon into her drink. "Everyone come in here!" she hollered in an unfamiliar happy voice. "I have a surprise for you!"

We all gathered except for Linc, who was at work at Kwiki-Mart on the corner.

"What's going on?" Tip asked, on guard as well. "What's the surprise?"

"We're going to Liberty Park for a picnic," Mom chimed. "It's a beautiful day and we should be outside in the fresh air. Go get your shoes on!" My sisters sped off, but I paused. Compared to Mom, I felt smelly and grubby.

"Can I please wear some of your perfume?" I asked cautiously, as if that would have covered the wet-puppy smell emanating from my entire body.

Mom had just gotten on the phone, so she didn't answer. As I put on my sandals by the back door, Tip gave me a piercing look. Mom was talking in a silly voice that confused us. She was laughing and giggling, shifting her weight from one leg to the other and pushing her hips from side to side. Rudely, Tip interrupted her.

"I'm not going without Linc," he announced. "I'm not going to be the only boy with all those stupid girls!" With that, Mom hung up and turned to him. "As long as you stay inside and watch TV, you don't have to go," she said.

Before long, the four of us squealing girls were climbing into the back seat of the Chevy, and Messer was singing her favorite song that she made up: "Run-run, get your coat and run-run, get your coat, as fast as you can, as fast as you ever can..." Beth sighed in exasperation.

"Wait, we didn't pack a picnic, Mom," she said. "I'm starving!" Mom smiled, quelling her worry.

"My friend is bringing Kentucky Fried Chicken, so you'll all have plenty to eat." She flipped the ignition and shifted the car into drive, her cat-eyed sunglasses framing her face.

Ten minutes later, we arrived at Liberty Park, with the sounds of carefree kids in the air through our rolled-down windows. We hadn't been to Liberty Park in ages—especially with Mom! She had barely put the car in park when we were already racing to the swing sets. It was a perfect sunny day, and there wasn't a cloud in the sky.

As Mom made her way across the grass, I spotted someone sitting on the green picnic table with their feet flat on the bench. I thought it was a man, but I changed my mind as soon as she stood up to greet Mom. She had very short brown hair and was wearing Levi's and a tight black T-shirt. The manly lady smiled at Mom before calling over her own three children, who rushed to the table. She had to be Mom's friend because there were two huge buckets of KFC sitting on the table next to her—and we were all so hungry that we abandoned the swing set with our tummies growling and ready to eat. Mom tried to calm us down, asking us to sit on the grass nearby so we could meet everyone.

"Girls, this is my dear friend, Lynn," she said. "We met at the hospital and have become very close. These are her children, Ricky, Samantha and Amy." After awkward "hellos," we dug into the food. I was the first to stick my grubby hand into the greasy bucket, looking for chicken legs because those were my favorite pieces. The chicken was half-cold, but it still seemed like the best thing I had tasted in my whole life, and I ate five or six pieces.

Once we were all full, Mom told us all to go play together, and Lynn's annoying kids begged us to push them on the swings and ride the merry-go-round with them. Beth kept looking over at Mom and Lynn, who sat closely on the tabletop talking in smiley whispers.

"We met her at the hospital once, right Anna?" Beth asked.

"Maybe," Anna replied. "I think she was there last week when we visited Mom. They were making those mosaic ashtrays. Remember?" Beth shrugged and kept swinging for a bit before getting off, complaining that she felt sick and dizzy. She ran over toward the table and plopped herself down under a nearby elm tree, picking dandelions until Mom sent her back to play with us again.

"I couldn't hear what they were saying," Beth said when she returned, "but it sure sounds secret."

Despite my annoyance with Lynn's kids, I got nervous because they were chasing ducks and playing too close to the pond. I looked over and Mom and Lynn weren't watching because they were too busy talking. I knew we weren't allowed to go to the pond without a grown-up, so I ran up to Mom and Lynn.

"Can I go with those kids to play with the ducks?" I asked them. Suddenly, Lynn was up and running, yelling, "Get back here, right now! Ricky! Get those kids away from the water!"

Mom stood up and dusted the crumbs off her shirt.

"Oh honey, I'm so glad you were watching them," she said, and I smiled as big as I could. Finally, Lynn came back out of breath to the picnic table, and Mom started ignoring me again, turning to her instead. When neither of them were looking, I reached over and tipped the KFC bucket, spilling the last crispy thigh out onto the blanket. I snatched it up and bit into the juicy chicken while running back to the swings, my mother's laughter disappearing in the wind behind me.

The next day when the school bell rang, I was folding papers and shoving them into my desk when Anna and Beth came to fetch me for the walk home. As the twins stood shyly waiting, my third-grade teacher Mrs. Taylor came over to speak to us. She was a solid woman with kind green eyes and massive ropes of braids piled on top of her head like curled snakes. She gently placed her hand on my shoulder and smiled.

"Girls, could one of you please comb your sister's hair before school?" she asked. "The other kids were teasing her today." We were all relieved that we weren't in trouble.

"Sure, Mrs. Taylor," Beth replied. My teacher handed a folded pink note to Anna, saying, "Please have your parents read this. Diana is falling behind in her studies, so I'm a bit concerned. She might need a little extra encouragement at home. Maybe you two girls could help her with her studies?"

Anna blushed pink, and the twins nodded in unison as Anna stashed the note in her schoolbag. It was no surprise that I had fallen behind in school. I had already been forced to change schools several times, and when the school across from our house burned down the year before, all of us kids got shipped to different places—and Mom and Dad definitely weren't helping us study.

We made our way outside with Messer and looked at the

brilliant fall colors around us. Halloween was around the corner, and Messer and I kept chatting about our ghost costumes all the way home. Each year, we cut two holes into old graying sheets for our costumes—Mom used to help us make costumes, but she had checked out on holidays a long time ago. Anna kicked up the piles of yellow and orange leaves and sang "Jesus Wants Me for a Sunbeam," a song for kids in primary that we had recently learned in Sunday school. I tried to join in, but I didn't know the words very well since our family didn't show up to church very often.

Anna and Beth had taken it upon themselves to walk to church every Sunday, and occasionally, they'd drag Messer and me along. Church was a new thing for us, and we all liked it because it meant a taking bath, getting to wear a dress and eating brownies and chocolate chip cookies after lessons on Jesus. We had to dress ourselves, and one time, in the middle of Sunday school while sitting on a cold plastic chair, I realized I had forgotten to put on my underpants. I didn't say anything to anyone until we got home, and my sisters and I giggled, retelling the story over and over. We had a lot of fun going to church together, and Mom and Dad even encouraged to go, but I think they just wanted us out of the house to do whatever they wanted.

When we got home from school, we saw there were cops at our house. We weren't worried—they'd been there many times before, normally with an ambulance. Tip was standing on the front porch and as we got closer, we could hear him saying something about Mom. He was talking really fast and then led the cops inside, ignoring us.

Inside, the conversation continued.

"Calm down, son," the cop demanded. "Tell us what happened." Tip took a breath. "When I came home from school, Mom was here. But her blue suitcase was on the porch, the one she always takes to the hospital." Choking back tears, he continued, "She was in the kitchen on the phone and she was crying. As soon as Mom got off the phone, I asked her if she was going somewhere. She said to the grocery store, so I asked if I could go with her, but she told me to go play in the backyard. I went outside just for a few minutes, but I knew something was up, so I ran back in the house and called Dad. While I was on the phone, I saw her walking down the street. She got on the bus with her suitcase."

"I'm sure she's fine," one of the cops tried to reassure him.

"Your dad called us and asked us to come. He's on his way home," said the other officer in a steady voice. "Why don't you all go wait in the TV room?" As they moved us down the hall, Anna stayed behind because she spotted a note on the table by the phone. She could clearly see it was Mom's handwriting, so she grabbed it and broke into a dead run toward the Kwiki-Mart where Linc worked, with me hot on her trail.

Bursting into the shop, she waved the paper at Linc, who was breaking down boxes in the back.

"It's a note from Mom!" she cried out. "The cops are at our house." She thrust the note into his hands, sounding alarmed. Linc dropped what he was doing and read the note. Without saying a word to his boss, he ran out the back door, and we followed him at record speed. When we made it home, we barged through the front door out of breath and found Dad, talking to the cops in an unusually low and strange voice.

"The FBI must have taken her. They've been following us for a few months now," he said. His eyes were glassy and distraught as he loosened his skinny black tie.

"Dad, it's not the FBI," Linc said. "You've got to read this." He handed him Mom's note.

The six of us stood in the front hall at the bottom of the stairs, waiting. As Dad read the note, he chewed his gum so hard it looked like his jaw might break. He tried to light a cigarette, but his hands were shaking so hard that he couldn't manage it. One of the officers held the lighter for him and kept his cigarette still. We couldn't take our eyes off our father, who was pulling huge drags off of his cigarette as he silently read the note over and over, pacing over the wooden floor.

Finally, Dad fell to his knees and let out a sound we had never heard before.

"Oh, my God," he said. After that, he started making sounds like a bear being attacked. The note fell out of his hand and he sunk even lower to the floor.

It was scary seeing him like that, but I ran over and picked up the note. It was just two short lines:

I tried, I really tried.

I'm so sorry, I have to go!

Chapter Five
November 1966

I was home with a fever one afternoon when I heard Linc chasing off a couple of gangly teens through an open window. They had been teasing Tip when Linc came to defend him.

"Get the hell off my lawn," Linc snapped at the boys. He was wearing bell-bottom jeans with holes in both knees and a striped brown and gold turtleneck sweater. He had a reputation of being a tough guy, so they didn't want to take any chances and took off.

When they were alone, Tip turned to Linc.

"I want to change my name," he said. "How do I do that? I mean, my real name is Thomas. Where the hell did Dad come up with Tip, anyway? I'd rather be called Tom. I'm going to tell Dad and everyone else that my name is Tom now. As of today."

"Might be hard to get used to, but I'll try to call you Tom from now on," Linc offered.

My brothers came inside and hollered in unison from the

foyer, "Dad, we're home!" Without waiting for a reply, they went straight to the kitchen to look for a snack and finally settled on stale graham crackers and powdered milk.

"I've also decided I'm not going to high school next year," said the newly named Tom, wiping away his milk mustache with the back of his hand. "I hate school, and I hate all my friends."

"You can't hate everybody," Linc said, turning to Tom. "That won't do you any good." Tom shrugged in response. He'd been growing his hair long, trying to copy Linc's cool, hippie look. They were both starting to look pretty similar—they also both had a lot of acne, which reminded me of the connect-the-dot puzzles Grandma gave us for Christmas.

"You just haven't met the right friends yet," Linc continued, chugging the last of his instant milk.

"Shouldn't Dad be getting ready for work?" Tom asked, changing topics. We hadn't heard a peep from Dad, even with all the commotion in the kitchen.

"He's been sleeping all day," I answered, with graham crackers stuck between my crooked front teeth.

"Yeah, but he's usually up by now," Linc said as he glanced at the kitchen wall clock.

We all went upstairs to check on him, Linc first. In his room, we found Dad lying face down on the wood floor. With the windows shut, the air was hot and smelled like dirty socks. I felt dizzy. Dad was white as a ghost and half naked, wearing just his khaki pants. His glasses had been knocked off his face and his oily hair was standing straight up. His entire body looked greasy.

My guts were twisting into a knot and my heart was jack-hammering. *Maybe he's dead,* I thought. I tried to wake him up by shaking his arm, feeling the slimy sweat on his skin. Linc knelt carefully next to Dad's body.

"Dad? Wake up," he pleaded as he shook him.

Finally, Dad let out a heavy *hmph* and rolled over, curled up like a baby as a little drip of foam spilled out of his mouth.

"Oh God, go call the police!" yelled Linc. A few minutes later, we were in the middle of an all-too-familiar scene. Two police officers came in the house followed by medics dressed in all white.

"Mr. Cannon, did you take or drink something?" one of the medics demanded in a loud voice. He shook Dad with his two big mitts (*He has really big muscles*, I thought). Dad mumbled something about tranquilizers, just as the other medic discovered Dad's bedside contraband. "Get a load of this," he said, pointing at the sprawling display of amber glass pill bottles in disarray.

Since Dad had been hospitalized several times, he had been prescribed lots of different medications to treat his mania and paranoia on top of his daily Ritalin. He kept them all in the open on his nightstand, which was so crowded it looked like a full miniature pharmacy. After inspecting Dad's stash and checking which bottles were empty, the two men lifted him and carried him out the door on a stretcher. Once again, we were left to fend for ourselves.

After the sirens faded down the street, Linc reached into his pocket, pulled out a little white pill and popped it into his mouth. I wondered if he had stolen it from Dad.

"The other girls will be home any minute now, and they don't need to know about this," he said, turning to me with an accusatory finger. "You got that, Di? It's between us. We don't need to worry everyone. Dad will be home soon. I've got everything under control."

When my three sisters bounded through the front door after school, Linc told everyone that Dad was away for work and that he was in charge. No one batted an eyelid or questioned his word because having no parents around had become the norm. Selfishly, I enjoyed having a secret with the boys. It made me feel special, like I was a grownup. Though I was dying to tell the girls, I swallowed that urge and zipped my lips for once.

Dad came home the next day looking the color of old sausage meat gone bad—gray and oily. His eyes were red, and he wouldn't look at us directly. None of us talked about it until a week later, when Dad attempted suicide again. This time, there was no hiding it.

I was struggling with my math homework and had my papers all over the dining room table when I heard the front door slam. My sisters had gone off to primary class for church lessons and after-school activities, but I was grounded for falling behind in my schoolwork. Tom sat across the table with his nose in a Mad magazine, snickering at the antics of Alfred E. Neuman (I never understood any of the jokes). His head popped up when Dad came through the front door early from work. We both kept quiet as he disappeared into the family room. The television clicked on.

"Who's home?" he croaked.

"I'm in here with Diana," answered Tom. "We're doing homework."

"I need my favorite bartender. Come take my order, Tip," Dad called playfully, kicking off his shoes.

"If you get my name right, I will fix you a drink," said Tom, testing Dad's mood.

"I just can't get used to this new name of yours. Give me a break and get in here, *Tom*," he said sarcastically. My brother jumped up. It seemed like he enjoyed making Dad's drinks. He had a talent for it since he'd been doing it since he was six and we lived in New Mexico. Tom grabbed his notebook and a pen and headed into the family room. I tipped back on my chair's legs and leaned over to watch—anything was better than memorizing multiplication tables.

"What can I get you, sir?" Tom smiled. Dad had his legs propped up on the coffee table. He pulled a cigarette from his shirt pocket, tapped it on the back of his hand a couple of times and flipped it into his dry lips.

"Good ol' Dad had a rough day at the office and is in serious need of a stiff drink. Here's my wish, bartender. Four cubes of ice in a tumbler, three-quarters Everclear and one-quarter white wine. Got that?" Tom pretended to write it down, gave him a wink and retreated to the kitchen to whip up the cocktail. He served Dad the drink with a fake smile and great showmanship, but Dad just grabbed the glass and guzzled half of it in one chug, ignoring my brother who was waiting for him to say something nice about his bartending skills. Dad just kept his eyes glued to the television until he eventually passed out, with the paper across his chest like a blanket.

Tom returned to *Mad Magazine* and I sketched daisies on my unfinished assignment, but the two of us kept an eye on Dad all the while. When his snoring went silent, Tom poked his head back in the TV room.

"Is he even breathing?" he asked, his voice cracking. I

shrugged while chewing on my yellow number two pencil. Tom was braver than me, so he tried to wake Dad up but got no response. Knowing the drill, he ran for the hallway phone.

"Shit, it's dead!" wailed Tom, slamming the phone down. Ever since Mom left, all kinds of things weren't working anymore, like the lights or the heater. Dad always forgot to pay the bills, even though it was obvious they stopped working and bills were piling up on the kitchen counter. Tom bolted out the door, running into Linc on the porch. I ran after him, not wanting to be alone with Dad.

"C'mon Linc, Dad's passed out again," he said. We ran all the way down the street to the corner payphone and called the police. Back home, we watched the white-coated men put our gurney-strapped father in the ambulance and drive off once again. But this time, Tom unexpectedly burst into strange laughter. Linc shot him a look.

"What the hell is wrong with you?" he asked. Tom, with sinister eyes and fingers curled up like a witch's, sang, *"They're coming to take me away, ha ha..."*

It was the crazy Napoleon XIV song he had been playing over and over on the radio and that was number three on the *Billboard* charts that year. Linc joined in they started singing it together, word for word. I only knew the chorus, so I joined in on the *ho ho's* and *ha ha's*. We danced around the yard like a trio of fools, belting out the lyrics and not caring a bit what the looky-loo neighbors thought. We kept on going until we caught sight of the girls racing home.

We gathered together in the messy family room and Linc let everyone know Dad would not be coming home for a few days. That night, Linc prepared the fanciest dinner we had ever eaten at our parentless house. Sitting around the dining room table, pretending not to notice Mom and Dad's empty chairs, we had silly conversation and scrumptious beef stroganoff.

"Compliments to the chef," chimed Tom, who held up his water like he was making a toast with wine. We all giggled and joined in, raising our glasses and feeling very grown-up.

Later, I heard Anna ask Beth, "When is Mom coming home? I miss her and we need her." She started crying.

Beth must have been in a foul mood, because instead of comforting her twin, she shouted, "Mom's not coming back, dummy! She left because we are bad kids. We made her have a nervous breakdown! I heard Dad talking to Grandma Dot, and that's exactly what he said."

Anna looked at Beth with big, terrified brown eyes as Beth continued. "Don't you get it, Anna? She's never coming back!" Beth stomped upstairs, slamming her bedroom door shut. Anna crumpled onto the couch.

Messer stood up and heaved herself onto my back for a piggyback ride.

"We haven't been bad, have we?" she asked nervously.

"I don't think so," I answered.

"What's a nervous breakdown?" whispered Messer.

Chapter Six
November 1966

The day after Dad drank too much alcohol, Linc got us all off to school with homemade lunches in tow (even if they were pretty small and sad). He said that we could manage fine with Mom and Dad gone. Everyone was on their best behavior—except for me. Later that day, I made off with a pack of my father's cigarettes to impress my pal Bodie, who was eight just like me and tough as nails. Bodie ate worms, potato bugs and mud pies. Under pressure and wanting to seem as tough as him, I started eating almost anything he dared me to try. By comparison, smoking a cigarette seemed easy!

We made our way to Bodie's rundown apartment building, a peeling white eyesore with a giant staircase on the side that led right up to the roof. Sprinting up the stairs, we reached the top, panting and laughing. We wandered over to the west side of the roof for a front-row seat of the sunset shining over all the tall buildings in Salt Lake.

As we lit up, we had a perfect view of the Mormon

temple with its golden angel on top. Bodie struck a match and held it out to me. Even though I had seen my parents smoke since I could remember, it wasn't as easy as I thought it would be. Taking my first drag, I coughed, sputtered and carried on in fits. Bodie wouldn't stop teasing me as he inhaled like a pro, the smoke seeping from his lips and nose like a dragon. I felt my stomach turn. I knew I was doing a bad thing and I suddenly wondered if maybe I really *was* a bad kid. Was it true? Had I driven Mom away?

I stomped out the butt and ran all the way home from the rooftop perch. Once inside, I washed my mouth out with soap to get rid of the nasty taste and to erase the whole thing like it never happened. I knelt by my bed praying and pleading with God to bring my mother back.

I promise I'll be a good girl, I told God.

The next day, Grandma Dot showed up at our house early in the morning. Being Saturday, most of us were still in bed. She must have known Dad was not around because she seemed very sad. I wondered if somebody from the hospital had called her. She didn't look quite right; she was missing her bright pink lipstick and her eyes looked like she'd been crying. As soon as she stepped through the door, she put a big bag of cleaning supplies on the floor, straightened her posture and put on a fake smile. We were all happy to see her, but we weren't so excited to see what was in the bags. We wanted chocolate chip cookies, not Comet.

"Dad's in the hospital," Messer tattled as she ran down the stairs to greet her.

"Yes, dear, I know," Grandma said. "That's why I'm here. Run and tell everyone to come to the family room so we can make a plan for the day." Once everyone had gathered,

Grandma gave us our assignments. "Start with your rooms, and then we'll go from there."

When it came time to inspect our work, Grandma Dot quickly discovered Messer and I tried to hide everything under our bed. As she pulled the dirty clothes out, her blue-and-white checkered dress rode up to her waist, revealing her large bottom and huge white underwear that came to her knees.

"Grandma," I gasped in disbelief, "are those your under-pants?" We had never seen such huge underwear in our lives and we burst out laughing. Grandma didn't think it was funny and quickly got up off all fours, scowling at us while pulling her dress down to cover herself.

"These are my temple garments and we mustn't make fun. They are sacred to me and God. I'm disappointed in you girls—it's rude to laugh at someone behind their back!" She pointed her finger at us, her bracelets rattling. We hung our heads with our shoulders rounded and fidgeted with our hands. Mom and Dad yelled at us all the time, but Grandma Dot had never yelled at us before.

"We're sorry, Grandma Dot. We'll clean our rooms really good now," said Anna, fighting back tears. At that, we all scampered off, not wanting to disappoint Grandma again, and started picking up, dusting things and scraping poop off the floor.

Later, I stood at the top of the stairs, watching Grandma Dot shake out the front door rug. For the first time, I noticed how truly beautiful the house looked when it was clean. I felt terrible for lying about our room being clean and for laughing at her. Tears spilled down my cheeks, which surprised me—of all the girls, I cried the least. I went over to

Grandma and apologized over and over for my bad behavior, promising to never do it again.

"Oh Diana, I forgive you," she said softly, peeling me off her and holding my hand. "Now, let's go see how your room looks."

A few minutes later, Messer and I passed our room inspection with compliments and hugs. We were rewarded with a sleepover, and since we didn't have any suitcases, I ran downstairs and grabbed two grocery sacks—one for Beth and Anna's stuff and one for Messer's and mine. We threw in our PJs, toothbrushes and one toy each, just like Grandma told us to.

"Don't forget to pack church clothes," Grandma Dot called from the hallway. "I'm taking you to my ward tomorrow and I want to show off my beautiful, sweet grandchildren." Faced with no clean laundry, Messer and I plucked a pair of dirty floral dresses from the closet hangers and stuffed them in with the rest of our things.

We piled into Grandma's car, girls in the back and boys in front. As she dug through her purse for car keys, she pulled out a pack of Juicy Fruit gum, our favorite, and gave us all a piece. We chewed away and snapped bubbles with the wind blowing through our greasy hair. I was having fun, but I wondered what Mom was doing at that exact moment. Did she miss us? Would she care that Dad was in the hospital? Just then, Tom turned up the radio, drummed his fingers on the dashboard and I stopped thinking about it. We were driving down Third Avenue, past all the towering oak trees and pretty brick houses to Grandma's, where we always felt loved and safe. Most importantly to me, I knew we would be well-fed.

"Diana, maybe this weekend we can talk about a date for your baptism," Grandma said into the rearview mirror with a smile. My baptism had been almost totally forgotten because of all the psych-ward admissions, Mom disappearing and Dad trying to commit suicide. Baptisms were supposed to happen right after a child's eighth birthday, so it wasn't too late. Once it happened, all your sins from before were wiped clean and from then on, you commit to a lifetime of moral, chaste behavior and devoted service to the church. I had only been to Sunday meetings a handful of times and didn't really understand what it all meant, but since my eighth birthday had now passed and all my siblings were already baptized, now it was my turn.

Four months after my birthday, on November 5, 1966, I was baptized with my cousin Sammie, who had also just turned eight. Since my father was not in "good standing" as a church member and had only recently been released from the psych ward, my Uncle Garn performed the baptism at the Salt Lake Temple grounds in a round building called the Tabernacle. They told me it was built in 1863 under the direction of church president Brigham Young and later was the home of the famous Tabernacle Choir.

The only thing anyone had prepared me for ahead of time was that I had to change into white clothes and get dunked underwater so all my sins would be washed away and I would be perfect again in the eyes of the Lord. My siblings teased and terrorized me, saying that 100 percent of my body had to be submerged, and if not, the dunking would continue until everyone was satisfied that not one teeny-tiny part of my anatomy had remained above water. Beth had pounded the details into my head over and over again.

As I looked out at the crowded room, I saw my entire family watching me and suddenly I was nervous that I would screw something up. Uncle Garn stood in the baptismal font, which looked like a small swimming pool to me. He sure looked funny in his white jumpsuit, and I swallowed an enormous guffaw as I joined him in the warm water. I didn't hear a word anyone said as my uncle held my arm at a right angle like I was taking an oath over a Bible. My other hand plugged my nose in terror and anticipation.

Naturally, I had to be dunked twice, since my big toe stuck out of the water on my first submersion. After the second soaking was over, everyone congratulated me, so I figured I must have done a good thing. Dad had returned from the hospital and he seemed happy, too, hugging Sammie and me and welcoming us into the church. Grandma Dot, Aunt MaryAnn and Uncle Garn stood nearby beaming and snapping Polaroid pictures. The twins giggled and teased me about not getting it right the first time because of my renegade toe. Walking out of the Tabernacle that day with wet hair and a racing heart, I had a lightness in my step. *I need to tell Bodie I can't smoke with him anymore,* I thought.

Chapter Seven
1966–1967

G randma Dot worried nonstop about Dad's mental state, so we started having Sunday dinners at her cozy house to everyone's relief. We all tiptoed around the subject of Dad's health, and we never mentioned the suicide attempts. Getting together each week fulfilled several purposes. Grandma Dot could monitor Dad firsthand, which was good because she was still lonely without Grandpa Ted, and she liked the company. For us, we couldn't get enough of Grandma's love and attention.

Spending time with Grandma was also good because she helped us catch up on our studies. She had recently received her teaching certificate from the University of Utah and taught fifth grade at Washington Elementary School. She was a marvelous tutor, both patient and kind. Every time we drove over, I was giddy, my senses on high alert. I could almost smell and taste the homemade food—I imagined beef Wellington with gravy or ham and mashed potatoes and just thinking about it made me drool.

It was snowing like crazy one night in December when we were all warm and cozy in Grandma's house, which was decorated with Christmas garlands and tiny white lights. The grownups were sipping cocoa in the living room by the warm glow of the Christmas tree lights. I was spying on them and something seemed suspect about their conversation and hushed tones. When they spotted my cousin Sammie eavesdropping, too, the discussion ended abruptly.

"What were you guys talking about?" Sammie asked, revealing herself.

Aunt MaryAnn hustled over to her daughter and started apologizing to Grandma, taking Sammie out of the room and whispering in her ear the whole time.

I slipped into the next room without being discovered, but Aunt MaryAnn saw all the others listening in.

"What are you naughty kids up to?" she demanded. Dad cleared his throat while smoothing back his hair.

"Is dinner ready yet?" he asked. "I'm starving!" Around the corner, I saw Grandma get up and brush off her apron.

"Oh Tug, I hope I haven't burned the rolls! Come everyone. Let's eat before everything gets overdone."

We rushed to the yellow kids table and fought over the best seats. That night's dinner was a feast of pot roast, mashed potatoes with gravy, Waldorf salad and Grandma's famous Parker House rolls drenched in butter, a family favorite. Whenever she made those moon-shaped morsels, Sammie and I would compete to see who could eat the most. That night, Sammie managed to eat 18 while I only made it to a baker's dozen.

After dinner, Grandma came out with a tray of fancy glass bowls filled with pistachio ice cream for dessert. As we gobbled it down, the grownups drifted toward our table and formed a semicircle around us. Grandma Dot blushed as she cleared her throat.

"I have something I want to share with everyone," she managed to get out. "In the last year, since Grandpa passed, I have had many suitors. I really don't want to get married again, but there's a gentleman who is being very persistent in pursuing me, so I've decided to marry him. He'll be a good companion for me. His name is Rex Williams, and he is a kind widower from my ward. We plan to get married next spring."

"Isn't that great, kids? Dad declared with a little too much enthusiasm. "We're so happy for you, Mother." Eyeing the room, I noticed that Aunt MaryAnn didn't seem as excited as Dad. Her eyes were sad when she looked over at Uncle Garn.

Taking Dad's cue, we all agreed and gathered around Grandma to hug her congratulations.

"Are you going to move away?" Anna asked.

"No, dear, just over to L Street into Rex's house," Grandma replied. "I'll be close. And I will still teach at the same school." Grandma patted her head and after taking her hand away, Anna's red frizzy hair sprung back up.

Once the grownups were back in the living room, we darted off to the family room to keep playing Old Maid. Nobody talked about what Grandma had said, but I knew we were all thinking about it.

After a few minutes, Messer blurted out, "I have the Old Maid," by mistake, ruining the game.

"No, *Rex* has the Old Maid," Tom said, and we all cracked up, laughing so hard we were rolling on our backs.

Just to think that Grandma had a boyfriend had us in stitches.

When I went to the bathroom later, I stopped near the living room when I heard Aunt MaryAnn.

"Are you sure you're not rushing into this, Mom?" But Grandma didn't answer and Dad changed the subject.

"I hear Joyce is holed up somewhere in Reno," he said, "where she's a compulsive gambler."

"No surprise there," Grandma Dot said with a snort.

Wow, I thought to myself excitedly, *a compulsive gambler in Reno*! I didn't know what a gambler was, but it sounded like a good thing—even kind of fancy. I wanted to write it down so I'd remember to look up Reno on the map at home. It meant that I finally knew where to find Mom!

I envisioned myself running away with a knapsack on my back, in search of this mysterious town. "Reno," I whispered, the "R" rolling off my tongue. With a bellyful of Parker House rolls, I couldn't stop picturing my great escape and triumphant reunion with my long-lost mother.

Excerpts from Joyce Cannon's Journals

WENDY
BORN OCTOBER 12, 1950
SALT LAKE CITY, UTAH

Our baby was due on October 12, 1950, which was nine months and nine days after the bogus date on our marriage certificate. Whew. Close but safe.

My body seemed to know how to be pregnant without any help—except for keeping food down for the first few months—but I didn't have a clue how to be a wife. My only models were my parents. I was the product of a bossy, narcissistic mother and a father who was passive, depressed and often sadistic. Since I was the oldest of five kids and a rebellious one to boot, I thought I got to be the boss in our marriage. I was disabused of this notion the first time I tried it, but it took years for me to give up on trying.

Ted's idea was that he was the lord and master of the household, and my job was to do whatever he wanted me to with no argument. This meant I didn't get to be mad when he came home late for dinner, as he often did with no explanation or prior warning. I was supposed to be delighted that he came home at all and to greet him with what he considered appropriate affection and gratitude.

On that morning, my water broke, and the doctor said to go to the hospital even though I was having no contractions. It took all that day and into the wee hours of the next for the baby to be born. In the process, they discovered she was coming out face first and had to push her back in, turn her head and start labor all over again. I was unconscious through most of this and only heard about it later.

When I was awake enough, they brought her to me to feed. She was a beautiful little girl with red hair. I tried to put her to my breast to eat but she wouldn't close her mouth (I found out later she couldn't), and I had trouble trying to maneuver her around because they had cut me from stem to stern and the stitches were very painful. No one had stayed to help me and I felt like a terrible failure because she wouldn't eat. When the nurse returned to take her back to the nursery, I told her about my problems, and she said not to worry about it. This was the only time I got to hold my baby.

The next feeding time, the doctor told me they weren't going to bring her in because she was tense from the hard delivery. I had no idea what that meant, and I was worried, but the nurses kept reassuring me.

Early the next morning, the doctor came in and said the baby had had a cerebral hemorrhage during the night and asked if I wanted to have her blessed, which in the Mormon Church includes naming. I said I did and asked if there would be time for my father to come from work to do it. The doctor assured me there would be time, but he was wrong. She died before he got there. To me, my first daughter is Wendy Joyce Cannon, and she is as blessed by me as any child ever was by the laying on of men's hands.

I was kept in the hospital for a week and Ted and his family held the funeral during that time. I never got to say goodbye or do my grieving. Ted's mother came to our apartment and removed all the baby clothes and furniture we had accumulated and told Ted she had been worried when she heard we were planning to name her Wendy because, in the story, Wendy flew out the window and never came back. Oh, my God. I killed my baby by naming her Wendy.

THEODORE LINCOLN CANNON III
BORN OCTOBER 28, 1951
SALT LAKE CITY, UTAH

On October 28, 1951, our oldest son was born. Ted had long ago informed me that his first son would be named Theodore Lincoln Cannon III, and since I'd been such a failure in the naming department the first time, I didn't fight him for long on this one. I had a hard time calling that cute little baby Lincoln, which is what we had decided to call him, or Linc for short. It seemed like way too much name for such a little guy, and for some time I just called him Honey or Sweet-pea. Ted's folks called him Champ, and he was (and still is).

I was determined to be a good mother, and for the first five months, I breastfed him. He gained three ounces a day and became a little butterball but cried day and night from a bellyache. The pediatrician said he must be allergic to something I was eating, so I tried cutting one thing then another from my *diet but nothing helped. Finally, I gave up and switched him to cow's milk. Almost overnight, he became a sweet, contented baby.*

THOMAS (TIP)
BORN JANUARY 2, 1954
SALT LAKE CITY UTAH

Our second son was the only child we actually planned. As usual, the time lapse between trying and succeeding was measured in nanoseconds. Two years apart was the accepted norm for siblings, so we thought that was the way to go, because God forbid the first child should get spoiled.

Thomas's expected arrival date was December 16, 1953. He arrived on his own timetable at 3:20 am on January 2, 1954, and I quickly discovered that two little boys were way more than twice as many as one. I was able to manage just marginally while nursing Tom, though two-year-old Linc saw that I was immobilized and took advantage of it to find ways to get my attention.

In those days, there were no support groups or help for mothers with post-partum depression—in fact, it didn't even have a name. I actually had more experience than many young mothers having helped raise younger siblings, but I was only about 22 and my family lived in another state. I coped as well as I could, but I was so depressed and had so little energy that Tom was badly neglected and became anemic and malnourished.

He slowly recovered strength, learned to walk and talk, and began to eat a greater variety of foods. At some point, he

developed a passion for spaghetti that remained for his entire
life.

ANNA & BETH
BORN SEPTEMBER 17, 1956
DURANGO, COLORADO

In the spring of 1956, Shell Oil Company transferred Ted
to Durango, Colorado, in the mountains of the Four-Corners
area. They provided us with a three-bedroom house for a
reasonable rent. It was the first time Ted had been away from
his family and we were delighted to be on our own.

Linc was four, Tom (who we now called Tip) was two and
I was pregnant, as usual. We found out a few weeks after the
move that we were having twins. Ted worried about how he
would support us, and I couldn't see how I was going to take
care of four kids. I was already far gone into depression and
struggling to manage two little boys and one large one.

In September, the twins were born three weeks early.
Anna and Beth were quite small (five pounds, nine ounces
and five pounds, one ounce, respectively), and had to be fed
every three hours, day and night. First Ted's mom came to
help for a week, then mine came for about 10 days. My sister
Carol even came and helped out for a while. Then I was on
my own.

The feeding ritual involved changing a diaper then
feeding one baby, stopping partway through to burp her, then
feeding and burping again. This took about 40 minutes, and
then the process was repeated with the other baby. I was immobilized for long periods of time and could scarcely find time to

*eat, go to the bathroom and holler at the boys when they misbe-
haved, let alone stay on top of an enormous amount of laundry.
Cloth diapers for twins, in addition to the regular family laundry, was staggering. In the cold Colorado winter, the diapers
would freeze as soon as they were hung on the clothesline, and
sometimes the temperature didn't get above freezing for days.
I'd have to wrestle the frozen diapers off the clothesline and hit
them with the side of my hand to fold them, then hang them all
over the house to dry. Meal preparation was squeezed in there
somewhere and sleep was just a faint memory.*

*Asking Ted for help was out of the question—this was the
'50s and most men would rather eat boiled okra than demean
themselves by washing a dish or changing a baby's diaper.
This was women's work—period.*

DIANA
BORN AUGUST 20, 1958
FARMINGTON, NEW MEXICO

*Diana was a sweet, happy-natured baby and remained
placid though having to be in a cast for several months for a
congenital dislocated hip, followed by pillow splints for
several more months.*

*When Ted began to talk about wanting to move back to
Salt Lake to go to law school, I could not have been more
enthusiastic. He passed the Law School Admission Test with
flying colors and we moved in early summer of 1960.*

Chapter Eight
1967–1968

"I don't know how those polygamist pioneer men did it,"
Dad announced to Linc one afternoon while doing his
daily proof of *The Tribune.* "More than one wife would do
me in. And those women in all their frumpy clothes and no
makeup are anything but sexy!" The two of them chuckled
as they sat at the dining room table drinking iced coffee, a
forbidden beverage in the Mormon Church.

I was working on my fourth-grade science homework
and losing my focus when their talk caught my attention.
The only two words I heard were "polygamy" and "sexy."
Growing up, I remembered hearing that our ancestors were
polygamists, but I never knew what it meant. Occasionally,
Dad would tell us stories about his great grandparents and
the Cannon family farm, which was a compound of 13
homes on the Jordan River. Grandma Dot's family were
polygamists, too, and she spoke with great pride about her
heritage, reminding us how much those pioneers had to
endure back in the day.

She loved to tell us stories of the Mormon pioneers traveling across the plains, always hungry and looking over their shoulders in fear of being attacked by "savage Indians." If that wasn't enough, they were dying of cholera, dysentery and snake bites, too. Everyone had to do their part, which meant the women pulling handcarts and handling weapons. None of it sounded like much fun to me.

Grandma would go on and on about how the women were strong and had to share the responsibilities of caring for each other and the children. It seemed like all the conversations about it were mysterious or scandalous and only whispered about in our family and friend circles.

I was curious why they thought the topic was so funny, so I pushed my chair out and ran straight upstairs to my dad's office. Books covered every inch of the wall above his cluttered desk, crammed onto shelves and desperately in need of organization. As I reached for the big, red Webster's Dictionary, his vial of mercury caught my eye.

It was snug inside in a little wooden stand, and its silvery beauty reminded me of a genie in a bottle begging to be set free. I glanced at the office door to make sure no one was watching and grabbed the heavy book to pull it off the shelf —and accidentally knocked papers and books off the shelf, which all came tumbling to the floor. I hurried to pick up the dictionary, snatching the mercury vial off the desk as well before sneaking off to my room. Someone was coming up the stairs, so I shoved the vial under my pillow, ignoring Messer, who was lying on her unmade bed, playing with her tattered ballerina doll. I plopped down on the tangled sheets and opened the dictionary, but my body was so full of adrenaline that I couldn't remember what I wanted to look up.

Dad appeared in our doorway and I buried my nose in the dictionary. But rather than searching for "sexy," I turned to a random page and memorized the definition of a funny word I couldn't pronounce—*ebullient*—just in case Dad wanted to know what I was up to.

He turned to me with a snarl and said, "So, it was *you* making all the ruckus in my study! Numbskulls are not allowed in there without permission, and you know that. Just what were you doing in there?"

Sitting up, I displayed the massive book and replied with stellar confidence, "I'm just doing my homework, Dad! Sorry about the mess. Should I go clean up?" By now, I had perfected the art of fibbing, reinforced by the school of hard knocks.

"No, just put the damn book back and keep out of my office!" He looked over at a frightened Messer who had disappeared under her covers. "Hey shlimp, you don't need to be scared. I'm not mad at you," he said, his face softening. Messer was the runt of the family, and Dad lovingly called her "shrimp." But when Messer pronounced it, she said "shlimp," which made her seem even sweeter than she already was, so the nickname stuck. Messer peered out of her blankets with her enormous hazel eyes, which made Dad grin from ear to ear.

"It's almost time for dinner. Why don't you come help your sisters get ready?" he said. Messer quickly obeyed, running past Dad and out of sight. Then, Dad glanced over at me. "If you need any help with your homework, I'm happy to assist." It was weird that sometimes he acted like a normal father because he never did it consistently or for very long.

"Okay, Dad, thanks!" I answered, keeping my eyes glued

to the tiny print. Secretly, I knew I would never ask him for help. I couldn't let him know how behind I was.

"Hey, did you hear about the Jacobsen family?" Dad asked. I perked up hearing my friend Nancy's last name. We were neighborhood playmates and the occasional Sunday school pals when Grandma got us to church. "They're moving to Colorado City. Got the whole damn house packed up and ready to go."

"But why would they move?" I asked, setting down the dictionary.

"Apparently, they want to practice polygamy," Dad whispered. He shrugged before thumping his way back downstairs.

Remembering now what had gotten my dad on the topic (and what had made me grab the book in the first place), I flipped to the P's. There it was in the dictionary:

Polygamy (n.): The practice or custom of having more than one wife or husband at the same time.

After that, I moved to the S's.

Sexy (adj): Sexually suggestive or stimulating; erotic, generally attractive or interesting, appealing.

I closed the book, still confused. *Nancy Jacobsen's mother is the opposite of sexy*, I thought, *so how can she be a polygamist?* I was a little sad Nancy was moving, so I took the liquid mercury out from under my pillow and played with it, tilting it back and forth and watching the silvery substance slide around inside it. I knew there would be hell to pay if Dad caught me, but I took my chances, hypnotized by the liquid metal. I wondered what Nancy's new life as a polygamist would be like. *Maybe it wouldn't be so bad to have more than one mother,* I thought. After all, we were trying to figure out life *without* a mother.

One June night in 1968, Dad came home from work late. Dinner had already been cleaned up and the six of us were getting ourselves ready for bed like we usually did. Messer and I were having a pillow fight when we heard Dad whistling as he approached our door. He poked his head in but stayed put instead of marching through our clothes and toys, and we both looked up simultaneously.

"Hi, Dad!" Messer chirped as she gripped her troll doll.

"Hi, girls!" Dad replied. He seemed happy. *Probably because he's drunk,* I thought, since he smelled like beer.

"I need both of you in my bedroom straight away, chop-chop. The rest of the kids are already there. I have some exciting news."

We bounced off our beds and ran into Dad's disorderly room, excited that we were allowed to stay up a little later. Not much in the bedroom had changed since Mom left. There was still a thick layer of dust covering her wooden dresser, along with all the meaningless trinkets she had left behind. The speckled glass of the mirror made my reflection look strange, so I stuck out my tongue at myself. I blushed when I noticed all the other kids were staring at me.

Dad sat down at the foot of his bed, lit a cigarette and took a huge drag. We all watched the curling, snake-like trail of smoke slip out of his mouth and float up into the light.

"Do you remember your Aunt Carol?" he asked casually. We all nodded in unison. He took another drag, unaware his belly was slipping out the bottom of his white T-shirt, and stood up to hoist the window open for fresh air. My eyes were still fixed on the smoke as it wisped away.

"Aunt Carol and your cousins, Debi, Mark, Pam and Danny, are all coming for a visit in a couple of days," Dad said. "We've got to get the house cleaned up because they may be staying with us. Isn't that great news?" Not exactly thrilled by this announcement, we all looked at each other and shrugged, not sure how to react.

"You mean Mom's sister?" Anna piped up. "She's coming here?"

"Why would she come without Mom?" Linc asked. Tom threw Dad's pillow up toward the head of the bed before saying, "When is Mom coming home?" Dad's face looked like a balloon losing all its air."

"Let's focus on the good news," he said. "We have guests coming, so I need positive attitudes and everyone's full cooperation. Saturday will be house cleaning day, got it? That's that! Now, go to bed and get some sleep. We have a big week ahead." After that, he scuttled us out of the bedroom and shut his door.

After Mom left us, her father, Grandpa Ross, told the rest of their family what happened. Mom had four siblings, two sisters and two brothers. Grandpa sent a letter to all of them explaining that their older sister Joyce had up and left her husband and six children, his words full of religious preaching. Grandpa Ross asked for everyone to pray for Mom. None of this information surprised anyone, especially Aunt Carol, who knew about my mother's history with depression.

Aunt Carol never replied to Grandpa's letter, nor did she

try to call Mom after hearing the news. Nine months later, she reached out to my father to ask if she could come visit us for a check-in. The truth was Aunt Carol had always been jealous of Mom because she'd had a crush on Dad ever since childhood. They flirted when they were young, but nothing ever came of it. Aunt Carol was getting divorced from Uncle Ralph, which I think was the real reason she wanted to visit us in Salt Lake on her way to see her parents in Denver.

Aunt Carol and Uncle Ralph had three children together: Mark, who was my age; Pam, who was Messer's age; and Danny, who was not yet a year old. The oldest was Debi, who was 14 and from Carol's first marriage. Even so, Uncle Ralph raised her like his own. It had been more than a year since we'd set eyes on any of our cousins from Phoenix, and we hadn't yet met Danny.

We cleaned the house as best as we could even though there were no adults around to make sure we did a good job. Dad inspected the boys' room and stashed the *Playboy* magazines they had scattered all over the floor. He also took their poster of Cheryl Tiegs off the wall, the one with her wearing a baby-doll dress and sitting on a red car with her legs open, showing her underwear. Somebody had drawn girl parts over her underwear. After that, I had to convince him our dumpster-diving rope was actually a jump rope and that the dried pee in the closet was from the dog and not from Tom's sleepwalking.

Aunt Carol pulled up on a Sunday in a brown and tan paneled station wagon. That day, there were no clouds in the sky and the sidewalks were hot enough to cook on. Messer and I watched everything from the front window.

When Aunt Carol got out of her car, she carefully fluffed

her blonde beehive hairdo, pulled her bunched-up turquoise dress back into place and stretched her upper back, pushing out her giant boobs. She pulled out a tiny mirror from her purse and the beads on the back sparkled in the afternoon sunlight while she put on her milk-white lipstick. I couldn't look away as she tugged at her eyelashes, trying to make them look longer and blinking open and closed to test them out. She almost looked like a cartoon character, and Messer and I had to bite our tongues so we didn't laugh.

Aunt Carol and her kids all wore fancy clothes, which made our hand-me-downs look even shabbier by comparison. As she got out of the car, Debi had her arms crossed tight, and by the look on her face, you could tell she was upset. She was curvy and had the grooviest haircut I had ever seen—platinum blonde and cut in a fashionable A-line, straight out of a Vidal Sassoon catalog. She wore a bright orange, polyester mini-mini-dress with some kind of white belt wrapped around the middle. She looked like she should be on TV selling dish soap!

Mark and Pam were pushing each other as they climbed out the back doors, and Pam landed on the lawn strip by the sidewalk. Mark towered over her, laughing. He was just a few months older than me and handsome, with the straightest teeth I had ever seen. His dark blonde hair had an enormous wave in the front. When he tried to help Pam up off the grass, she punched him in the gut and jumped up, brushing off her blue terry cloth shorts and white tank top. I couldn't tell how long her blonde hair was because it was piled up high on her head like she was on *I Dream of Jeannie*. She was only seven, but she seemed way beyond her years. She was wearing white lipstick just like

Aunt Carol and strutted toward us like she owned the place.

Aunt Carol had baby Danny on her hip as everyone moved toward us. We all stood around not knowing what to say or where to look until Dad finally burst through the front door and boomed, "Well, aren't you a sight for sore eyes!" He never sounded more chipper.

Aunt Carol's face lit up like a sunrise. "Oh Ted, you're still your charming and handsome self!" Then she started blushing.

They were only going to stay for two nights, but Debi acted like it was an eternity. She avoided us all while complaining to her mother that she didn't want to be there the entire time.

"This house is old, and it stinks," Debi said. She took refuge in a corner of the parlor next to the couch, making a cozy nest for herself with a clean blanket. She slept there, surrounded by *Tiger Beat* magazines and pictures of David Cassidy.

Mark and Pam were friendly to our faces, but I heard them complaining to their mom behind our backs.

"Where are we going to sleep, Mom?" Mark asked.

"Yeah, Mom, where?" Pam chimed in, folding her arms across her chest. "This place is gross."

"It's haunted and disgusting. I'm sleeping in the car." Mark said and made a military-style turn on his heels, huffed and walked right into me, startled that I had heard the whole embarrassing conversation. Red-faced, he bolted out the front door and plopped down in a wicker chair on the front porch.

So everyone would get along better, I eventually

suggested we all go on a walk to grab a free Popsicle from Kwiki's. Pam perked up and pulled out a five-dollar bill, waving it at us with a smile—I couldn't believe she had her own fiver! We all loped to the store like rabbits and loaded up on penny candy, equally surprised and thrilled by Pam's generosity. After that, we booked it to Bodie's house.

Pam, our new favorite cousin, carried a small white paper bag bulging with licorice rolls, Jolly Ranchers and Tootsie Pops. It wasn't hard to lure Bodie out onto the roof to share our sweets with us. With cigarettes in one hand and suckers in the other, all four of us sat quietly and enjoyed our freedom until Messer had a coughing fit that reminded me of an earthquake. My little sister had tried smoking a couple of times now but never quite got the swing of it. I did my best puffing to impress Pam, who seemed shocked we had the nerve to light up.

Back home, Dad hustled about in the kitchen, peeling the tinfoil off frozen Swanson TV dinners. We were thrilled at some of the new varieties, but I could tell from my cousins' expressions that TV dinners weren't special at their house— not even close. We didn't care; our stomachs were growling, and Dad was in a fine mood, humming along to his favorite album, *Whipped Cream and Other Delights* by Herb Alpert & the Tijuana Brass. The more Dad whistled, the more Debi scowled, eventually pushing her dinner away and running off.

To our enormous relief, Aunt Carol's long-awaited departure time finally arrived. While our cousins were loading up the car to continue their trip to Colorado, Dad sent us out to wave them off. We all said our phony, smiley goodbyes, thinking it was the last we would see of them for a long time—but it sure wasn't.

Shortly after, Messer and I found ourselves at Aunt Carol's in Arizona for the weekend, astonished that she had a maid, a pool and a tidy house. A few months later, she returned with her entire family again, and Dad called us all together.

"I've asked Aunt Carol to marry me," he said. "We wanted Debi and Linc to give their permission as the eldest of each household. They have given their blessing, and now we want to know how all of you kids feel about it."

My stomach dropped as I looked at a sullen Linc. *He sure doesn't look like someone who's just given his blessing,* I thought. Aunt Carol stood before us batting her spidery eyelashes and smiling as my father put his arm around her waist.

"Come give me a hug before we head back to Arizona to pack up the house. We'll all be together again soon," Aunt Carol said, extending her arms out to me. I didn't want to, but there was no way out of it, so I walked over. As she squeezed me tight, she said, "I guess you don't have to call me Aunt Carol anymore!" I smiled through my clenched teeth.

"Bye, Carol." I would never call her Mom.

Chapter Nine
April 1968

Now that Grandma Dot and Rex Williams had been married for more than a year, Rex asked us to call him Gramps, and we didn't have a problem with it. He was a sweet, baldheaded man with a beaming dimpled smile, plus he was gentle and said things that made us laugh, so he easily filled the role.

Grandma Dot moved into his brown brick bungalow, which had a beautiful backyard with flowering gardens and a gazebo where we all gathered on our weekly Sunday visits. The two of them were faithful church-goers and always had on their Sunday best, with Gramps sporting a suit and tie and Grandma Dot in a matronly dress with pearls. Following in her musical father's footsteps, Grandma Dot served as the ward pianist, organist and choir leader, and when we visited on Sundays, she would often let us sit by her side as she played the organ at their home.

Each time, two or three of us would squeeze onto the piano bench in our ragged play clothes. Dad's attempts at laundry were few and far between, but we knew she loved us despite our smell and appearance. I was mesmerized as she pumped the pedals with her dainty feet and reached for the keys on three levels, all while looking straight ahead at a sheet of music. As she played, Gramps would sit quietly in his rocking chair, tapping his toes and singing along to the hymns.

Because she was always so generous, when Grandma Dot moved out of the house on Third Avenue that she'd lived in for 40 years, she gave it over to Dad. It was his childhood home, and it was a much nicer place for us to live—she even paid for a new addition so Linc and Tom would have their own rooms. When the remodel was finished, we couldn't wait to move in. It seemed strange to see our mismatched worn furniture in such a pretty storybook house. Even the scent of her violet perfume seemed to linger in the air. I couldn't believe Grandma's house was ours!

Dad and Carol's engagement hadn't been announced yet, and Carol was determined to remain "chaste," obeying church covenants, so she and my four cousins moved into our old house on Second Avenue until the wedding could take place. We were forbidden to tell anyone about their arrangement—especially Grandma Dot. During their hasty engagement, I noticed that my father gave up smoking and drinking. All of a sudden, he had transformed from a boozing, cigarette-loving, cursing father to a buttoned-down and practicing Mormon. Clearly, it was all for Carol.

Carol, as we now called her, was a stickler for the church's rules and culture. She was obsessed with keeping up appearances and wholesome living, so she and Dad spent their time discreetly planning the wedding and thinking about how they were going to combine their two families. There was one giant hurdle to jump before they could do all that: they needed to get Grandma Dot's blessing. They actually had *two* giant hurdles since my parents weren't even divorced yet, but nobody seemed worried about that.

One afternoon, we were all busy unpacking boxes and nesting into our new rooms when Messer and I heard the back door slam, followed by some yelling in the kitchen. There was only one wall between us and the argument, so we snuck up to the doorjamb with our backs to the wall to listen.

"What in the hell is Carol doing living in my house?" Grandma shouted. Messer and I shot each other a look— Grandma knew. Also, we had never heard her cuss before.

"I went there this morning to clean only to find that witch in the kitchen, barely dressed and her three out-of-control children running around!"

I motioned to Messer to stay put and peeked around the door to get a better look. Dad was on all fours putting pots and pans away in the lower cabinets and groaned as he stood up.

"Not to mention she was very rude to me, acting as if she was queen bee of the house," Grandma continued with her hands on her hips. "I couldn't believe my eyes! Ted, you should have told me! What's going on? I want an explanation and now!" Dad's face reddened as he stuttered out a sorry excuse.

"She needed a place to stay for a while. I should have told you. Please, Mother, come sit down. Let me explain." He took her hand and guided her to the table. "This is probably as good a time as any to tell you something, and you're right. I should have told you much sooner." I waved Messer over with my other hand to my lips, silencing her so we could both hear Dad's confession.

"There's just been so much going on with Dad dying, Joyce leaving and your re-marriage," he said nervously. "I just didn't know how or when to break the news." He took a breath before continuing. "Carol and I have been courting all summer and we're planning to get married in just a few months. Maybe November." Grandma gasped.

"Oh Ted, this is asinine. You've got to think this through! You've been on a good path and finally, after all this time, you've moved on from Joyce. Why on earth would you want to marry her *sister*? This seems like a crazy decision, and I'm not happy about it at all!"

Messer and I gawked at each other. "Holy shit," I whispered. "Juicy stuff!"

"Carol has always been infatuated with you," Grandma Dot continued, "and now she has her claws in you and our whole family."

"Whoa," said Messer quietly. "Carol has claws?" I suppressed a giggle. After that, we heard a deep-chested, heavy sob.

"I need to go home and be alone," Grandma said, her voice quivering. As she drove away, we spied on Dad on the floor, looking as worried as we had ever seen him.

"What have I done," he muttered, over and over. He suddenly looked so small and sad in his splotched khaki pants and wrinkled short-sleeved shirt. His head fell into his hands. I felt sorry for him.

Despite Grandma's protests, Dad and Carol had a simple wedding on November 9, 1968, just one day after

Dad got a signed divorce decree from Mom. *So much for continuing the Cannon polygamist tradition,* I thought. The ward bishop married them in a short ceremony, but I hardly listened. I was more concerned about Grandma Dot's reaction. I watched her every move as she stood quietly while Dad and Carol took their vows. Then, I saw her grab Grandpa Rex's hand when it was time for Dad to kiss the bride. Carol and Mom's parents, Grandpa Ross and Grandma Jane, watched the ceremony with blank faces. They clearly weren't fans of the union—or of my father. Grandma Jane had the biggest round brown eyes I had ever seen and silvery-white hair piled up high on her head. She always seemed to wear too much white powder on her face, making her teeth look yellow. Grandpa Ross was a slender man with a military-style crewcut. They both looked around nervously at the crowd.

I tried to think through what it all meant as I gazed around. *My aunt is now my stepmother,* I realized, *and my first cousins are my stepbrothers and stepsisters. Now there are 10 children!* We were already related and loved each other, even if we didn't know each other very well, so that part made perfect sense. The more I thought about it, I guessed that maybe the same was true for Dad and Carol, too. What struck me most was how Dad kept kissing Carol and smiling. I had never seen him so happy or affectionate.

When the ceremony was over, the bishop quickly excused himself along with Grandma Dot and Gramps, and the 12 of us headed off for a celebratory dinner at Sizzler Steakhouse, which was by far the nicest place I had ever eaten in my whole life. We each got our own piece of meat and a steaming hot baked potato followed by a trip to the ice cream bar. *Things are really looking up*, I thought, inhaling my second hot fudge sundae. Even though the older kids were being mean about it, I was happy my younger cousins were going to be around on a full-time basis. Linc was sitting next to me and the twins and leaned in.

"Next thing you know, we'll all be moving to Colorado City to join the polygamists," he said. "This is bullshit!" We held our tongues as to not encourage him or draw attention, but I snickered under my breath.

I thought that maybe going to an honest-to-goodness steak house was a sign from God, one that meant that our lives were finally going to change for the better. I moved my spoon around in my sundae, watching the ice cream melt. *Are Carol and Dad polygamists?* I wondered.

Chapter Ten
1968–1969

When Carol and her crew moved into the Third Avenue house with us, the reality of everything hit us for the first time. It was a tight squeeze, to say the least, and Linc and Tom were furious when they found out they had to be bunkmates again after enjoying their own newly remodeled bedrooms. Meanwhile, Mark got to have his own room, which infuriated my brothers to no end. The more special treatment Mark got, the more Linc and Tom secretly called him a spoiled brat. My brothers' way of dealing with the new family was to avoid everyone, often shacking up at friends' houses whenever possible. Sometimes they were gone for days at a time, but no one seemed to mind—it meant fewer mouths to feed.

Anna and Beth shared a tiny room and were still joined at the hip, and Grandma Dot made them feel special when she told them that Aunt MaryAnn had slept in their room when she was a girl. Before everyone else moved in, Messer and I had been enjoying our spacious room with the queen-sized brass bed Grandma left for us, but now we had to squeeze together to make room for two more kids.

Pam moved into our bed and acted like she owned the place, bossing us around and taking up more room than she needed. Danny's crib took up all the other leftover space, so much so that we had to shimmy through the bedroom if we wanted to move around. If Danny cried and woke up during the night, it was suddenly our responsibility to feed him a bottle or change his cloth diaper. Every night, the three of us girls slept in a line with Messer sandwiched between us. Messer and I were fine with this as we were used to cuddling together. Naturally, Pam hated this arrangement and constantly complained. Whenever one of us accidentally peed in the bed, she became furious, ranting and raving to Carol that she wanted her own room—but she never got her way.

While Mark and Pam struggled to integrate with our family, Debi, who was a cheerleader in her junior year of high school and one of the popular girls, refused to move to Utah and be a part of our Brady Bunch family. She chose to live in Phoenix with a family friend instead. She wanted nothing to do with us or the chaos. She didn't trust our dad and was grossed out by the new marriage—so much so that eventually, even Carol gave up and let her abandon the family.

Luckily for me, I thought of the chaos as my friend. I figured that with more kids in the house, it would be even easier for me to go unnoticed while failing at school. But when I started at Longfellow Elementary School in The

Avenues, the teachers had no clue about our family history, so I lost my sympathy card.

From the outside looking in, we all looked like a completely normal family, so my bad grades confused my teachers. Because I had terrible study habits, my teachers forced me to do a bunch of tests, and I was mortified when they stuck me in a classroom with several other academically challenged kids. Each day, I sat in a private cubby with headphones over my ears, working on remedial reading and math. I was terribly behind, but somehow I managed to keep that embarrassing news from my ever-growing family. With 12 people in the house, it was easy to hide in the shadows. I liked being invisible, particularly when it came to school and all the trouble I was starting to get into.

A week after taking their civil vows and moving into the house, Dad and Carol couldn't pack fast enough for their honeymoon in San Francisco. While they were away, they put Linc in charge and asked Grandma Dot to check on us occasionally; thankfully, Aunt MaryAnn offered to take Danny. Relishing our freedom from parents, we stayed up late the second night and played cards at the kitchen table—except for Linc and Tom, who were out roaming the neighborhood.

As Mark threw down his winning ace, he leaned in.

"Pam and I have something to tell you, but you can't tell Linc and Tom," he announced. "We're leaving for a couple of days to go see our dad, and we'll be back before you know it. Linc and Tom won't even notice us being gone since they're never here anyway."

"How the heck are you getting there?" I asked, fidgeting with my fan of cards.

"Never mind all that. We're leaving in a few hours. Go get packed, Pam—the rest of you should go to bed." We all went off to our rooms, happy to do what Mark said because we all wanted him to like us. He was athletic, handsome and funny. In my eyes, he was cooler than all of us put together. Besides, we felt bad for Mark and Pam, too—they obviously missed their dad just like we missed Mom.

Uncle Ralph had a sister named Bonnie who lived a few miles north of Salt Lake, and Mark had arranged for her to take them to the airport. Messer and I finished helping Pam pack her patchwork denim overnight bag when Mark came for her.

"Bonnie is here," Mark said. "You ready?" Pam climbed up onto our squeaky brass bed and gave Messer and me a quick hug. As they walked out of the bedroom, Mark turned back and winked, putting his index finger up to his mouth to tell us to hush. The house was quiet except for some muffled rock music coming from Linc and Tom's room. When we heard the front door close, we sprang out of bed and went to the front window to watch the taillights of the shiny black car disappear into the night like two matches burning out.

Three days into their honeymoon, Dad and Carol got a call from a panicked Grandma Dot telling them that two of the kids were missing. They immediately booked plane tickets to Phoenix to find the two runaways. Even though Carol had custody of her four kids, Uncle Ralph seemed to have more power over them, and he literally bribed them with money, cars and boats to leave our family and live with him. Carol and Dad spent what was left of their honeymoon in a lawyer's office, drawing up paperwork to get her children back. On the last night of their ruined trip, they boarded a red-eye flight accompanied by Mark and Pam and returned to Salt Lake. As if things weren't already bad enough, their flight was diverted to Ogden due to poor visibility, so the miserable foursome ended up having to endure a lengthy bus ride together.

When they all finally got home, we were all getting ready to go to school. As he walked in the door, Dad slammed his suitcase down and headed straight for his bedroom. Mark and Pam did the same, which made me wonder if they were grounded. Meanwhile, Carol stomped into the kitchen where we were eating breakfast. She looked terrible because she hadn't gotten much sleep for days. "How the hell did this happen?" she said, huffing. "Linc, you were in charge. Tell me how you let this happen!" Linc didn't look up and answered between spoonfuls of Cap'n Crunch.

"They took off in the middle of the night," he said. "How was I supposed to know anything?" He shot Carol an innocent look and shrugged his shoulders.

"Were you home all night?

"Yup," he answered, clearing his bowl and setting it in the sink with his back to Carol. Our stepmother turned to us four girls.

"Who is going to tell me what the hell really happened?"

Since Beth was the bravest of us all, she replied, "They told us they missed their dad and wanted to go visit for a couple of days. They said they would be back before you got home—that it was no big deal."

"It was late at night when Bonnie came to pick them up," Anna added. "We all had gone to bed, and then Grandma came by the next morning on her way to school to check on us. When she asked where they were, we told her." Unable to contain her fury, Carol snapped.

"I am so disappointed in all of you!" She grabbed a Diet Pepsi, slammed the fridge door and stormed off.

We showed up late for school that day, and Mark and Pam got to stay home. I found my usual spot in the small room with cubbies and put headphones over my ears. Moments later, I felt a gentle tap on my shoulder. When I turned to look, my fifth-grade teacher Miss Nance was standing behind me. She was young, tall and slender with a quiet voice. "Diana, would you like to come join the rest of us in class today?"

You mean I'm done with dumbbell math already? I thought. I smiled and nodded yes. It had been a crappy morning, but it was turning into a good day. After that, Miss Nance took me to a normal classroom with students my age —and better yet, it was Mark's class, too! Having my step-brother a few rows over was going to make school a much happier place for me. All the girls seemed to have crushes on him, so my association with him upped my status in fifth grade.

But naturally, this good fortune didn't last. Three weeks later, I was sitting in math class wondering why Mark's chair was empty. Shortly after that, I heard my name over the intercom telling me to go to the office. *Oh shit,* I thought. *Now what have I done?* When I walked in, Carol was waiting for me. She and the principal asked me what I knew about Mark and Pam being absent, but I didn't know anything—nobody did. It didn't take long to verify that they were both missing.

Later that day, Carol paced around the kitchen red-faced

as she told us what had happened. She had gotten a call from her ex-husband that Mark and Pam were back on an airplane to Phoenix, and after that, she had rushed to the school to see if they really were. Now, it was all confirmed.

"I have custody, those kids belong with me. I'll see that son of a bitch in court!" she yelled, slamming her fist on the counter. Danny was in earshot in his crib and started to sob, and his cries tugged at my heart. The honeymoon was definitely over, and Carol's true colors were showing from underneath her fancy bouffant hairdo, rosy cheeks, batting eyelashes and shiny white lipstick.

I ran to Dad's office, wishing there was a door I could shut behind me for some privacy. His office, which was now in a corner of the family room, was a mess of unpacked boxes. His globe was resting on top of the highest box, and I climbed the teetering pile as carefully as I could to get it down. Sitting in the middle of the floor, I opened my notebook and pretended to study as I slowly spun the globe, realizing how little I knew about geography. As I blankly looked at the colorful round ball, it was all I could do to locate North America.

When Linc passed through to get to his bedroom, I flipped a couple of random pages in my notebook.

"Hey Linc, what state is Reno in?" I asked. I quickly added, "It's for my homework." He shot me a suspicious look as he kept walking.

"Nevada."

"Is Nevada in North America?"

"Yes, dummy." I heard the sound of his bedroom door close and his stereo blare to life.

"Thanks, Linc!" I shouted over the noise. Within a few

minutes, I had found Nevada on the globe, and it didn't seem too far away. I ripped a piece of paper out of my notebook and wrote in my best cursive: *Reno, Nevada*. What a relief— it was only one state away! If Mark and Pam could run away to their dad, why couldn't I do the same to my mom?

Chapter Eleven
July 1969

Just when I had started improving my grades and making friends in the neighborhood, Carol's constant complaining about "too many drugs and hippies" in The Avenues led to another moving truck appearing in front of our house. Even though we lived in a conservative Mormon community, the counterculture was finding its way in anyway.

Carol and Dad made an offer on a larger house in a wealthier part of Salt Lake City, and without even consulting Grandma Dot, they sold Dad's childhood home. The new owners tore the house down and replaced it with a modern-looking apartment building, which broke Grandma's heart. I felt bad for Grandma Dot. She'd given us a house and had been providing for us in many other ways our entire lives. After it was all over, Carol and Grandma Dot's relationship got even worse.

But neither Dad nor Carol could be bothered with any of that—after months of legal battles and headaches with

Uncle Ralph, Carol was thrilled to finally have Pam and Mark back in her house. Dad was also applying for law school for the second time, and they joked that if Uncle Ralph kept trying to take the kids away, they would at least have free legal counsel.

Our new home felt like a mansion, and I couldn't believe we got to live in it. Carol never stopped repeating stories about the home's legacy, either. It had been constructed for Joseph Fielding Smith and his second wife, which was a big deal to Carol since Joseph Fielding Smith's grandfather was the nephew of Joseph Smith, the founder of the Mormon Church. Anytime we had visitors over, Carol made sure they knew these churchy historical facts before they had even crossed the welcome mat.

Our new house had seven bedrooms, three bathrooms, a formal living room, a dining room, a study with a balcony and a large kitchen tragically painted black and purple. Carol complained incessantly about the distasteful colors and the prior owners' lack of taste (they were non-Mormons, which only made her complaints worse). She made imme-diate plans for a remodel and manically sewed white sheer curtains for the bottom halves of the windows. She also painted the walls lemon yellow, and it seemed like she did it all solo—none of the kids helped her, and I never saw Dad lift a finger, either.

A musty basement downstairs sported a TV room, laundry area, bathroom, Dad's workroom and Linc's bedroom, which was actually the old coal storage room that looked like a scary cave. When Dad put in an above-ground swimming pool out back shortly after we moved in, we spent afternoons laying out and playing Marco Polo with the neighborhood kids. Carol spent endless hours scolding Messer for scaling the majestic willow trees in front, but Messer ignored her; they were begging to be climbed.

Carol's favorite thing about our new home was that it was near the upstanding Garden Park ward, where several of the Mormon Church's important, highfalutin general authorities were members. As I had learned through classes at our church, in Mormon society, a ward was made up of several blocks of church members, and all those wards were part of a larger stake, and most stakes were made of four to five wards. Our stepmother loved to brag that in our ward, we had neighbors like Hugh B. Brown and Richard L. Evans, who were Mormon bigwigs. Spencer W. Kimball, the church's prophet at the time, also lived near us. As we began to understand, living among church celebrities was considered a big deal.

All visitors were immediately directed to the entryway of our kitchen, where a black-and-white photo hung on the wall of Grandpa Ted Cannon shaking the hand of former prophet David O. McKay. The first time we hung it up, Dad stood proudly by the photo, taking a long look around the house.

"Wouldya look at that," he exclaimed, shaking his head slightly. "In the blink of an eye, we have miraculously become holy high rollers."

Though all 12 of us fit comfortably into our new home, and we lived in a much nicer part of town, it didn't fix the underlying tension and dysfunction. Linc spent most of his time at home listening to music in the cave and burning patchouli incense. Tom's door was always closed, and we knew better than to bug him. Pam, Messer, Mark, Anna,

Beth and I hid from our parents and roamed the neighbor-hood, climbing trees and playing kick the can until our curfew.

The rest of the year in the new house went smoothly until the second day of summer break, when I heard loud noises outside. I ran down the long stairway and into the kitchen to investigate where I saw Carol standing at the back door with both hands on her hips, watching some kind of commotion in progress.

"What's all that noise?" I asked.

"Just go to your room, Diana," Carol replied coolly. "This is between your dad and Linc."

Now worried, I ran upstairs to Danny's room, which had a full view from the second floor to the driveway. Below, Dad and Linc were in a full-blown brawl like in a Western movie. Since he'd turned 17, Linc was a boiling pot of rage and testosterone and tall enough to take on Dad. Dad slugged Linc in the gut, making him stagger backward and nearly fall over—but then he recovered, charging forward and knocking Dad to the ground. It was hard to tell who had the upper hand. They pummeled each other with tight-fisted punches to the face and chest until Dad finally made it to his feet and gave Linc a kick in the side.

"Get out of my face, you ungrateful shit!" Dad yelled, spitting with anger. "You have 15 minutes to pack your stuff and get out!"

I stood frozen at the window. I couldn't go down and risk a beating, but I wanted to do something. Linc had looked out for us all these years, and now I couldn't do anything to help him. I was powerless. I fell to the floor and cried, waking up Danny, who stood in his crib smiling behind his binky and holding out his arms for me. I carried Danny halfway down the stairs when I overheard Carol say, "You did the right thing, Ted. He's on drugs, and he can't be trusted. We can't have that riff raff around this family and this neighborhood. It's time for him to move on."

My knees got so weak that I thought I might drop Danny, so I hurried down the rest of the stairs to hand him to Carol and ran back to my room without saying a word. I was terrified for my oldest brother and wondered where he would go. I smashed my face and fists into my pillow and screamed as loud as I could, "Don't leave, don't leave, don't leave!" It hit me with utter clarity: the one person who had always held my family together was being forced out the door.

I watched him slowly walk down the driveway in his dirty white tank top and Levi's, his head hung low. He had his guitar strapped to his back and paused for a minute at the sidewalk. He looked both ways as if making up his mind which way to go, then turned and made for the bus stop. When he disappeared from sight, a little piece of my heart went with him.

The rest of that summer felt stagnant, intensified by those searing hot, 100-degree Utah desert days. There was no breeze, no sounds of life, just that stand-still choking kind of air that left your chest feeling heavy. Just like when my mom left, we weren't allowed to talk about the day my brother got kicked out, so a ball of fire burned inside my gut.

I knew something wasn't right with my family, but I had no idea what to do other than start planning my own escape —especially since Carol's short fuse and cold command of were proving unbearable.

Now that Carol was in charge, our cleaning regimen had swung from nonexistent to white-glove level scrutiny. Every Saturday, we spent four or five hours on our assigned jobs so that every square inch of the place would be spit-shined. Carol inspected our work by donning a white glove and running her fingers up and down the banister, china hutch and every other surface within reach. If it didn't pass her expectations, we cleaned it again and again until she was satisfied.

One day during a particularly tedious cleaning session, I daydreamed about the letter I was going to write to Mom, outlining my plan to run away and live with her in Reno. The minute I finished my work, I stole away to my bedroom and started writing. Messer, who was putting the last of her clothes away in her drawer, saw me.

"Whatcha doing?" she asked.

"Shhh! Come here," I replied, motioning for her to sit next to me on our bed. "I'm writing a letter to Mom. I found out where she is, and I want to go live with her. I hate it here. Wanna come with me?" Messer stared at me and then looked away, earnest in her thoughts. "How do you know where Mom lives?"

"I heard Carol and Dad talking about her."

"You can't leave without me. I'm going with you!" I was happy because truthfully, I knew I could never leave my little sister behind.

"We have to write this quick though, before Pam comes in and catches us," I whispered as I sharpened my pencil.

I began the letter by telling Mom a little about us—that I was now 11 and just starting sixth grade, and Messer was eight and entering the third grade. We only had time to fill a page when we heard Pam chasing Danny up the stairs, but it was enough to get our point across that we missed her and were coming to find her. I grabbed the letter, folded it sloppily and shoved it in my pocket.

"We just need an envelope, an exact address and a stamp, and we'll be able to send it off," I whispered.

The next day after church and family dinner, everyone was lounging around in the basement watching *The Beverly Hillbillies*. Dad, still in his shirt and tie, snored in his new black recliner chair, which was a wedding gift from his blushing bride. Carol had taken off her church dress and was ironing in her underclothes; shockingly unattractive sheer garments squished by her bra and nude nylons. Not a pretty sight. She was chomping on her gum so hard, I wanted to scream, "Non-chompus!" but was afraid I would wake Dad.

It was time to make my move. Nonchalantly, I made my way up to the main floor where I stealthily retrieved an envelope and stamp from Dad's desk in the study. Then I ran upstairs to my room to get the letter tucked under my side of the mattress. I carefully placed the letter in the envelope and sealed it. It was now secure. The last hurdle was that I needed Mom's exact address.

In my heart, I believed that Carol would be sympathetic. After all, Mom was her sister. I thought she'd want to help once I explained about the letter. Confidently, I waltzed back down to the basement and walked right up to Carol, who was still chomping and ironing, and said, "I need Mom's address. I know she lives in Reno, Nevada." I held out the blank envelope. "Do you have her address, and will you please help me write it on this envelope?"

Carol glanced over to the TV area, and I followed her

gaze. Dad was still asleep. She carefully placed the iron on the board, and without looking at me, she snatched the letter out of my hand.

"How did you find out she's in Reno?" she demanded, her voice strangled. Her piercing eyes made it clear that I had made a grave mistake. My gut told me to grab the letter and run like hell, but I was too scared. I could only stand there and remain mute. She turned the envelope over a couple of times before sliding her long, red fingernail along the top and opening it.

I started to panic. I had foolishly written to Mom about how mean Dad and Carol were, and now she was reading those exact words!

After calmly reading my letter, Carol looked at me blankly while slowly crumpling the paper into a ball. She walked to the family room fireplace and threw it into the crackling flames. I turned and ran back upstairs, but this time, instead of crying, my fists balled up and I felt my face get hot. The burning fire in my stomach was now a raging inferno, and I damned her to hell.

After the letter, I fancied myself a little bit of a rebel and started hanging out with a girl named Renae, one of the "bad kids" who wore heavy makeup and reeked of cigarettes. We got busted smoking in the bathroom at school and a fuming Carol ordered me to "get my ass home." The walk home was only six blocks, but I wished it were 50. I knew I was in for a beating after witnessing what Dad had done to Linc. I only hoped Carol would be more lenient and let out a sigh of relief when I saw that Dad was still at work.

Carol had placed an interrogation chair in the archway, separating the living room from Dad's den. The yellow metal kitchen stool sat about five feet in front of the chair, and I was ordered to take a seat in it. She took her place on the stool, towering over me, and I shrunk into my seat and listened to a bunch of mumbo jumbo about giving in to Satan's temptations, embarrassing her in front of all the neighbors and why couldn't I act more like the twins. It all sounded like the teacher from Charlie Brown—*wah, wah, wah.* I did, however, sit up straight and pay attention when she stood up, walked over and hit me across the face, filling my left cheek with an instant rush of heat.

"Are you listening to me?" she demanded. "I talk and talk until I'm blue in the face and I still feel like I'm talking to the wall! You're not listening! Just you wait 'til your father comes home!"

Carol ordered me to my room. I tried to distract myself by listening to the radio while I waited, but as soon as I heard Dad's booming voice downstairs, I immediately peed my pants—and with no time to change, I was called downstairs.

I stood sheepishly in my dripping pants at the top of the stairs. Dad was surprisingly quiet and calm.

"Come on down, Diana, I need to talk to you," he said. I came down slowly and as Carol tried to join in on the conversation, Dad made her leave the room.

"I'll deal with this," he said as he waved her off. After waiting for her to leave, he saw the bright red hand mark on my cheek and continued. "Did she hit you?" He reached over to touch my face and I flinched, not daring to say a word.

"That wasn't very smart of you, Diana," he said. "I expect better from you." After that, he walked out of the room. I couldn't believe he had let me off the hook! I wondered if he understood my curiosity for cigarettes because I had seen him in our backyard sneaking a puff or two on several occasions. One time he caught me watching him, but we never spoke of it. My Dad and I now had a silent common bond in our rebellion against Carol's pious command.

For smoking in the bathroom, I got suspended for three days and grounded for two weeks. My sisters couldn't believe I had started smoking again, especially since we had started going to church and had been lectured about the Word of Wisdom (a health code that required abstinence from coffee, tobacco, tea and alcohol). Their brows furrowed over my nonadherence, but Pam gave me a big thumbs up, which was way more important to me. I guessed she was impressed by my rebellious spirit, which only energized me to win her over even more.

Once Carol had physically hurt me, I started avoiding her at every turn, retreating to my room. When I showed up for meals, it was at the last minute. My body may have been at the table, but my mind was elsewhere. Still, I started to notice that Carol had also been hiding in her room most of the time, only coming out to get dinner ready for us. When Thanksgiving was right around the corner, her spirits finally lifted again and she started baking, decorating and making holiday party plans, which slightly doused my burning hatred toward her—but only slightly.

We had been invited to Thanksgiving dinner at Uncle Garn and Aunt MaryAnn's house. That morning, we were told to get showered and dressed up in our best Sunday clothing. Once the car was loaded up with the ignition running, Dad honked the horn for Tom. He finally graced us with his presence, but his body language said all that needed to be said. Tom was now a junior in high school, and he hadn't been the same since Linc got kicked out—I didn't think he was even bothering to go to classes anymore. He dropped into the back seat of the car with his long hair hanging over his bloodshot eyes.

"You look like a damned sheepdog," Carol said to him. "I'm going to make an appointment for you to get that mop cut off this week. You should be embarrassed showing up for Thanksgiving dinner looking like that." Tom had already been wearing his hair long for a few years like most of the teenagers during that time, but Carol couldn't stand looking at the dirty hair covering his face.

"Carol's right," Dad said into the rearview mirror. "You look like a derelict."

Dad and Carol took turns badgering him about his hair for the entire 15-minute car ride. Tom hung his head low and kept his gaze in his lap, remarkably calm. It was lucky I was the only one who heard him say "Fuck off" under his breath.

After we devoured dinner and cleaned up the dishes, we all sat in the living room to "visit" as the adults liked to call it. Just as we took our seats, Uncle Garn asked Tom how he was doing in school. Tom mumbled something unintelligible, still hunched over and seeming angry.

"Sit up and speak up, Tip!" Dad barked. "Or is all that hair growing into your ears, too?"

Everyone chuckled at Dad's words except Tom. After an awkward moment, he exclaimed, "It's *Tom*, not Tip, goddammit!"

His words hung in the air and we all froze, wondering if

Dad would strike back. Tom jumped up and darted outside. Before Dad could get to the door, long-legged Tom had made it halfway down the street.

Later that night, I heard Dad and Carol's voices downstairs in the kitchen. I had gone to bed early but couldn't sleep, so I snuck to the top step to eavesdrop. I caught snippets of the conversation—they had finally found Tom wandering around downtown with his guitar and a small backpack.

"He must have made it home to gather a few things before we found him," Dad said. After listening for a while, I heard that they had lured Tom into their car, promising that they weren't mad and that he could come back home. When he got in, they drove him straight to a boys' ranch for juvenile delinquents instead and dropped him off. As I sat on the top step listening, my throat tightened. Another sibling gone. My world was falling apart a little more each day.

The next morning, Carol sent me downstairs to wash Danny's poopy cloth diapers in the basement toilet. In between flushes, I heard a strange ripping sound down the hallway. I couldn't see anything when I peered my head out, so I kept washing the soiled mess. When I finished, I grabbed the full bucket of diapers and headed toward the laundry room, leaving a trail of drippings behind me. As I passed the TV room, I spotted Dad pulling off a big strip of silver duct tape. His beloved chair had a giant gash in it, and he was ripping the tape with his teeth and meticulously covering the damage. Apparently, Tom had slashed it on his way out of the house, and now the chair looked like the ratty ones we saw on *The Beverly Hillbillies*. It was almost certainly the wrong time to ask about Mom's address in Reno, but I did anyway.

"You are not going to go live with that bitch whore!" he yelled. "She doesn't want you! You have it pretty damn good here, and I'm sick and tired of all of you ungrateful little shits." I saw a blur before I felt a powerful backhand smash into my cheek. He hit me with so much force that I sailed five feet through the air and stopped only when my back crashed into the wall. I slid down and landed on the floor with a thud.

Through the waves of pain, I heard Dad retreat upstairs, but I was too stunned to move. I lay there for what felt like an eternity, my red-hot cheek pressed on the cool cement floor. I was starting to realize that I might not ever see my mother again.

Chapter Twelve
July–August 1970

D ad and Carol's first wedding anniversary was fast approaching, and all their attention was focused on temple readiness and the pressing Mormon goal of building an eternal family. Forget about the fact that Linc was long gone to God knows where, that Tom was locked away at a boys' ranch and I was once again nursing a parent-inflicted wound. Dad and Carol's priority and year-end aspiration was to be sealed for all time and eternity in the Latter-Day Saints Temple.

When they first got married, the church did not consider them worthy of the temple; it was a privilege awarded only to devoted couples after scrupulous interviews with bishops and stake presidents. Every couple who made it had to be deemed morally clean and chaste, abide by the Word of Wisdom, and pay a full tithing—10 percent of one's income —among other requirements. Apparently, when they were asked, "Do you follow the teachings of the church of Jesus Christ in your private and public behavior with members of your family and others?" they must've conveniently forgotten that they were using their daughter as a punching bag.

Dad and Carol were sealed in the temple in August 1970, but that was only the first step to an eternal family. After going through the rituals, adult members of the church received temple garments they had to wear under their regular clothing 24/7 as a physical reminder of their covenants and relationship with God. Later, the children needed to be sealed to the couple as well, though that had to happen later. Most importantly, it was time for them to go on another honeymoon, and this time, they decided to celebrate in Aspen, Colorado. When they returned a week later, Dad and Carol discovered Mark and Pam had fled once again, though Beth and Anna took the heat this time, since they were in charge.

In just one short year, Linc, Debi, Tom, Mark and Pam were all gone, and our big house in the fancy Garden Park Ward felt a lot emptier with five kids in it instead of ten. Messer and I moved into Tom's old room, which was the largest upstairs and a significant upgrade. One lazy weekend morning, Messer and I were in bed discussing how we could delay our Saturday's work. As if on cue, Carol walked in with a list of chores in her hand, wearing her usual cleaning attire of paint-splattered Bermuda shorts with her temple garments hanging well below the hem and the previous night's mascara smeared under her eyes. Carol seemed more chipper than usual, so we immediately grew suspicious.

"You girls better get up and get busy!" she said. "You only have a couple of hours to get your work done, so I've cut your list of jobs in half, just this time. Beth and Anna will have to do theirs when they get home." Messer and I shot each other a look and wondered whether Carol had lost her mind.

"Guess who's in town and wants to take you to lunch?" Carol continued.

"Who?" We chirped in unison.

"Joyce—your mother! She wants to pick the twins up at 11 am and take them first, then she'll come get you two at one o'clock." Messer and I flew into an embrace, flabbergasted by Carol's unexpected announcement. We hadn't heard a peep from Mom in four years! Just then, Beth and Anna barged in and joined in on our celebration. We were all giddy with excitement and squealing with joy.

"Calm down," Carol interrupted, dampening the mood. "Let's not get too carried away, girls. Now, get cleaning if you want to go."

The twins swept, scrubbed and shined in record time that morning, alight with the news of Mom's impending arrival. While gathering more cleaning supplies from the basement, I saw Dad grab a tennis racket from the top shelf of the game closet. He was wearing embarrassingly short shorts that were light blue, highlighting his milky white legs. Dad's garment-wearing rules were laxer than most, and he boasted many times that we were "liberal Mormons." I didn't know what he meant, but most of the time it just meant that he thought the church's strict rules simply didn't apply to him—especially if they weren't convenient.

"You're not going to be here when Mom comes to pick us up?" I inquired.

"Hell no," he answered, starting to walk out the back

door to make himself scarce. "I don't want to ever see that two-bit bitch whore again."

Messer and I worked fast that morning, but it was hard to keep focused with our upcoming lunch on my mind. The last time I had seen Mom, I was eight years old, and now I was 12. It felt like I had lived just as much without Mom as with her. In fact, I barely remembered her. We hadn't seen or heard anything from her, and I wondered if she had ever even tried to get in touch with us. *Maybe Carol and Dad intercepted her mail,* I thought. *Maybe she's coming to check on us and take us away with her. Or maybe she's planning to move back to Salt Lake.* I shut my eyes tight and strained to picture her face, but nothing came to mind.

Even after our required baths, we were ready an hour before Mom's expected arrival time. We sat patiently on the couch in the living room, careful not to mess up our hair or our neatly ironed dresses that Carol had laid out for us.

A million questions raced through my mind, the biggest one being: *Can Messer and I come live with you?* As soon as I thought of it, I took off running up the stairs to grab a couple of items just in case she said yes. Dad had told us all repeatedly that she didn't want us, but maybe he was lying. I grabbed a toothbrush, my favorite yellow-haired troll and the unmailed letter to Mom that I had rewritten after the first one was burned, shoving them into my small white purse.

Messer was kneeling on the couch and looking out the front window.

"Where did you go?" she asked. Before I could answer, she pointed and shouted, "Look! Mom's car just pulled up!"

We watched Mom help the twins out of the back seat. Anna was smiling as she gave Mom a big hug around her waist, but Beth ran straight for the front door, and it appeared as if she had been crying, her cheeks flushed and eyes red. We made a move to greet Beth, but before we could get a word out, she flew up the stairs. Messer and I looked at each other confused, shrugged our shoulders and approached Carol, who was standing at the front door watching Anna say her goodbyes.

"Okay, you two, it's your turn," she said. "Go on out and have a good time."

Messer and I sped out the door in a flash. Anna still had a tight grip around Mom's waist, and Mom was gently trying to peel her off. She glanced up at Carol, who had changed from her frumpy work clothes into tight black pants and a turtleneck sweater with fresh makeup on her fake smiling face. Neither of them waved to each other, and I wondered why Carol wasn't coming outside to greet her. *Weren't they happy to see each other?* I thought.

As Messer and I reached the curb, Anna finally released her grip and wiped the tears from her face. She stood watching us as Mom leaned down to pull Messer and me into a hug.

"Are you hungry?" Mom asked. "I hope so because I want to take you to lunch. Is that okay?" Wracked with anxiety, questions and excitement, we smiled and politely nodded.

"Time to come in, Anna," Carol called out. Our deflated sister reluctantly headed toward the house, walking backward with her eyes fixed on Mom.

Before we pulled away, Mom rolled down the window and lit a cigarette. I couldn't take my eyes off her; she looked so different. Heaps of dark hair were piled up high on her head, sprayed into a giant beehive. Short stiff bangs framed her big brown eyes, and she wore pretty makeup, which was perfectly applied. She also looked thinner than I remembered. I wondered if we looked different to her, too.

We drove past Liberty Park, and I noticed that as Mom smoked, her fingers shook ever so slightly. We didn't say much as we headed downtown and pulled into the lot behind Dee's Family Restaurant. My ever-famished stomach rumbled in anticipation. I hadn't eaten all day, but I suddenly felt like I might throw up.

Once we were inside the diner, we settled into a brown booth with Mom sitting across from us. Messer and I clasped hands under the table.

"How do you like your new house, honey?" she asked. "How is school?" A lump formed in my throat.

"It's good," I replied, but I was having a hard time answering her simple questions. All I could manage were one- or two-word responses. I didn't want to talk about little things. I wanted to know why she left us, when she was coming back and most importantly, if we could move away with her—but none of those sentences came out of my mouth. Instead, I bit into my hamburger and forced down a few fries.

"What's it like in Reno?" I eventually found the nerve to ask. "How's your job as a compulsive gambler?" Mom laughed.

"Is that what you've been told?" she said. I nodded as she shook her head.

"I can climb clear to the top of our willow tree!" Messer chimed in.

"That sounds dangerous, Melissa. Please be careful,"

Mom warned. No one had called Messer her given name for a long time, so it sounded foreign to us when it spilled from her lips.

During our lunch date, Mom ate nothing. She just smoked constantly and sipped her coffee, leaving a mocking pink half-smile under the cup's rim. Unable to control the urge any longer, I went over to her side and snuggled up against her, wrapping my arms through hers.

"We don't know where Linc and Tom are," I said with a sigh. Mom ran her fingers through my stringy hair and tipped my chin up.

"Oh honey," she said. "Carol didn't tell you? Tom is living with me now. He called me from the boys' ranch a few weeks ago hysterical because he had heard he was being sent to a working farm in the middle of nowhere. He begged me to come get him, so I drove up one night and got him released. I didn't let Carol know until I had him safe at home with me. I thought they would have told you kids."

Before I could say anything in response to this information bomb, she added, "He's not staying long though. He's angry and hard to live with—all he does is sleep and play guitar all day. I can't take much more."

Our rail-thin waitress, sporting too much eyebrow pencil, appeared with the check, and Mom dug into her purse to pay. Messer, oblivious to our conversation, was swiping the last bit of ketchup off her plate with her index finger. I took one last bite of my burger, but midway down it got stuck in my throat—much like the rest of the questions I had for my mother.

Afterward, we walked over to the large department store called Grand Central that sat on the corner of Ninth South and State Street. I had only been inside a couple of times with Carol, so I was excited to explore. I inhaled the beloved aroma of bubble gum and plastic as we went through the door. Inside, the bright lights made everything look new and shiny. We walked up and down the aisles and cruised the jewelry section. My hand lingered a little too long on a delicate silver necklace with a turquoise pendant. I looked around to see if Mom was watching, but in a flash, I remembered the candy-stealing incident and quickly withdrew my hand as if the charm were a hot potato. I didn't want Mom to know about my thieving desires.

After Mom bought her cigarettes, shampoo and lotion, she asked us if we would like a souvenir. "Something to remember our visit?"

"Yes, please!" we exclaimed.

There was a coin-smashing machine that stood in the store's lobby. When Mom dropped a quarter in, we watched it fall through a maze of colorful obstacles, finally landing onto a small flat surface. The machine sandwiched the coin, smashing it into an oval and printing the day's date on it. When it was spit out of the slot, it was still warm. I pressed it to my cheek and examined it. I stashed it in my purse with my other things and silently vowed I would keep it forever.

"Okay girls, time to go home," Mom declared, sighing with exhaustion. Her eyes had a faraway gaze. At that moment, it became utterly clear that she had every intention of dropping us off with our little souvenir rather than taking us to Reno. I realized Dad might have been telling the truth —maybe she didn't want us. Five minutes later, we were pulling up in front of our house.

Messer and I got out of the back seat and waited for

Mom to open her door. When she didn't, I grabbed her handle trying to be helpful, but she held it tight and rolled down the window. "Oh honey, I have to go. I'm not going to get out. Come give me a kiss."

Mom glanced up at the house and saw Carol on porch patrol. Carol held up her hand for a quick wave and half smile, but Mom looked away. Messer and I leaned in through the window to kiss her on the cheek, politely thanking her for lunch and our souvenir. I couldn't believe our time was already over! I had waited four long years to see her, and all we got was two measly hours and a two-bit coin. I wanted to tell Mom about the letter I had written to her. I wanted more time, but when I saw the tears welling up in her eyes, I turned away. Messer had already gone in the house, running under Carol's arm through the open door. I started up the walkway but abruptly turned back.

"Wait, I have something for you," I said. Both of Mom's hands were gripping the steering wheel tight as she turned to me, forcing a smile. I hoped Carol couldn't see what I was doing as I reached into my bag and handed the crumpled letter to her, relieved to deliver my message. I dropped it in Mom's lap and turned to run toward the house without looking back.

Later, the four of us had all changed out of our fancy luncheon outfits into grubby play clothes, hoping we might feel like ourselves again, but it was impossible. Everything was different now that Mom had made an appearance. I went to my room and taped the coin to a page in my tiny diary where I usually just rambled on about boys and crushes. Finally, Messer and I made our way to the twins' room and tapped on the door.

"Go away!" Beth hollered.

"Leave us alone," Anna followed.

Messer and I slid down the wall, thudding onto the hallway floor. Leaning in toward Messer, I whispered, "I gave Mom the letter." Messer's teary eyes met mine.

"She doesn't care about us anymore," she whispered.

Our hushed voices must have intrigued Beth and Anna, because soon they came out of their room and joined us on the floor. Their faces were red and puffy.

"What are you guys being so secretive about?" Beth asked, closing the cover of her journal as she waited for an answer. The twins were more dedicated to journaling than I was; it was a habit strongly encouraged by church leaders. Beth's journal was a red velvet book and Anna's blue, both prettier than mine.

"What do you think?" I said with a sneer.

"She looks so weird," Messer mumbled.

"Did you know Tom lives with her now?" I said a little too loud. Anna and Beth simultaneously started blubbering again.

"I hate her!" blurted Beth, causing Anna to close her eyes, plug her ears and rock back and forth in place. The stairs creaked as we saw Carol's shadow moving across the wall. We went silent, and I wondered how long she'd been listening.

"So, how was the visit with your mom, girls?" she asked. In no mood to talk to Carol, Anna and Beth burst into tears and ran back into their rooms, slamming the door behind them. I heard a faint "It was awful" from Beth, but I don't think anyone else caught it. Messer shot a nervous look at me. All I could mumble was: "It was good."

"Look what we got," Messer said as she held up the souvenir coin.

"Oh, that's nice," Carol replied with a hint of sarcasm.

"Did you know Tom lives with Mom now?" I asked nervously.

"Yes, your mom called us about a week ago to let us know he had run away from the boys' ranch and taken a bus to Reno." I knew she was lying, but I let her finish. "Poor Tom. I don't know what he'll do with himself. Now that he's an adult, he'll have to figure it out on his own." Her voice trailed off as she walked down the hall, picking pencils and scraps of paper off the floor.

Dad never even asked us about Mom's visit, and from that moment on, we knew instinctively to add it to our list of unmentionables. Besides, it was obvious that Mom wasn't coming back—she may as well have been dead and buried. Our hopes, like our cheap souvenirs, had been smashed for good.

Chapter Thirteen
June 1971

As Dad and Carol became regular temple-goers, a wave of drastic changes rippled through our household. Carol was a devout Mormon, so she put a great deal of energy into guiding my heathen father and his motley troops toward the light. Seemingly overnight, new rules were instituted like going to church every Sunday. Our appearances now mattered greatly, especially since Dad had formed some lofty political aspirations while he was in law school. We were expected to dress well, act appropriately and show up at Sunday school with big smiles on our faces. It was all a far cry from the years in The Avenues, where I was the ratty, tough, bug-eating street kid. And now that my long-haired, unkempt hippie brothers were gone, Carol reined us in and whitewashed our lives with a vengeance.

Despite the appearance of having a traditional marriage, Carol had a lot of power in our family—especially when Dad wasn't around, which was more often than not. He was too busy with law school and his big plans.

"If I'm going to graduate at the top of my class, I've got to eat, sleep and drink the law," he'd exclaim over dinner, waving his pork chop like a judge's gavel. Apparently, with the "loads" of money she'd gotten from her divorce settlement, Carol was able to pay for my dad to finish his degree.

I resisted Carol's new world order more than Dad, Messer and the twins. I even tried to persuade my sisters to jump the line now and then by saying things like, "Who does she think she is, coming into our family and trying to change us?" I focused on winning Messer over to my side, but she had evolved into the peacemaker of the family and never wanted to make waves. Since my sisters seemed to enjoy our new church-infused lifestyle filled with ward picnics, social volleyball games and sleepaway summer camps, my rebellion was squelched before it could ever take off.

Carol's new motto was "shape up or ship out," as swiftly demonstrated by the "shipping out" of my two brothers, and in that environment, I was only getting angrier and angrier. Everything I was feeling made me want to break the rules even more. Fortunately, my neighbor Sarah, who lived three houses down in a two-story Tudor house with all the trimmings, gave me plenty of opportunities to do just that. My parents didn't approve of me playing with Sarah because even though she was Mormon, she and her family rarely attended church, which made Carol suspicious. I idolized Sarah, but I was also intimidated by her family because they drank and smoked (and on occasion, so did she). I had seen plenty of it growing up, but Carol talked about church teachings so much that I was starting to think maybe she was right—maybe those kinds of vices *were* evil. Even Dad had recommitted to his garment-wearing church obligations and had once again stopped smoking, drinking and cursing.

One Saturday, I finished all my chores earlier than usual. Debi had come for a visit, so Carol's mood was elevated by having her eldest kid around, so she was feeling especially generous and agreed to let me sleep over at Sarah's house. I stuffed my smiley-faced bag with my best (though slightly tattered) PJs, a toothbrush and a hairbrush. Slamming the door behind me before Carol could change her mind, I raced all the way down the street to Sarah's, ignoring the cramp in my side and the fact that my Keds were too tight. With so many pairs of feet to fit in our house, new shoes were a scarce commodity, so I had learned to live with the dull ache of cramped toes. As I rang the doorbell, I wondered what we'd do that night or how I should act. I didn't have much experience with Saturday night sleepovers.

After she came down to get me, we disappeared upstairs into Sarah's bedroom, where the sweet scent of cheap strawberry perfume lingered. Lying on her flowery bedspread, I surveyed the room with its pink shaggy bean bag chair, white vanity and collection of trolls in the bay window. It all seemed so frilly and fancy, like a princess's suite compared to the unadorned, cluttered room that I shared with Messer.

As Sarah and I began planning our evening, her groovy mom, Val, in a psychedelic paisley mini-dress, came upstairs to check on us with a plate of cookies and the newspaper in hand.

"Why don't you girls go see a movie?" Val suggested from the edge of the bed.

"Far out," chimed Sarah, grabbing the newspaper and spreading it before us. "There's a movie at Tower Theatre at six o'clock." She pointed at the page and then looked up at me with mischievous eyes. "We could walk there."

Walking around at night without a grownup seemed like a red flag, and I knew my parents wouldn't approve, but I nodded yes anyway because I didn't like conflict. Before I knew it, we were strolling through our quiet neighborhood, headed toward the theater. Feeling rather grown-up, I took a big deep breath and tried to allow myself to enjoy this first taste of freedom.

We gabbed nonstop as we moseyed down the winding streets that led to the Tower Theatre. The marquee was advertising *Bananas* starring Woody Allen. I had no idea who Woody Allen was; I was just happy to be out of the house. I bought buttered popcorn and chocolates with my babysitting money, eager to impress Sarah. We settled into our seats, and I was charged with nervous energy as the theater grew dark.

The movie was kind of funny, a little raunchy and way above my head, but I was thrilled to be in that dark space eating Milk Duds with my friend. In certain scenes, Sarah's face lit up and I watched her smile and laugh, which made me do the same. When we finally left the theater, it was just getting dark.

"Let's go back to your house and play games," I suggested, feeling a bit uncomfortable. I knew darn well I was not supposed to be out after dark. Sarah hesitated a little.

"Why don't we go find Kenny and his friends?" she suggested. "They're hanging around somewhere nearby."

Again, I didn't protest. I was both nervous and curious to learn from her since she was so much more experienced with boys. My gut was telling me that something bad was going to happen and that I should just go home, but I ignored it and went along.

As we walked, Sarah rambled on about her boyfriend, Kenny. I couldn't understand the appeal of hanging out with boys, but she was determined to convince me that they all weren't all noisy, smelly troublemakers.

"They can actually be really fun and nice," she said. I still thought boys were cootie-covered scalawags that were best to just avoid. Rounding a corner, we saw three figures in the distance. All five of us gathered in the shadows next to a streetlight. We were all around the same age. Kenny, who was a year ahead of us in junior high, dominated the conversation. He was flexing his teen-boy wit like a bird flaunting its plumage.

Lanky with gray eyes, glasses and long, greasy red hair, Kenny looked like a hood—just like the type who smoked outside our junior high school building and that I tried to avoid. He sure looked ugly to me, but Sarah seemed smitten as she laughed and laughed with him (even when he wasn't remotely funny). Standing there hanging out with the bad kids, I wondered what my friends from church would think. Kenny's buddy Ed offered me a cigarette a couple of times, but I passed. My warm memories of sneaking smokes with Bodie had been replaced by the vivid, traumatic memory of being caught smoking in the fifth grade and the backhand and suspension that followed.

Someone suggested doorbell ditching before one of the boys bragged he was house-sitting for a neighbor.

"Why don't we go swim in their pool?" he said. Everyone thought this was a grand idea—everyone but me, that is. We headed over to his neighbor's house and entered the back-yard, trying to keep our voices low. Still, our laughter and shushing was loud enough to make the neighbor's dogs bark. Undeterred, we started jumping in the pool, fully clothed. When it was my turn, I felt a stabbing sense of dread in my belly, but I knew I had to join in or risk being labeled a "goody." I leaped into the pool, my nose suddenly burning from the rush of water. We splashed around until the neighbor's back porch light flicked on, prompting us to flee. My hands shook as I hid in the bushes. Finally, the investigating neighbor went back inside, and we all started walking back to our homes.

We were coming back well after the movie ended and were now soaking wet, so Sarah and I devised a story to tell her mom. I knew it was important to get our stories straight in case our parents checked with each other. I wasn't too worried; Sarah's mom was much cooler than my parents, and I thought of myself as a professional liar.

As we tiptoed through her back door, we found her mom waiting for us in the kitchen.

"What were you two doing?" she asked seriously. Immediately, we shared the story we'd rehearsed: on the walk home, some kids had turned on their sprinklers and got us soaking wet. Her mom didn't seem too upset until she turned to me with a serious face.

"Your parents want you home," she said. "I called them because I was worried and thought maybe you two had gone to your house." My entire insides felt like sludge as I slung my smiley face bag over my shoulder and said goodbye.

I should just keep walking, I told myself. *I can't go home;*

I'm soaking wet. They're going to kill me. I should just run away right now.

As I approached the long driveway, I felt a warm stream of pee running down my already cold and wet pants, right into my shoes. As soon as I reached the back porch, I saw Carol sitting on the yellow metal stool by the stove. She seemed as angry as a hornet, and her face was beet red. *Stick to the story*, I thought. *As long as she believes it's not my fault.*

As I came through the door, everything went into slow motion. Both Carol and Dad barked, "Where the hell have you been?"

"Remember, there's nothing I hate worse than a liar," Dad yelled before I could answer, "*so tell the truth!*"

"After the movie, we walked around the neighborhood and found some friends," I calmly lied. "On the way home, someone turned on their sprinklers, and that's how we got all wet." Dad's face turned a deeper shade of purple, like a pressure cooker about to explode. At the time, my father was still in his first year of law school and planning his career as a prosecutor. In his best court appearance voice, he warned that if I didn't tell the truth, he would hook me up to a lie detector.

"All my friends are judges, and I'll make you testify under oath to get to the truth if I have to," he said. I stuck to my story as more pee ran down my leg. Once I thought everything was under control, I convinced him to call Sarah to verify everything. Dad picked up the phone and spoke to her and her mom briefly, but as soon as he hung up, I could tell he saw through our paper-thin alibi.

Carol had heard enough. "Ted, go get the belt," she hissed. Dad looked at her and then stared back at me, unnervingly quiet. He stormed out of the room, apparently convinced he could beat the truth out of me. As Carol waited for Dad to reappear, she kept her eyes fixed on me. Her lips were pinched, and her face was full of contempt. When Dad came back, he was holding a brown leather belt that was doubled up. In all my 13 years, I had never seen either of them use a belt on anyone in the family before, so I assumed they were just trying to scare the truth out of me.

Dad pushed his red hands together, making the belt form a circle and then quickly yanked them apart. The belt made an awful loud *snap!* The muscles in my body tensed and twitched at once. Still, I tried not to flinch. Abruptly, Dad pushed me toward the kitchen sink and forced me to turn my back.

"Take off your shirt," he commanded. "Now, take off your pants." I stood there in my wet bra and underpants with goosebumps all over my pale skin, hanging my head in utter embarrassment. My dad put both my hands up on the cabinets above me.

"Spread your legs," he barked like a cop. He was standing close enough that I could feel his hot breath on my neck. Then I felt a sharp, searing pain on my back as a loud *snap!* exploded in my ears.

"Tell the truth, goddammit!"

Snap!

"I'll have you arrested!"

Snap!

"I'll have you thrown in jail!"

Snap!

I bit my tongue so hard that I had to spit a huge mess of

blood into the sink. *I won't cry,* I thought over and over again. *I won't cry!*

He whipped me nine more times—one for each year of my life, I suppose—and I could feel the welts forming across my back and upper legs. Even though my skin was burning, my mind was empty and I felt numb. Whatever strength I had left faltered, and I crumpled to the floor.

"That's enough, Ted," Carol announced, still sitting on the stool with her arms crossed tight and face unemotional. "Go up to your room. We'll deal with you in the morning."

I got up, wiping the bloody drool from my mouth, and pushed my sweaty hair from off my face. As I walked toward the stairs, I could hear muffled sobs coming from above. When I made it to the top, I found Anna, Beth and Pam lying on the floor in a huddle, bawling.

"Watch out," I tried to warn them, my voice quivering. "Dad's coming. He'll hear you!" They didn't waste a single second, racing to their rooms. As I struggled to change into dry clothes, Messer woke and came over to see why I was sobbing. Seeing the welts, she burst into tears. She handed me a baggy T-shirt to put on and I gingerly crawled into bed with her, trying to find a way to position my body so I wasn't lying on my now-oozing wounds. Face to face with my little sister, we vowed that we would run away, just like the others before us.

"I hate Carol!" I spewed. "And Dad's gone crazy. We've got to find Mom's house in Reno so we can go live with her!"

"I'll go with you," Messer exclaimed with big, empathetic eyes.

I never told the truth about where I was that night, and no one ever spoke about what had happened to me. I expected sympathy from my siblings, but something was happening with my older twin sisters. I could see that they were starting to see me like Carol did: as "the bad kid" in the family. I started to think maybe they were right.

Feeling happy in my family felt like it would only ever be a memory—but when I tried to think back, I couldn't even remember any memories of my mom and dad happy together. Maybe seeing Dad and Carol together was making them fade, or maybe they never existed at all. *If Mom and Dad were always so miserable, why did they even have me?* I thought. *I wish that Dad never married Carol, or that I'd even been born—I wish Mom and Dad had never even met!* I didn't say anything like that to Messer; instead, we just hugged each other. She held my hand while I cried myself to sleep, but I think she cried even harder.

Excerpt from Joyce Cannon's
Journals

Falling in Love, 1949

Though Ted's family had lived around the corner from us for years, he and I didn't run with the same crowd. My life was bound by school, church and family, and, since he didn't go to church and was a year ahead in school, we rarely saw one another. When I was 17, he started coming to church. He was in college by then and seemed much more sophisticated than most of the boys I dated. He was also in the ROTC, which was considered extremely nerdy by my friends, but when he invited me to the University of Utah Military Ball, I couldn't say yes fast enough.

It was a formal affair and he wore his officer's uniform, in which he looked very handsome. I wore my frilly pink dress with my first orchid corsage pinned to the shoulder. We double dated with friends of his and the evening was a blur of dancing, laughter and fine dining. Ted was at his funny, charming best, and I was dazzled.

My other boyfriends suddenly seemed boring, and I could hardly be bothered with them unless I wanted to go to some high school shindig that Ted wasn't interested in.

Ted was always a perfect gentleman, and as we went on date after date, I became increasingly bewildered. Most of my dates with other boys ended with either some heavy necking, me fighting my way out of the back seat of a car or both. So what was up with Ted? (No pun intended.)

One evening after we'd been playing tennis (our sixth date), he kissed me. It was the sweetest, most romantic kiss I'd ever had—no tongue, no hands. He said goodnight and left. I staggered into the house, closed the door and leaned on it to catch my breath, as I'd seen Doris Day do in a dozen different movies. I floated (I swear it) up the stairs to my room and fell onto the bed, heart fluttering. I suppose I eventually got into my pajamas and went to bed, but I'm not sure I didn't stay awake daydreaming. I was smitten.

The day came when he invited me on a special date for lunch at a private club (his father was a member), which required dressing up, including a hat and gloves. Since I owned neither, I went shopping. It was far more glamor than I was used to, and Ted was witty and charming, as usual. When we got back to my house, he walked me to the door and said, "This was a goodbye date. I'm getting too involved. I have plans to go to West Point and make a career in the army and there's no place in my life for a woman." He kissed me goodbye and left.

I had never been formally jilted before. My self-esteem plummeted. I spent the next week or two alternating between crying jags and racing to answer the phone when it rang, hoping he was calling to apologize.

Somehow during this time I managed, just barely, to graduate from high school and make plans to go to business college in the fall. I slowly got on with my life, and by the time Ted called to say he'd missed me and wanted to resume dating, I was able to be a little cool. But not for long.

Once we got back together, things heated up quickly. The first time we actually had intercourse—in the back seat of his 1940 Chrysler convertible—he used a condom. It had been in his wallet so long the outline of it was permanently etched into the black leather. The second time was on the couch at home while I was babysitting my younger siblings, and apparently he had used his total supply of condoms the first time.

Growing up, I had heard women talk about getting married and then trying to get pregnant. It always sounded as if it took months of hard work before it actually happened. Well, boy, not me. I learned over and over during the next 12 years that my ovarian on-off switch was permanently stuck in the on position. If there was one live sperm anywhere in the neighborhood, it would find me and implant itself in my nurturing womb. My body craved motherhood. I, however, was ill prepared to be a mother or a wife for that matter. In those days (1949–50), you either got married or were labeled a fallen woman.

Ted did the honorable thing, faced my parents, explained the situation and told them that he loved me and wanted to marry me. I sat in a chair and cried. At that moment, Ted was an authentic hero.

My mother took me to her obstetrician and together they made arrangements for us to get married in Burley, Idaho, where he knew a doctor who would do the blood tests and waive the two-day waiting period. He apparently had a *contact at the Burley Courthouse as well, because after a judge pronounced us man and wife, with only our fathers as witnesses, the clerk backdated our copy of the wedding certifi-cate from the actual date of January 30 to January 3, a much more convenient date.*

Ted and I settled down in a tiny basement apartment and tried to figure out how to make a life together. It was less than a month before my 18th birthday and Ted was not yet 19.

UNEDITED LETTER FROM TED CANNON TO JOYCE, 1953:

Dear Honeypot—

This is just a little note on the subject of what time to awaken the lord and master of the 'ouse'old.

1. The time for awakening of said sterling individual to be not later than 12:00 o'clock midday, on the fourteenth day of March in the year of our Lord one-thousand nine-hundred and fifty-three and 99/100% pure.

2. Be gentle but firm. Be diplomatic. He must be up at that hour. Promise him that he can go back to bed after he finishes that damned paper...even make the supreme sacrifice and tempt him out of bed with the lure of your unsullied virtue et al (unless of course you-know-what has started in which case try another tack—use your initiative)...

CAUTION: No ice cubes or cold H2O pls! And remember: "It's all for the cause!"

I LOVE U TRULY

Luv
"The Chief"

Part Two
The Ballad of Ted and Joyce

Chapter Fourteen
1971-1973

After the belt incident, Carol insisted that I wear oversized T-shirts and pants all summer long, even when I was swimming. Because we were one of just a few families in the neighborhood with a pool, we always had lots of kids asking to come over and swim. It wasn't a fancy pool, just one of those above-the-ground types, but friends and family would still appear to get in it on most summer days. Normally I would listen to the radio and perfect my tan, but that summer, I covered up. Carol didn't want anyone to see the welts, scabs and eventual scars. Still, I didn't care about that. The pain in my heart hurt much deeper.

Dad "campused" me for the rest of the summer—he loved to use the word "campused" instead of "grounded," because it made him feel superior, like usual. I missed out on family picnics, lagoon trips, movies and barbecues. My friends teased me about my dad's quirky vocabulary, but I didn't find it entertaining in the least.

Something was burning deep inside of me that summer

of '71. It felt like my welts would never heal, but I was strong. I refused to let anyone see the wounds, inside or out. The man who had once protected me once against Carol after I got caught smoking was no longer there for me. He had betrayed me, moving his allegiance to the other side. *So be it, then*, I thought. *If the alliances are shifting, then so will mine.*

I soon found out that being campused meant that I witnessed more behind-the-scenes family drama than the rest of the kids who were off playing with friends. One day, I heard the sound of Uncle Ralph's sports car approaching the house, so I tossed my teen magazine to Messer's side of the bed and peeked out the faded curtains. Uncle Ralph was bringing Danny home from their Yellowstone Lake vacation. He stopped in front of the house and hoisted Danny, who was now three years old, out of the passenger seat. Danny giggled as Uncle Ralph pinched his chubby cheek, and the two of them walked hand-in-hand to the front door.

I lost sight of them as they disappeared under the stoop, but suddenly thunderous yelling broke out. As if I had balcony seats to a Clint Eastwood movie, Dad and Uncle Ralph tumbled back into view as an intertwined ball of fury rolling across our lawn. I couldn't help but lean forward for a better view.

"You two-bit, sonofabitch," Dad yelled, trying to separate himself from Ralph, "get the fuck off my property!" Uncle Ralph was on all fours and wobbled like he was dizzy as he struggled to get back to his feet. He was leaning to one side and looked like he might fall over again, but instead, he took a step toward my dad and threw a punch square at his face.

Dad stumbled back, catching himself and barely staying upright before disappearing under the stoop again.

"You crazy motherfucker!" Uncle Ralph raged. "I know you've been beating these kids! I heard what you did to Diana! I'll have you arrested for child abuse!" My dad didn't bother to respond, and though I couldn't see him, it sounded like he may have retreated into the house. Uncle Ralph stepped back into view, attempting to smooth his black hair into place and brush grass off his pants.

I thought the brawl was over until my dad came back to confront Uncle Ralph, only now he had a shotgun pointed at him.

"I guess you didn't hear me the first time, asshole," he said. "I'll tell you once more: get the fuck off my property or I'll shoot!" Dad took another step with the shotgun still leveled at Uncle Ralph, who threw his hands into the air and slowly backed toward his car.

"Jesus Christ, Ted, you're gonna shoot me?" Dad didn't bother to answer. But he didn't lower the shotgun either. Uncle Ralph quickly opened the car door with one hand, keeping the other in front of his face. He gazed up and spotted me hanging halfway out the window, and I withdrew so quickly that I hit my head on the window jamb. Now hidden, I watched Uncle Ralph start his car and rev the engine, peeling out and leaving a patch of rubber on the road behind him. For good measure, he flipped my dad the bird as he sped off.

I learned later that I wasn't the only one watching the R-rated movie scene playing out on our front lawn. A few of our neighbors were peering through their curtains as well. *So much for making a good impression in the Harvard-Yale neighborhood*, I thought. Playing the role of good Mormon didn't seem to be Dad's priority at that moment, as he lowered the gun, mumbled "Fuck off" to the looky-loos and wandered inside.

Later that night, Messer and I were upstairs listening to *Abbey Road*, a recent purchase from my babysitting stash. We were on "Maxwell's Silver Hammer" until it was interrupted by the raucous ringing of the family dinner bell. Messer and I jolted up in bed and ran downstairs. Carol was standing under the balcony of Dad's office, slinging the bell's chain around like a cowgirl in a rodeo. When we sat down to our creamed chipped beef on toast (or "shit on a shingle" as both Dad and Carol called it), we listened to Dad lie about his swollen, oozing eye.

"Wayne and I played a tennis match at Liberty Park today, and he hit a hell of a smash ball," he said, gingerly feeling around his left eye and wincing in pain. "That's what happens when you don't keep your racket up!" Carol rolled her eyes and left the table in a huff. The rest of the meal was as quiet as a funeral.

I thought the whole thing was over until six months later, those of us still living at home were summoned to court by Uncle Ralph. He was suing Dad, claiming attempted murder and assault. He was still fighting for custody of Danny, and he needed to prove to the judge that Dad and Carol were unfit parents. I was sure that neither Dad nor Carol knew that I had witnessed the fight, so I figured I'd better keep the information to myself.

Our family attorney sat us all down to prepare us girls to take the stand and explain that we had never been abused (even though we all knew otherwise). On the day we were in court, our lawyer turned to me and asked me to point to the man who hit my dad. I never wanted to be invisible so badly. I was forced to look directly into the eyes of my Uncle Ralph and when our eyes locked, I thought I might vomit. Uncle Ralph shook his head at me, silently communicating, *Please don't do it.* I quickly glanced at Carol, who was smiling at me and nodding reassuringly. *You're doing the right thing,* she seemed to say. I could barely lift my arm to point at the so-called perpetrator.

Thanks in part to my testimony, Uncle Ralph was charged with assault and battery and lost the custody suit, and Dad and Carol later whooped in victory. It was determined that Uncle Ralph had thrown the first punch and that Dad was simply defending his family and his home from this crazed animal, but I certainly knew otherwise.

After the chaos with Uncle Ralph died down, Carol spent hundreds of laborious hours designing the perfect family tree for her newly established professional genealogy business. She threw herself into the project with vim and vigor, determined to map our history like so many other dedicated Mormon women who spent hundreds of hours researching and organizing their family genealogies (second only to journaling and scrapbooking every aspect of their lives).

In the Mormon world, it seemed like there were few things more important than anything related to genealogy. If you went into someone's home and *didn't* see a family tree hanging on the wall, it would be surprising. The image on Carol's genealogical tree was simple: black ink on ivory-colored paper depicting an entire family's foundation and growth. She even sold her template to the Mormon Church, and her distinct design became part of their official Genealogy Family Tree line of products. They were a hot commodity in the church community and a shining achievement for our stepmother.

As I stared at our family tree, it seemed strange to see Mom's name next to Dad's. I wondered if it bothered Carol, or if Mom would even want to be a part of this family. She had been MIA since 1966, except for that one measly lunch date at Dee's Diner. I was tempted to scratch her name off but decided against it.

Three years had passed since our sad little lunch, and I hadn't heard from Mom other than the occasional birthday or Christmas card. It was clear that I was stuck with Dad and Carol, and I didn't have any fight left in me.

Dad had graduated from the University of Utah law school and joined a small firm in Salt Lake City, which ironically specialized in civil and domestic suits. My sisters and I immersed ourselves in the ward by playing church sports, singing in the choir, heading community service projects and praying daily. The twins dove into church life with zeal, feeling that "burning within" meant you were on the right path. To make matters worse for me, they were perfect students, too. I wasn't about to measure up spiritually or academically, so I focused on being cool and popular.

I tried to distinguish myself from their churchy ways, teasing them relentlessly when they joined the seminary choir, which I thought was the all-time nerdiest thing on the planet. Early each morning we walked in the dark to seminary class (a daily church education program held before school started). While optional for most, Carol insisted we go, so naturally, I enrolled but hardly ever attended. The twins performed with the seminary choir all over the valley on Sundays, adorned in matching high-collared, red-and-white gingham dresses. I told all my friends they were "Sem-Queers," a nickname they didn't find funny whatsoever.

Coinciding with my academic failures, my church studies were even more disastrous. I found I was loving the church social scene and was making some great friends, but when it came to understanding any of the scriptures or lessons, I simply checked out. Unfortunately, that spacey habit also applied to lessons on temple work that would've been helpful to pay attention to.

I was 13 when I nervously made my first trip to the temple with all of the other kids from our church class—both boys and girls, all the same age—for the Baptism for the Dead. As our church leaders had once explained to us, our job as young people was to serve as a proxy on behalf of those who had died but failed to get baptized while they were alive. Sister Delvy had explained that this temple work was both a privilege and a blessing.

"Once a Mormon child turns 12 and is considered worthy of baptism by a bishop," she said, "only then can they enter the House of the Lord to perform this sacred ordinance." I was with her on being old and worthy enough to do a sacred ordinance—even if I didn't totally understand what she was saying. It didn't matter; I'd heard enough, and my attention wandered after that. Now that my car was pulling up in front of the temple, though, I was straining my hazy memory for a little more detail.

After a worthiness interview by the bishop, deeming us righteous enough, we all sat in a row in our temple white jumpsuits. Boys sat on one side of the room and girls on the other. I watched intently as my friends were called up, so I could learn what to do. One by one, their names were called, and when they entered the font they were plunged under-water in a giant tub that was shouldered by 12 golden oxen—I know for a fact they weren't watching for every inch of skin to be covered by holy water this time, because my best friend's hair was not even completely wet when she was done. *There are so many dead people to baptize,* I considered. *I guess there just isn't time.*

I started to worry I wouldn't even have time to catch my breath between dunkings. There were two men in the font baptizing, and one stood on a platform calling names of deceased people from all over the world. Thankfully, I had been called up toward the end and only had to be dunked 15 times. Some of the people we were being baptized for had been dead for more than 150 years. If this was what it took to be a good Mormon, then I was happy to do my part—but that didn't mean it wasn't still unsettling.

I also tried hard to read the Book of Mormon, a sacred text of ancient scripture written by the original Mormon prophets and published in 1830. With strong encourage-ment from family, church leaders and seminary teachers, I would tell myself I could do it. The problem was that even when I would read one or two scriptures out loud in front of my Sunday school class, or worse yet alone, the sheer boredom of it would quickly fatigue me. But as a regular church-goer for the past five years thanks to Carol, I found myself deeply entrenched and participating in the social life of a good Mormon girl. That meant I needed to do what everyone else at my age was doing to gain my own testimony of the gospel. I was on the hunt for that "burning within" which signified the Holy Ghost was telling me something was true.

"Heavenly Father has spoken to me, and I know in my heart that the Book of Mormon is the word of God," swooned Anna, while straightening her hair. She had taken to ironing her frizzy auburn locks to look more like her twin.

"Diana, I am so proud of you for searching for your own testimony. I had the most spiritual experience of my life and I hope you will, too" declared Beth, taking my hands, her green eyes full of compassion. Beth, now 16, wore her brown hair long and straight with a part down the middle and two bobby pins holding back her bangs. I listened intently to both of my older sisters, who seemed much wiser than me. Maybe they were onto something.

I had also heard fellow church members stand up during our monthly fast and testimony meeting, bearing their souls before God. I found fasting to be the worst part because we had to skip breakfast. The idea behind fasting was to strengthen one's spirituality, but I was an utter failure at it most of the time. If I felt the least bit of a tummy growl before walking to church, I panicked. On most occasions, I'd sneak a piece of bread or whatever else I could get my hands on. If I didn't eat, skipping breakfast made attending three hours of church even more miserable. I preferred the testimony meetings to regular sacrament meetings because Carol brought Cheerios for Danny to keep him quiet, and he would always sneak me a few. Munching on the O's, we'd listen to various members stand at the microphone and tell stories of their spiritual experiences and how their testimonies of the church had been strengthened that week or month. Inevitably, there was a lot of crying and sniveling.

You could also count on the women to publicly declare, "My cup runneth over!" followed by "I have a testimony that this is the one and only true church of God," while fanning their faces and choking back tears. This weekly hour proved to be more entertaining and far better theater than listening to a member give a boring talk and read from scriptures during the sacrament meeting.

I listened to young children, family and friends bear witness that they had experienced the "burning within" and knew right then and there that the Mormon Church was the only true church according to God. I was curious about it, but I could barely make it through the first two paragraphs of the scriptures without waking up with drool running down my chin.

Now that I was 14, I felt a little pressure to figure this all out. I mean, Joseph Smith had already been a prophet at 14, but I hadn't even managed a spark of feeling, let alone an entire burning bosom. Determined, I got comfy, stripped down to my underwear and got under the covers in my white canopy bed, which used to be Debi's before she outgrew it. I picked up my scriptures and settled in for the long haul, letting my fingers wander. Skipping the introduction, I went straight to the book of First Nephi (a prophet from around 600 BC) and read about five pages, surprising myself that I had actually made it that far! In fact, I was even comprehending snippets of it! My heart beat faster as I read on and on, too excited to remain still when something happened—all the energy building inside me released and I felt the promised burning within! There was no denying it: God had truly touched me. *So this is what everyone has been talking about all this time*, I thought breathlessly, *and after only five pages of the boring religious book!* I had received my promised testimony. When the feeling passed, I shot straight up and scribbled in my journal as fast I could: "I'm so happy today. I know that God lives and I know the church is true, with all of my heart!" Amen.

Chapter Fifteen
1973–1976

As I started going to East High School, I found some true friends and gave in to church life and the daily routines of my insular community of modestly dressed, family-oriented Mormons. It turned out that living life on the "straight and narrow" was the best way to keep out of trouble, even though I was not thrilled about being labeled "straightlaced." I was still scared shitless of Dad and Carol, especially now that Dad was a prosecuting lawyer. The scars on my back constantly reminded me what they were capable of, so I kept my head down and my mouth shut. Slowly, the raging fire in my belly simmered. I had learned the hard way that it was best to stay out of his path and wrath, and I never wanted to encounter the version of him that was a crazed, belt-wielding maniac ever again. I prayed that I could behave like a good child of God, like the one in the primary song I learned in church when I was young:

I am a child of God, and he has sent me here
Has given me an earthly home, with parents kind and dear
Lead me, guide me, walk beside me, help me find the way
Teach me all that I must do, to live with him someday.

While I enjoyed the melody of that tune and most of the other hymns I'd heard thousands of times growing up, I rarely paid attention to the words, especially when I was little. As I matured and started really listening to what I was being taught in church, I was starting to get confused. So many things made absolutely no sense to me.

I couldn't get past the lyrics in "Child of God." If my parents were given to me by God, and I supposedly chose them while in the spirit world, why did my one "kind and dear" parent leave? The two parents I was living with now didn't exactly fit that description. I wondered exactly what I was supposed to learn and do to live with God again. I seemed to be the only one of the girls in our household that had these questions swirling around in my head. The rest of my family was swallowing the Mormon Kool-Aid with zeal while I choking it down to fit in.

I didn't dare profess my confusion and qualms, since my father had made it perfectly clear that kids were to be seen and not heard. Only *his* opinion mattered, and we were to go along with whatever he said. Frankly, I knew my father didn't really care much about the Mormon Church or their Word of Wisdom–inspired dietary restrictions. He seemed happy to ride on Carol's spiritual coattails and cash in any political benefit that came with being a true-believing Mormon and member of the faithful community. Truthfully, he could never give up the ritual and romance of a good cocktail. Every once in a while, he would turn on the Tijuana Brass and mix up a "virgin" gimlet, which was about as virgin as Carol.

On the other hand, Dad was a proponent of the strict family rule, dictated by church standards, that there would be no dating until we were 16 years old, which made all our 16th birthdays that much more significant. Messer and I fantasized about what it might be like to hold hands with a boy as we watched Beth and Anna, envious that they were free to explore the world of young men—and they did. Beth had more dates than Anna, and when she got serious with one guy, her face constantly started breaking out from making out, so we all teased her relentlessly.

Dad and Carol continued to battle, but as we got older, we got better at tuning it out. They argued about countless things, but one of the biggest triggers was the composition of our family. Within just a few short years, Carol had basically lost three of her four children. Debi had gotten married and moved to Idaho while Mark and Pam lived with Uncle Ralph in Arizona. Only Danny, now seven, remained under our roof at Douglas Street. He was a quiet, fretful kid who got lost in the disruptive dynamics of the household. He mostly entertained himself with crafts, coloring and watching TV. He loved being in the company of us "girlers" as he called his four remaining sisters, a nickname that stuck. We would spend hours in the basement playing board games and dress up, complete with a big box of fancy hand-me-down clothes. We loved transforming him with gobs of makeup, long flowing dresses and high heels. Carol grew very protective of him, and I can't say I blame her. Danny was all she had left of her original family, so she held on to him tightly, while at the same time keeping him a safe distance from Dad.

Beth and Anna held real jobs at a local fast-food joint called Arctic Circle. It meant that they could afford to buy their own clothes, so Messer and I would sneak into their closet and steal their new tops to wear to school—but since the twins and I attended the same school, that also meant I had to try to avoid them, which I didn't always manage to do. More than once, we got into wicked catfights when we got home. Even though I was tougher and could beat the snot out of the two of them, they put up a good fight, digging their nails anywhere they could. Anna always gave up after drawing blood, satisfied to have made her point. But that gave me an advantage. Once I had only one twin left to deal with, I would roll on top of her and beat her newly developing chest with my fists.

The family drama had mostly died down, but there were still the occasional storms that ripped through our household. When Carol and Dad fought, it often ended with Carol storming out of the house in a huff. She'd climb into the green Ford Maverick, slam the door and blast out of the driveway like an Indy 500 pro, sometimes not returning for a day or two. We always wondered where she went but didn't dare ask. One time, Dad ran through the kitchen after her, wearing nothing but his white temple garments while I stood paralyzed in the corner. I wasn't used to seeing him in his funny underwear with bottoms that sagged at the butt and hung to his knees.

When he threw open the screen door in the back of our house, I thought for a minute he might chase her down the street with his garments flapping in the wind. Much to my relief, he just stood on the cement slab and spit out a long string of expletives. I had never heard him use the c-word before, so I figured something awful had happened. As I snarfed down a chunk of cheese, I wondered if Carol would be gone for good, secretly hoping so. *Had she taken a little suitcase with her?* I wondered, hopefully.

Messer was still a sweet little girl, so she despised all the cursing, often plugging her ears when the barrage of bad words filled the house. But one day she made the grave mistake of divulging to me the word she hated the most: tits.

She could barely utter the word, so offended by its ugliness and skin-crawling sound. Determined to live up to my role of being the family pest, I tormented her relentlessly. Messer could be minding her own business or doing homework, and I would lean in and exclaim in rapid-fire bursts: "Tits, tits, tits!" Never one to fight back, she put up with my annoying antics.

One Sunday, as we were both sitting stiff in a sacrament meeting, I decided to up the ante. I leaned in and whispered into her small, innocent ear, "Tits, tits, tits!" Messer jerked her head forward to get away from my cursing. Then, to resettle her feathered hairdo, she swiftly threw her head back with dramatic flair and hit the window casing behind us so loudly that the entire congregation turned around. When Carol and Dad looked over at us with daggers shooting out of their eyes, Messer and I got the giggles. Two seconds later, and almost reflexively, Messer's hair-flipping habit kicked in again, and this time she hit her head so violently that she started bleeding. Carol shot us a death stare and motioned for us to meet her in the foyer behind the window. When we got there, she ordered us to walk home, declaring we'd be dealt with later. Unfortunately, it was the other kids who ended up getting punished for our misbehavior that day.

When we got home, all the kids huddled together on the gold and green floral couch in the living room to endure a long lecture.

"You will never *ever* embarrass us like that again in church, do you hear me?" Carol said with her voice quivering. "You all act like you were raised in a barn!" She raised her hand and smacked us across the face, one by one. I couldn't take my eyes off her plum purple face and the throbbing vein in her neck. "Don't you understand how important it is for people to respect your father? To respect this family?" None of us responded as we sat silent as stones, our cheeks burning. "I talk and talk until I'm blue in the face and then I still feel like I am talking to the wall." We all gave her blank stares and she stormed off, defeated.

Later, we were called downstairs to find two older men with short, slicked-back hair and rumpled suits. They were ward "home teachers" who traveled in pairs to different families once a month to check on their spiritual and temporal well-being. As if we hadn't had enough preaching for the day, we all congregated back into the living room where our foul-mouthed stepmother had erupted at us and slapped us across the face. Now, however, she beamed as she showed off her brood. We obliged and sat obediently like little wing-fluttering angels, listening as the men talked about how Jesus loved little children. *If Jesus's "love" was like Carol and Dad's, no thank you,* I thought.

Despite our hectic, dysfunctional home life, Dad secured a job as assistant prosecutor in the Salt Lake City attorney's office. He immediately began making headlines as a ferocious anti-pornography crusader by targeting several theaters in Salt Lake City that ran X-rated films.

Occasionally, he'd recruit the four of us girls to gather our church friends and stand on State Street in front of seedy theaters to picket for his cause. Despite being clueless what *Deep Throat* was about, my friends' parents were happy to let their daughters do something good for the community. They believed Dad was acting as an instrument of God to eliminate pornography. His efforts eventually led to a city ordinance banning X-rated films in Salt Lake City theaters, all to the delight of conservative churchgoers and upstanding citizens.

Dad's career took off like a rocket after that, fueled by vehement public speeches about moral decency. He was often quoted in the paper and appeared on the local news, which added an electric current to the household. By 1976, he had joined the attorney general's office as a rising star, specializing in pornography and obscenity prosecutions. Church authorities watched Dad closely and took note. They couldn't have been happier to have him on their side, which greatly improved Dad's standing and reputation within the church. Carol was delighted, of course. And really, who cared that he had called my step-mother the c-word or that *Playboy* magazines were hidden throughout the house, or that his drawings of female body parts could be found on tablets or random pieces of paper strewn about his desk, or that he was sneaking gin on the weekend? My father, Ted Cannon, relished his new role as a man about town who was bringing pornographers and other sinners to their knees. We were proud of him, too, and eager to help with his campaigns by going door to door with anti-porn flyers—and we thought it was especially cool that he regularly appeared on television as well.

I had just turned 16 and was going into my junior year of high school when my friends started teasing me about my dad's job. Everyone in town seemed to know that Dad had to watch *Deep Throat* starring Linda Lovelace as a requirement for his work; it was all over the local news. Notations like "Tell Ted to keep fighting porn!" and "Movie night at your house?" smattered the pages of my yearbook. Most of it went over my head, as I didn't understand what the big deal was about Linda Lovelace. Still, I knew that underneath their jokes was the accusation that I was overly innocent and prudish, which made me burn with excruciating embarrassment.

At home, after my dad fought for righteousness in the public sphere, our house would swing from profanity-fueled arguments to pious scripture lessons on Sundays. My sense of faith was completely topsy-turvy, and all I could think was if we were truly God's children, he must have been extremely disappointed and worried about our family's salvation.

Chapter Sixteen
1974–1976

S omehow, with only one year of dance class under my belt and no formal training, I made the cut into the school dance company during my junior year, and I finally felt like I had a safe place to hang out in my high school. It bolstered my self-esteem, and I fell in love with the art of dance and watched my body grow stronger and leaner. My earlier childhood experiences of having to go hungry were coming in handy for once because, as a dancer, I needed to stay lean. At five feet 10 inches, I felt like an Amazon woman on the dance floor next to my petite classmates—boys included. Even though I only weighed 120 pounds, I probably could have lifted the two male dancers in our company more easily than they could elevate me. Whenever they tried, we usually ended up in a crumpled heap on the floor. Our teacher, Mrs. Hepworth, had to remove the lifts in our dances, which fully embarrassed me. I was already self-conscious enough about my height and weight.

On top of being late to mature emotionally, until the end

of my sophomore year, I also had the build of a 12-year-old boy. Once my body finally did change, however, it felt like my boobs would never stop growing. I earned the dreadfully embarrassing nickname "Diana's Cannons" because I was skinny as a rail with big boobs. I felt awkward in my unfamiliar body, but I tried to push aside my negative thoughts. I loved dancing too much to retreat. I had finally found a way to express all the frustration and pain that had built up inside of me and channel that energy into a creative form. Being in the dance company required a great deal of time and discipline and gave me an acceptable excuse to be away from the chaos.

One day, I picked up the ringing basement phone and heard an operator announce a collect call from my stepbrother Mark. I raced upstairs, calling for Carol. Once she heard it was Mark on the line, Carol practically leaped to the kitchen phone. Within seconds, she burst into tears. Pausing on the basement stairs to listen, I could tell Carol was making plans for Mark to move home and live with us again. I nonchalantly slid into the chair next to Carol at the kitchen table, thrilled at the prospect of seeing Mark, who had been gone for five years. Carol slowly put the phone back on its base, seemingly dazed.

"Mark will be coming back in two days," she said. "Ralph sent him to military school in Texas and he hates it. He says the other boys have been beating him up, so he wants to come live with us and go to school with you girls at East." I could hardly contain myself. I was so excited!

"What about Pam, is she coming, too?" I asked.

"No, Pam is staying with Ralph." With that, Carol picked up the phone to begin planning for Mark's flight back. I ran upstairs to tell my sisters the good news, and we all jumped up and down on the bed. We loved Mark, and his presence was always a good tonic for Carol's mood swings.

Mark arrived home on September 14, 1974. Oddly enough, Dad and Carol had gone bowling with their league on that anticipated evening and left the task of fetching Mark from the airport to Anna and Beth—and after begging and begging if I could go with them, they finally relented. We waited for him at the gate, and as soon as we saw his smiling, handsome face, we ran up and embraced in a big group hug. Mark seemed a little embarrassed by all the attention. Once we were in the car, with Beth at the wheel, Mark told us he had been sent to Texas against his will to a horribly strict military school for boys.

"It was like being in jail," he said, his voice cracking ever so slightly. "And my crazy Dad has Pam all messed up, too. She's doing drugs and he doesn't even care." His fury toward his father grew apparent as he got worked up over the state of his sister. "I feel sorry for her. Dad cares more about his new wife than us."

"Oh my heck," said Anna quietly, biting her fingernail in the back seat. Mark leaned over to turn up the radio. I noticed how much better-looking he had gotten, despite the little acne on his face. He was taller and had a bronze tan from the Texas sunshine.

"Where's Mom, anyway?" he asked loudly, his voice competing with the Doobie Brothers. "Why didn't she pick me up?"

"It's their bowling league night and they couldn't find a substitute, so you got stuck with us," I responded with a reluctant smile.

Mark broke into a wide grin, showing off his movie-star straight teeth. He had been in braces for two years and now had a picture-perfect smile, aside from a slightly gray color. Luckily, Messer and I didn't need braces. Poor Anna and Beth had been told by the dentist multiple times that they did, but Carol and Dad said they couldn't afford them, so Anna and Beth ended up with crossbites. It was why Anna always held her hand over her mouth when she laughed or spoke.

Mark had no problem adjusting to a new school. He kept up his academics, and his social life picked up in a hurry. He started hanging out with me more, mostly because I could introduce him to my cute friends, who were of dating age. I was the youngest of all my friends and had to wait until the end of summer before my senior year to start dating. Mark's charisma and good looks magnetized most of the 11th-grade class, so he seemed to have a date almost every night. On those occasions, Carol would loan him her mossy green Ford Maverick. Even though it was an incredibly ugly car, it was still a car, and it pissed us girls off because she rarely tossed us the keys. The only time we were allowed to drive was when Carol needed someone to run errands for her.

On Christmas Day 1974, Linc and Tom came home, marking the first time the six of us were all together in years. Linc was on leave from the Army and Tom, all skin and bones, looked famished and lost. Still, to mask the awkwardness, we all had secretly agreed not to talk about anything that had happened in the past.

I wanted to know how life was "on the outside," so I pestered them both with questions, but they barely responded or even looked at me. Tom strummed the guitar in his lap, staring at the frets through his greasy bangs. I wondered how he could see anything through such a mangy mess. Despite everyone's attempt to make them feel welcome, the boys didn't stay long. There was just too much tension in the house whenever they returned. Inevitably, Carol and my dad couldn't help themselves and would harp on the boys about the very thing that drove them away—their "goddamn hippie ways." Once again, Linc and Tom high-tailed it out of the family home.

Mark felt more like a brother to me than Linc or Tom did. Since we were the same age, I could relate to him more. As a preppy jock with clean-cut hair, he had little tolerance for lazy hippies and had no respect for my brothers. For me, Mark made Douglas Street fun and added a much-needed element of excitement. He was also a good influence on Danny, who loved having his big brother around. He followed Mark around the house like a shadow and gradually came out of his shell in his big brother's presence. Despite our differences, I hoped Carol would get to keep at least part of her family intact.

Ever since the day we testified against our Uncle Ralph in court, he had made it his mission to obtain custody of Danny. The first time I realized that something felt odd was when a strange man approached me in the school hallway and started asking me questions. After dropping Danny off at elementary school, Mark and I had split up to go to our various classes for the day, so I was all alone as the man fired a string of questions at me.

"Does your father hit you?" he asked. "Does he hurt anyone in your family? Where are your parents, and why don't they take Danny to school?"

The man had clearly been following us, so I turned and ran to my class, convinced he was Ted Bundy, the serial rapist who was all over the nightly news. The whole city had been living in fear of him, knowing that there was a kidnapper, rapist and murderer stalking the city.

That evening after dinner, we all splayed out on the floor and couch to watch television. Dad hunched over the squatty console, turning the dial and cussing that there was an emergency broadcast on every station. As soon as it mentioned Bundy and our local school, we all sat on the edge of our seats. The reporter announced that there had been an attempted kidnapping of a girl at East High earlier that morning, but thankfully, she had managed to get away.

"You hear me," Dad said, pointing his freckled finger at the four of us girls. "This filthy rotten guy is luring young girls by pretending to be injured, and then he throws them in the back of his tan VW Bug." He turned to Beth with fear in his voice and continued, "And he prefers brunettes, so you're a bigger target. This Ted Bundy fellow is a handsome guy, so girls are being tricked by his charm. Be on the lookout."

Mark nodded in agreement and interrupted Dad. "Diana and I thought some guy was Ted Bundy who was following us around at school today, but guess not."

"What guy?" Dad asked, again interrupted when Anna turned up the TV to hear more about Bundy.

Anna, Beth, Messer and I shuddered at the thought of becoming one of Ted Bundy's victims. We cuddled together that night, fretting over this evil man skulking around our neighborhood. The next time the same mysterious man appeared, Mark and I had just dropped Danny off and we were still making our way to school. A car pulled up and the man approached us.

"I'm not going to hurt you," he said, holding out both hands. I was clinging to Mark, who was now over six feet and much taller than the man walking toward us.

"What do you want?" Mark asked in a deep, defensive voice.

"I just want to ask you a few questions about your parents." When we didn't answer, he pulled a badge out of his pocket, flipping it open, just like I had seen on *Dragnet*. "I'm a private detective, and I've been hired to make sure you kids are safe and that everyone is treating you and your little brother Danny well. I need to know if anyone is hurting him." He seemed nervous, looking up and down the street.

"We are not allowed to talk to you," said Mark as he stiffened and puffed his chest up a little. "We're late for school. Now leave us alone."

The dark-haired detective didn't push us any further and stepped aside so we could keep walking. As I turned around to make sure he wasn't following us, he winked and pointed his trigger finger at me, which sent a chill down my spine.

That night, as we were all chowing down on tuna casserole loaded with peas and crispy buttered cornflakes on top, we reported the incident to Dad and Carol.

"It's that pig-headed ex-husband of yours," Dad shouted. "He's spying on us, trying to find evidence that we're not fit parents!" Carol pushed her chair away from the table blubbering and disappeared into her bedroom without even asking to be excused. That was a big no-no in our household —somewhere between the "non-chompus" edict and putting your elbows on the table.

Dad explained that Carol had "given in to the depths of depression," as he scooped up another bite of tuna casserole. Apparently, Mark's return was not enough to save her from these dark moods Her sudden departures continued, and sometimes she would check out for two or three days. She'd eventually reappear from her room, barely putting one foot in front of the other. With weary red eyes and a stoic expression, she'd give everyone the silent treatment for days at a time. It felt all too familiar, reminding us of Mom's depressive behavior years back.

In spite of whatever other drama was going on, I was so engrossed with dance that it invaded my day-to-day life at home and even in my dreams. To me, the machinations of our integrated family, six years in, had morphed into their own dance of drama and avoidance.

When things got more intense, I started having recurring dreams where I imagined myself floating on the ceiling, observing from the best seat in the house as the family choreography unfolded. Like in most homes, the dance usually started and finished center stage: the kitchen. *Dun du-du-dun-dun, da dun, da dun.* I could hear Johann Strauss II's "The Blue Danube" clearly in my head as I watched my family members gracefully enter and exit the stage, some returning and some not. Dad and Carol would appear with different costumes and masks. The beat picked up and got louder as chairs glided in and out from the table, sometimes thrown across the room with a glass dish or two. Slamming cabinets echoed like drums. *Dun du-du-dun-dun, da dun da...*I had learned long ago to tune out the words and the noise. *Just watch the performance,* I would tell myself as bodies, objects and furniture moved throughout the house.

In my mind, my dance teacher, Mrs. Hepworth, would praise me over how we made use of the entire space as she taught us to do in class.

Having dance in my life was critical to my survival at home, and it gave me more confidence in all areas in my life. Finally, I had positive role models and more friends. I felt myself walking and standing a little taller, having found my niche. The older boys had turned to music, the twins to the church and Messer to athletics (even though Carol disapproved of her un-ladylike activities). I had turned to dance.

Mark and I had a couple of classes together, so we often quizzed each other and did homework in tandem. He was a welcome example of good study habits, so I didn't want to embarrass myself in front of him by getting low grades. Thanks to Mark, I started doing better in school.

One afternoon while studying for a US history exam, Mark asked, "What did the United States Constitution replace?" I squirmed in my chair and thought hard.

"The Articles of Confederation?" Mark held his hand up and I smiled, high-fiving him and giving him a hug.

"Good job, sis!" he said, before pulling back uncomfortably. I turned to see Dad and Carol spying on us.

"You two get into the living room, now!" bellowed Carol. Her venomous tone instantly made our stomachs plunge. Dad cleared his throat and then stuttered while trying to figure out how to start the conversation.

"We think it's inappropriate for you two to be spending so much time together." Carol sat on the arm of the couch looking down at her feet as Dad paced, chewing his gum so hard I could see the muscles of his jaw bulging. "We are worried you two will be tempted to become sexually involved, if you haven't been already."

Mark and I looked at each other in complete shock. Mark coughed and then released an awkward laugh. Though I wanted to join him in laughing at the absurdity of it all, I was too scared. I just sat there, staring at my sweaty hands in my lap and picking at my fingernails.

"Well, what do you have to say for yourselves?" Carol finally chimed in.

"Nothing," I said. "Nothing except that you're both gross!" Mark couldn't contain himself any longer and doubled over in laughter. I got up from the couch and ran upstairs to my room, throwing myself dramatically onto my perfectly made bed with its pristine white coverlet and frilly pink canopy. We had come a long way from the stained bedding of my youth, but now a different kind of filth permeated the household, all hidden beneath the veneer of social standing and Christian ethics.

I was sick to my stomach. Confused and embarrassed by their accusations, I skipped dinner that night and hid in my room to avoid any further awkwardness. *I HATE THAT WITCH, I HATE THAT WITCH, I HATE THAT WITCH!* I scribbled in my journal in giant letters.

Sadly, Mark's and my relationship changed for the worse after that day. I couldn't act natural around him anymore, convinced that Dad and Carol were suspiciously watching our every move and just waiting for the inevitable. We avoided each other, and once again, my heart was broken. I was furious at Carol and Dad for destroying our friendship. To make it worse, one night I caught Carol standing over my nightstand reading my journal. I stood stunned and embarrassed in the doorway. She flung it onto my bed. "You should be more careful—it was sitting out, right in plain sight!" she lied, staring me down as she passed me out the door. I vowed that it would be the last time I ever recorded my deepest, darkest thoughts while living under their roof.

Five short months after Mark moved back to Douglas Street, he got a late-night call from Uncle Ralph, who offered to buy him a brand-new boat and a sports car if he moved back to Phoenix. What teenage boy wouldn't be tempted by an offer like that?

On February 9, 1975, Mark sashayed stage right for good.

Despite Mark's absence, things improved during my senior year when I started dating my steady boyfriend, Todd, who became my first love. He was one of the popular kids who lived high on the hill in The Avenues, which Carol referred to as "Pill Hill," referencing the wealthy snobs. Like many of the rich kids at East, Todd drove a brand-new Jeep CJ5. We'd often skip class, take the soft-top cover off and go four-wheeling in the hills above his house. He was funny, wild and crazy, and so were his friends.

Even though I felt out of my element in his crowd, I wanted so badly to break out of my nerdy reputation. I adored his unkempt brown curly hair and warm eyes and his kind and loyal soul, but it wasn't all picture-perfect. Because he was a junior, six months younger than me, I took a lot of crap from my friends for "robbing the cradle." More serious was that he smoked pot. During adolescence, I had developed a huge fear of any drugs, including marijuana, due to a combination of the church's stand against them and the scary-as-hell movies we were forced to watch about the horrors of LSD and other hallucinogens in our school assemblies. I almost broke up with him over it, but he promised he would quit. He had ambitions of going on an LDS mission, so he knew he would have to stop before he took off as an ambassador of the church, anyway.

Few things were more important to devout Mormon families and young LDS boys than preparing for a mission. Fresh out of high school, these young men would dedicate two years of their lives to proselytizing around the world, dressed in dark suits and white shirts and armed with the Book of Mormon and the Bible. The church assigned each missionary a destination that could be anywhere from Arkansas to India. Some, however, put off preparing until the last minute, which seemed to be just as acceptable as living sin-free until the day they left.

No one in our family had served a mission since Grandpa Ross, my mother and Carol's father. Carol's only hope for family missionaries lay with Mark and Danny, so she worked hard to ensure they would have the opportunity. Nothing would have made her prouder, but Mark wasn't missionary material now that he lived with Uncle Ralph. It was all up to Danny now. He was expected to attend church like the rest of us and to begin the church's training for a mission, but I had a feeling he was a lot like me—just along for the ride and waiting to exit stage right. Bravo!

Chapter Seventeen
1976

As I neared the end of my senior year, as much as I was ecstatic about the thought of escaping my crazy household, I knew I had a dilemma. My girlfriends had financial support from their parents, and I didn't.

My only trepidation about college was how I would pay for tuition, books and room and board. I had saved about $200 from babysitting and planned on working all summer to make enough money to attend university. Dad had made it clear that we were on our own to pay for college. It didn't look promising, but I was determined to find a way.

Thankfully, my senior-year instructor, Mrs. Hepworth brought me an application one day after class.

"Utah State is offering a dance scholarship," she said, "and I would like you to apply for it. I think you have a great chance." I took it as a sign from God that I was supposed to join my friends for college in the fall, so I got to work. With a lousy 2.8 GPA, I didn't feel confident that I would qualify, so with the help of Mrs. Hepworth, I began choreographing a complex modern dance routine to prove my worthiness. I practiced hour after hour with Mrs. Hepworth as my coach and mentor until I could perform my routine in my sleep.

"You're ready for this, and you deserve it more than anyone," Mrs. Hepworth announced after a grueling session. Drenched in sweat, I stared at myself in the mirror. I looked svelte as I'd been eating nothing but apples for two days, but my old black leotard and tights looked worn. I couldn't afford a fancy costume. Like she had at the beginning, Mrs. Hepworth approached and handed me a nicely folded new black shawl for a prop. I smiled as I clutched it. Her small acts of kindness were exactly what I needed to keep going.

Two weeks later, I auditioned in front of Utah State's dance department head and four other judges. Thanks to Mrs. Hepworth's tireless help, I pulled off a strong performance. I just prayed I had done enough to secure my escape plan and my future. A few weeks later, I got home from school to find a sealed envelope addressed to me from Utah State University on the kitchen counter next to my list of chores. No one was home, so I grabbed the letter and ran to my room. Shaking with raw excitement and nervousness, I opened it. All I saw were the first two words: "Congratulations, Diana!" Right away, my tears were flowing and blurring my vision. I immediately called Mrs. Hepworth, who hooted, "Hot damn! I'm so happy for you!"

It was the first time I ever truly believed in the power of prayer. I now believed in my heart that the Heavenly Father loved me as one of his children and wanted this fate for me as much as I did. Even though I still didn't know much about church doctrine, I felt there was someone watching over and protecting me. It finally clicked—all the hardships we had endured as children and young adults were simply a test from God. If I could just overcome my challenges, be forgiving and strive for perfection, I would have a chance of succeeding and ultimately obtaining eternal glory.

The front door slammed, snapping me out of my newfound revelation. Anna and Beth had returned from a day of classes at the University of Utah where they were freshmen. To save money, the twins still lived at home. When I blurted out my big news from the top of the stairs, shrieks and high shrills filled the house as they ran up to hug and congratulate me. Messer, on the other hand, immediately burst into tears when I told her the news.

"You're really leaving?" she asked, her words riddled with fear. "You can't leave me here, I'll die without you!" We hugged and cried together. The thought of living without my little sister caused me visceral pain, so we decided she could come visit every weekend with Todd. At the dinner table that same night, I had the congratulations letter tucked under my leg, waiting for the right time to share my victory with my parents. After the mandatory blessing of the food, I took the letter out from under my leg and held it up. As I read it out loud, my voice crackled nervously.

"That's great, Di," said my dad, stabbing his broccoli.

"Congratulations," chimed in Carol, who kept her full attention on eight-year-old Danny as she fixed a plate of food for him. Danny, with his crooked, almost-buck teeth and wild wiry hair, smiled at me.

"You're the first one to move away for college!" Beth said.

"It's only 80 miles away," I replied. I hoped I was acting nonchalant, even though I was practically bursting with excitement to get the heck out of Dodge.

"When I'm done with high school, I'm going to Utah State too," Messer whispered.

"Me too," said Danny. "I want to be a dancer like you."

"Boys don't dance, dummy," Dad said, turning to me. "And what the hell are you going to do with a degree in dance?" I tried to ignore the condescending question, swallowing my fear.

"Look at me when I'm talking to you," he continued. "Are you deaf *and* dumb?" His tone made my skin crawl. I tried to ignore the cramp in my pelvic floor and the feeling that a flow of urine was about to burst from my bladder. In a flash, he had transformed into someone else. He looked over the top of his glasses at me and slouched in his chair. His shirt was gaping at every button, as if about to pop under the pressure of his fat, white belly.

"I dunno," I stammered. I was frightened by the abrupt change in his personality, but I looked him straight in the eye. "Maybe I'll teach dance classes, or be a professional dancer."

"And how are you going to pay for the rest of your expenses?" Carol said, pouncing on me as well. "You'll still have room, board, food and books to pay for. You do realize you're going to have to keep a GPA of 3.5 or better, right?" She, too, had gained weight in the past few years and had stopped wearing false eyelashes and makeup. Her "all is perfect" Mormon wife façade had been broken by her hellish day-to-day reality. While these were all valid questions, I answered with a newfound confidence and determination.

"Don't worry," I said. "I'll make it work."

That summer, I worked two jobs and babysat, saving $800. I didn't have much time for dating, and despite my relationship with Todd, I was detaching from him, knowing our separation was imminent. I was so busy I didn't even care when my friends told me that Steve, an older guy who worked at the gas station across the street from East High, had a crush on me. Twenty-two seemed way too grown up, and I couldn't imagine going out with someone who was five years older than me and already a returned missionary. I purposely avoided him by changing my route, opting for a longer way home. I kept doing the same thing for weeks until one day I forgot about him and walked by the gas station, too busy daydreaming about college life. Before I had finished passing by, I heard someone call my name.

I turned to see Steve walking toward me. *Shit, how could I have forgotten?* I thought.

"Hey," he said as he approached. "I've been wanting to ask you out for a long time. Would you go on a date with me?" Caught off guard, I stammered out a few excuses as to why I couldn't—Todd, my jobs, getting ready for Utah State —but he persisted. "How about I take you to church this Sunday?" His wide smile and hopeful eyes broke my resolve.

"Sure," I responded. Church seemed harmless enough; it certainly didn't seem like a date.

That Sunday, we went to church at his mother's ward in the south part of Salt Lake, followed by dinner at her modest one-level home. She had gone to great lengths to welcome me, setting the small table with fine china, roses from her garden and candles. Over roast pork and crispy potatoes, Steve and his mom got into an intense argument, much to my embarrassment. She asked when he was going to be able to pay her back the money she loaned him, and he immediately got defensive.

"I just bought new tires, and I've got rent due next week," he yelled. "I can't pay you now! Get off my back!" I had never heard or seen anyone talk to a parent the way he did. I hated to think how black and blue I would have been if I had ever spoken to my parents like that. I felt uncomfortable and sorry for his mother because of his lack of respect. I cried on the car ride home. Steve attempted a weak apology before dropping me off, but that was it for me. I decided to never go out on a date with him again.

When summer was over and it was time to go to college, Dad and Carol helped me load a few belongings into the back of Dad's red Ford truck. I had one suitcase full of clothes, a few pots, pans, dishes, my pillow and a couple of family pictures. Eager for a new adventure, I raced around the house, pulling together last-minute things to take. I couldn't wait to be on my own!

True to her character, Carol made me do the typical list of chores that morning before we left, but she also surprised me with a lovely handmade tied quilt, white with green and turquoise flowers and just the right size to fit my dorm room's single bed. I jumped off the couch and practically leaped into her arms to hug her. She stiffly patted me on the shoulder.

"I'm glad you like it, honey," she said. As happy as I was to finally be getting the hell out, I was touched by her thoughtfulness and grateful to have a piece of her to take with me—even if I could tell she was just happy to be rid of another kid.

When it came time to say goodbye to Messer, both of us cried and grasped on to each other for what seemed like an eternity. Once we separated ourselves and wiped the tears from our cheeks, I whispered, "Tits, tits, tits!" and we both had a good laugh. The twins gave me a group hug, expressing their jealousy that I was escaping our parents' watchful eye.

I hung halfway out of the truck window and smiled as they all waved me off. Dad started up the engine, chomping on a cinnamon toothpick to quell his cigarette cravings, while Carol fidgeted with her Bermuda shorts to cover her garments. I sat quietly, overcome by the moment. I remembered playing Truth or Dare on our front lawn, Messer racing up the weeping willow tree and my first kiss on the front porch with Todd. Of course, then I remembered the sharp sting on my back as Dad cracked his belt across it and the sight of the blood-splattered sink as the Douglas Street house disappeared from my view.

Ninety minutes later we arrived on campus, which to me looked like heaven on earth. The pretty northern Utah mountain town campus lay at the base of the majestic Logan Canyon, and a hint of fall filled the air. The quad, a large grassy section of campus surrounded by historic stone buildings, was crowded that day with students sitting on blankets, playing Frisbee and lining up for ice cream. Amy, Cindy, Liz and I met there with our parents to pick up our welcome packets before unloading our belongings into the Merrill Hall dorms. The scene buzzed with nervous energy as students hustled by, moving boxes in and out of their rooms and singing their friendly greetings.

I breathed in the collage of new faces. The four of us, plus two roommates from California, were going to share a tiny, three-bedroom cinder block dorm, which we decorated right away with disco posters, family photos and ferns. I made up my single bed carefully with my bright new white quilt, which would keep me warm and connected to my siblings and the rare good memories of "home" during the coming winter months.

Other parents lingered in the hallways, fighting tears as they dropped their kids off and said their goodbyes. I pretended to be sad when I hugged Dad and Carol, but I secretly hoped I would never have to go home again. As they pulled out of the parking lot to make their trek home, I let out a yelp. The only tug on my heart was the realization of how much I would miss Messer and to some extent Todd, who kindly promised to bring my little sister up frequently for campus visits. They had their first trip planned for the following weekend.

College proved much harder than I expected at first, I fell into a rhythm in a few weeks and buckled down. I opened a checking account, learned to live on a budget and savored my freedom to come and go with no one looking over my shoulder or worrying I would be *campused*. Independence suited me.

Just a month into school, I got a letter out of the blue from Mom. It had been five years since I'd seen her, and to my surprise, she asked if she could come to Logan to visit me. A few weeks later, my mother and her friend Marcia, whom she introduced as Mart, were standing in my doorway. After awkwardly embracing, the smell of Mart's body odor and cigarette smoke made me wince.

"Why don't we take a tour?" I suggested. I needed some fresh air. As we meandered around campus, passing the school's oldest stone building from 1890 and its shimmering red and yellow maples, I felt more like a tour guide with a pair of prospective students than a daughter reuniting with her long-lost mother.

We sat down for lunch at the school cafeteria, which started out unnervingly quiet as we moved robotically through the assembly line of trays, utensils and glassware.

"Well, honey, how do you like school?" my mom eventually asked.

"Oh, it's great!" I said. "I love it here. There are so many cute boys. I've been dating a lot, and I love my roommates and my dance program. Did you know I made the cut for both the modern dance and jazz team? I'm even choreographing a dance for our concert. You guys should come." Finally taking a breath, I realized I had been talking nonstop —a nervous habit of mine. Mart sat unobtrusively by my mom's side, eating a patty melt and fries. I had barely touched my salad and noticed Mom picking at hers as well.

"That's great, honey," Mom replied with a little too much vigor. "Who knew that my baby with two dislocated hips at birth would become a beautiful, strong dancer?"

Mom looked different from what I remembered. She had turned more granola, a far cry from her blue eye shadow, pink lipstick, giant beehive hairdo and plunging neckline days. Now, she wore her graying hair short and looked like she was ready for a hike in oversized shorts, sandals and a sweatshirt. I didn't have the courage to ask about where she had been the last six years. Instead, I embarrassingly watched as my mom and Mart kept smiling and winking at each other. I was glad we were in a corner, far away from the crowds so no one would smell or notice us. It all seemed strange as hell to me, but I tried to ignore the awkwardness and focus on the fact that my mother, five years sight unseen, was sitting right in front of me.

"Do you have enough money to make ends meet, Diana?" she asked.

"Yeah, I'm doing fine," I lied.

Before they left, Mom handed me an envelope with a $100 bill, which seemed like a small fortune to me. I didn't even attempt to refuse it. As they drove off, I wasn't sure why they had come. She made no mention of returning or why she hadn't been back since I was twelve. I regretted not asking anything about the psych ward or her job, and for passing up the chance to know her better. I had been so overwhelmed by her surprise visit I had even forgotten to inquire about my brothers.

The truth was she didn't feel like my mother. *Who is this person who appears occasionally, takes me to lunch and seems vaguely interested in me for whatever reason before disappearing again?* I thought. I felt numb toward her, so I pushed the visit to the back of my mind. Instead, I focused on more important things: school, dance, dating and my growing social life.

Chapter Eighteen
1977–1978

I relished the experience of being exposed to people outside of my small protective bubble for the first time. Students from all over the world came to attend Utah State, and I could hardly believe the cultural diversity. After attending a student dance with my roommates, I was dizzy with all the choices of good-looking guys. I finally broke up with Todd a couple of months into my freshman year. We both knew it would be too difficult to keep our relationship viable, so we agreed to date other people and let our relationship end without drama (except for the fact Messer no longer had a road-tripping buddy).

"I'm glad you two broke up," my roommate Amy said as we walked to our early-morning physiology class together. The morning's frigid temperatures had created ice crystals under our noses and on our eyelashes by the time we reached the science building. Amy had an over-sized knit hat on and scarf so that all I could see were here blue squinting eyes. "Now you have more time to hang out with me!" Amy giggled and put her arm around my shoulders pulling me in close.

While it sounded good, our dedicated girlfriend time came to an abrupt halt when Amy fell head over heels for Rick, a handsome guy from the Midwest who was small in stature and an avid tennis player. Despite sharing a tiny room with her, I hardly saw her. Occasionally, I'd get home from class to find her and Rick in her single bed. "It's so cold outside. We're just snuggling to get warm," she'd giggle as she peeked out from the covers, making me wonder if they were naked. After a few days of this act, their shyness and embarrassment wore off, and I would walk in and catch them rolling around, their clothes in a bundle by the bed, hardly noticing I was there.

Thankfully, I soon met a blue-eyed beauty named Tex—his actual name was Brad, but my Merrill Hall roomies and I referred to the boys we met by their home states. Smitten by his arresting good looks and Lone Star charm, I got swept up and quickly forgot my annoyances and jealousy of Amy and Rick's lip-locked passion. Tex planned to apply to law school and seemed to know what he wanted out of life. He was witty and smart, with a sexy Southern drawl to boot. After a few months of dating, we agreed to stop seeing other people, and before we knew it, we were madly in love.

As our relationship progressed, I brought him home to Salt Lake on a couple of occasions to introduce him to my family. He had other friends who lived in Salt Lake, too, so he had an excuse to come and a place to stay when he visited. Everyone liked him, even Carol, although on our second visit she pulled me aside and said, "You better end it before you break his heart. He is not one of us, so it will never work. You're expected to marry in the temple. This is part of God's plan, Diana."

"But we love each other," I tried to explain.

"I can see you care a lot for each other, and I quite like him, too. But if we want to be a family forever, you *will* get married in the temple."

The phrase "families are forever" was a major part of Mormon culture and its belief system, and I'd been hearing it ever since I was a young girl. As part of the doctrine, the LDS Church taught that the family unit could continue beyond the grave. Any children who were born to a "sealed" couple were automatically sealed to their parents, but this only happened with temple marriage and by living the promises made in the temple ceremony. There was very little discussion—or maybe I just wasn't paying attention—about how all of this got accomplished. That was, until Dad and Carol announced that we were all able to be sealed to one another in the temple in the coming summer.

Beth got engaged to her boyfriend Robert and abandoned college. She had been determined to go to nursing school, and we were all surprised when she ditched her dream career. Their upcoming summer temple wedding dominated our household discussions, but when I asked specific questions, like, "What happens in the temple?" I was shut down with evasive answers like, "It's too sacred to talk about" or "You'll just have to wait and find out for yourself." How could I push for more information when it was "too sacred" to talk about? I figured someday I would understand, so I rallied for Beth and her wedding plans. The excitement of it had shifted the mood in the Cannon household, and I was too in love to care about anything else.

When I went back to school, I spent as much time with Tex as possible. I wasn't going to let Carol's warning deflate my newfound bliss. I didn't have the courage to talk to him about what Carol had said, since I barely understood it myself. We spent our days and nights together, taking long drives through small farm towns and hiking and picnicking in Logan Canyon. When he could afford it, we'd go to movies as well. He spoke lovingly about his family, and I could tell he cared deeply about them.

"They would love you," he declared. "You would fit right with my family." I hoped to have the chance to meet them someday.

At 18, I finally gave into my passion for Tex, but I still felt the ever-present pressure of remaining unsullied for my temple partner, who I hoped would be Tex. I fantasized that he would convert and we could marry in the temple, making everyone happy. One evening, we found ourselves alone in the dorm and made our way onto my tiny single bed. Lying on top of Carol's home-made quilt, we almost went all the way. When I was a few days late for my next period, I panicked and went straight to the library, where I learned that a woman could get pregnant without penetration. Always sweet and supportive, Tex did the right thing and took me to Planned Parenthood in Logan, where I took a pregnancy test and got the happy news that I wasn't pregnant. It was enough to scare the holy shit out of me, however, and I vowed that I wouldn't go all the way with anyone until I was married. At the time, birth control pills were out of the question, and even though I knew my girlfriends were all "getting it on," no one ever said a peep about it—and I certainly didn't tell them about my trip to Planned Parenthood.

After moving away from nosy Carol, I started keeping a journal again. That night I wrote:

Monday, April 11, 1977

I can't believe this is happening to me! I am so evil, I hate myself! Why am I so weak that I can't resist temptation? I don't deserve all these fantastic things that I have been blessed with. How can the Lord be so good to me when I am so rotten in return? I am too ashamed to write down what has happened, and I really don't know what to do. I have no one to talk to. I hate myself, I hate myself, I hate myself!

I tried to talk to Tex about my feelings, but as much as he tried to sympathize, he simply couldn't understand or relate to my shame and guilt. He also couldn't believe that I used the word "intercourse" to refer to our sex life.

"You sound like my Aunt Mabel," he said. Tex was raised Baptist and knew nothing about the temple, our strict codes of conduct or our insular Jell-O-with-pretzels Mormon world. He didn't share my newfound commitment to celibacy (and who could blame him?), but luckily for both of us, the school year was nearing an end.

As my savings account dwindled, reality was kicking in. I knew I wouldn't have enough money to finish out the year. My scholarship paid tuition, but I was running short when it came to books, rent and food. To help cover the difference, I took babysitting jobs on the weekends when I was home, but toward the end of the year, my situation looked bleak.

Messer knew of my dire finances, and occasionally I would get a letter from her with a check for $5 or $10, which was truly a lifesaver. She had a part-time job at the university pharmacy, and I knew what a sacrifice it was for her, but 10 dollars meant I could eat for two weeks!

Each Saturday, the six of us roommates would pool our money and rotate who would do the shopping and cooking that week. We mostly ate cheap cold cereal for breakfast, a scoop or two of peanut butter for lunch and ramen or macaroni and cheese for dinner. There were a few times I couldn't contribute anything for the week, but my friends were sympathetic and helped chip in more to cover for me, supported by their parents.

By the end of the semester, I was completely out of money and had to bum a ride home with a friend who was headed to Salt Lake. Though I hated the thought of moving back home after experiencing my first taste of independence, I had no choice. My plan was to secure a job, work all summer long and join Tex and my friends for another year at Utah State. I knew it was going to be a challenge. They only offered my scholarship for one year and it was not renewable, which meant I would have to save about $2,000 to return.

I took multiple jobs, determined to return to college and Tex. I worked in retail at Jack Wolfe Ranchwear, a high-end cowboy store in downtown Salt Lake, and was quickly promoted to manager of shipping and receiving. I also waited tables at a family diner, picked up shifts at a local candy shop and babysat whenever I could, stockpiling cash in my savings account as I went. I was exhausted by the time I made the bus ride home each night, but I was determined nothing was going to stop me from getting back to the Logan campus.

Toward the end of summer, I made my second trip to the temple with Anna, Beth and Messer to be sealed for eternity to Dad and Carol, to complete the rituals that they'd started years before. The ceremony involved only the four of us girls, since Debi was already sealed to her husband and Linc and Tom were long gone. Uncle Ralph called bullshit on the whole matter, refusing to let Mark, Pam or Danny have anything to do with the "crock of shit" ceremony. Ralph had grown up in Bountiful, Utah as a Mormon, but once he'd left home, he became agnostic. He and Carol lived the party life-style for a while until she decided to get back into church and asked Ralph to take her to the temple. He'd refused. Instead, she had decided to go on her own, which was likely one of the first cracks that eventually led to their marital divide.

Anna took it upon herself to write a letter to Mom, asking for her permission and blessing to be part of the cere-mony. Surprisingly, Mom wrote back immediately, and we all gathered together on my yellow smiley-faced bedspread to read her response:

July 28, 1977

Dear Anna,
Enclosed is the letter you asked me to sign. I have signed it
with mixed feelings. I feel that you are my daughters and
nothing can change that, but I won't stand in the way of
something that you feel is important in your life. I'm sure that
you are all old enough and responsible enough to decide
what's best for you and that is just what I would wish for all

of you the very best that life has to offer! Please give everyone a
hug and my love, and keep a lot for yourself.
Love, Mom

At first, we were all relieved that Mom gave us permission to partake in the ceremony, but then Anna, the most adamant about the sealing, burst into tears unexpectedly.

"Just great," she mumbled. "It was so easy for her to leave us, and now she's just giving us away!" She kept sobbing, despite our attempts to console her. Personally, I had mixed feelings about the whole sealing ceremony and didn't understand why it was such a big deal to our parents, especially since most of the time I wondered when Dad and Carol were going to get divorced. They had separated a few times, and Dad had told Carol repeatedly that he didn't want to be married anymore. They seemed to fight non-stop, and just days before the sealing, she made yet another crazed escape. Then, there she stood, sipping a Diet Pepsi for breakfast the following morning as if nothing had happened. Messer also had her reservations. A couple of days before our sealing, she and I were eating cereal when she teared up. "Why would we want to be together in the afterlife with Carol? And, what about Mom?" she asked, between bites. "I don't think we have a choice, Messer." I replied, wiping the tears from her cheek.

On the day of the ceremony, we were escorted down a short hall and called up to an altar in the middle of a white room with many mirrors that multiplied our reflections. While it was meant to represent the idea of eternity, it felt more like the funhouse at Lagoon, a popular amusement park north of Salt Lake. My favorite attraction had a long hallway of mirrors that distorted our faces, bodies and limbs. I kept searching the temple mirrors, waiting for the funny distorted figures to appear, but these were serious. It was just a million images of me, the last one the size of a pin.

Directed to come together, we all held hands at the altar, which was covered in a pale pink satin quilt as an older heavyset man with thinning white hair jabbered on about eternal families. Sweating profusely, he kept wiping his forehead with a handkerchief. As I stared down at the cluster of hands in front of me, I wondered if anyone noticed how sweaty mine were. Gazing again into the eternal mirrors behind us, it hit me hard that Danny was absent and would not be with us for eternity, and a lump began to form in my throat, constricting my airway. *Breathe*, I told myself. *Just breathe.*

After the ceremony, everyone else in my sealed family was spouting spiritual tears of happiness, but I was weeping because my brothers weren't with us, and I didn't understand why. Looking at Messer, I couldn't determine exactly what her tears meant. I wished we had talked more about what it all would mean before the ceremony started.

The sealing was over in a flash, and our eternal family drove off to celebrate once again at Sizzler. In the back seat of the car, I grabbed Messer's hand.

"So, what did you think of all that?" I whispered to her. She beamed.

"It's the most beautiful place I've ever been...so quiet and peaceful. Are you happy to be sealed to Dad and Carol?" She looked up at me with a perfect pearl of a tear in her eye. "I'm happy to be sealed *to you forever*," she whispered.

I felt tears forming in my own eyes. Messer was my

whole world, and I couldn't bear the thought of being without her when I went to college, let alone being without her in eternity. In spite of all my other heartbreak, I was warming to the promise made to Mormons everywhere that families were forever.

Tex had gone home to his family for the summer, but we channeled our affection for each other into letters and occasional late-night long-distance phone calls. I never told him about the sealing. I just knew he wouldn't understand. We made plans for me to drive to Nassau Bay, Texas to meet his family, and Anna even agreed to go with me. I tried to save enough money to make the drive, but it never happened—my earnings just didn't add up.

I had plenty of opportunities to date other boys that summer, but I turned them down because I was in love and too busy with work, so I'm not sure why I accepted another date from gas station Steve. His persistence and Carol's relentless expectations probably just wore me down. We double-dated with some friends of his, even though my heart was still devoted to Tex. I didn't really like Steve because he came off way too strong, although he did manage to impress me with his apartment in Holladay and his brand-new truck. He also caught my attention by spending a lot of money on our dates.

After just a handful of nights out, Steve professed his love for me.

"I have a feeling we're going to get married," he insisted. "I prayed about it and got an answer from God." That night, he surprised me with a Timex watch, which I refused to accept. I was adamant about pushing him away, telling him I planned on going back to college in the fall and was not *ever* going to get married. He was certainly cute enough, and I enjoyed the material attention, but I didn't feel anything close to what I felt for Tex. I prayed that I would know the right thing to do, and that I would receive a clear answer like Steve had.

After spending the summer in Texas with his folks and working at a law firm as a file clerk, Tex drove straight to Salt Lake to see me when it was time to return to school. I was working at Jack Wolfe's when he walked through the door, and one look at his steel-blue eyes made my heart skip a beat. After patiently waiting for my shift to finish, he whisked me off to dinner. Once we were inside a local pizza parlor, we talked non-stop about the summer and how much we had missed each other. Three hours flew by in a flash when the conversation suddenly turned to marriage. I knew he was someone who loved me and who would take care of me. I didn't think about all the serious ramifications of marriage, and Lord knows I had never witnessed a healthy one myself, but I knew we loved each other, and that was good enough for me. The thought of moving out and starting a life with him made me dizzy with excitement.

After Tex kissed me goodnight on the front porch, he walked backward while singing in his deepest voice and snapping his fingers.

"*Da da, goodnight, sweetheart, well it's time to go...*" he sang. Ever since we'd first met at Utah State, he sang this 1950s song to me every time we parted, and I always giggled at the show. I flew into my house swooning, giddy with love. Foolishly, I shared our evening and conversation with Carol, and her face blanched.

"He's a nice boy, but you *will* get married in the temple,

and that's that," she said. "He's not Mormon, so unless he's willing to convert, you better break up with him tomorrow."

That night I lay in bed, distraught over what to do. *We'll run away and elope*, I allowed myself to dream for a moment before quickly realizing Tex would never go for such a plan. He was determined to finish college, so I knew he would consider early marriage a roadblock. After crying myself to sleep that night, I woke up the next morning feeling strangely clearheaded and wrote Tex a "Dear John" letter that I planned to give him that day. I figured it was my only choice—I needed to free him from me, marriage, our faith and my crazy family. I knew I had to do the right thing to stay faithful to God and my parents.

As I stood in the parking lot at work, ironically dressed in my required cowgirl work duds of a Western shirt and cowboy boots, Tex told me that I looked like his idea of a perfect Texas girlfriend, which only made me sadder. I didn't have the courage to give him the letter, but I shared my dilemma. Holding his hands, I surprised myself with my blunt words.

"This can never work between us," I said. "My parents have made it very clear that I am beholden to their expectations and rules of a temple marriage." I had to look away as I saw his eyes begin to tear, so I hugged him close. "If I don't marry a Mormon in the temple, I'll screw up the whole plan of our eternal family. I can't bear that load on my own." He broke away from my embrace and held my arms, his blue eyes more piercing than ever.

"But I love you," he said. "Isn't that enough?" Confused and distraught, Tex struggled to find words to convince me to change my mind. For a moment, he even considered joining the church, wondering if that would be enough. But it was obvious his Baptist family wouldn't approve of our love, either. My shoulders slumped and I thought I might vomit.

"It'll never work," I managed to get out. And that was that.

As Tex pulled away in his beat-up truck, I stood alone in the parking lot sobbing, the weight of the world crashing down on me. Through his windshield, I could see that he was crying, too. I felt ridiculous in my Western wear, standing there baking in the hot sun. I left work early and rode the bus home in total devastation.

Messer came into my room later that night, and I was still a mess. I lay on my bed with a pillow over my face to drown out my screams and curses, barely hearing Messer's jovial voice as she returned from her date with her new crush.

"I have so much to tell you about Nick!" she exclaimed before catching a look at my blotchy face and swollen eyes. She quickly switched gears. "Uh oh, what happened?"

"Just make sure you fall in love with a good Mormon boy who can take you to the goddamn temple," I blurted. Messer stepped back, clutching her chest, and gasped. She looked at me as if I was possessed.

"Why would you say that? You can't swear about the temple!" I put the pillow back over my face and screamed. Timidly, she came to my bedside to console me. We stayed awake until the wee hours of the morning with her bearing her testimony to me about following the teachings of the church so we could be a family forever.

"Forget about what Dad and Carol want," she said. "We just need to do what our Heavenly Father and the prophet wants." I had lost all confidence in my gut feelings, but since I trusted Messer implicitly, I went along with her beliefs and relied on her faith. It was the only thing I had to hold on to.

Just one day after our family sealing, Beth and Robert were married in the temple. While I was happy for her, I just couldn't imagine myself in those shoes.

It became clear at summer's end that I wouldn't even come close to having enough money to return to Utah State. I didn't bother to ask Carol and Dad for help; instead, I rode back to Logan with my former roommates to help them move into their off-campus condominium, green with envy over the fact that I wasn't joining them. As I stood on the balcony of their condo overlooking campus, all my hopes and dreams of college life and becoming a dancer faded before my eyes.

Chapter Nineteen
1977–1978

After moving back to Salt Lake that summer, I started drinking and even had a fake ID made so I could get into bars around town, a major offense in the land of temple-goers. By mid-fall, my other dorm mate, Liz, lost interest in college and joined me as a carousing partner in crime. She was by far the most daring and adventurous of all of us and was always looking for a party. Liz had long, golden blonde hair and a cute figure in a flat-chested kind of way. She had been dating a handsome fellow student named Will, who fixed up old cars and sold them.

Crude and funny, Will had a black Lab named Boner and had nicknamed Logan "Logasm," which made me blush. One weekend, he told me about a 1958 white Karmann Ghia that he had just finished restoring. We drove to his shop in Logan and, as soon as I saw the car, it was love at first sight. Will wanted $1,000 for the sporty beauty. I had never owned a car, but I sure could see myself in that one. I had $1,200 in my checking account, and with college out of the picture, I pulled out a pen, wrote him a check and drove it home. Even though its maximum speed was 55 mph and it had no heater or air conditioner, I was exhilarated at having the freedom of my own car. I named him Bennie, after my favorite song at the time, Elton John's "Bennie and the Jets."

When I pulled up in front of our house on Douglas Street, where I'd been living all summer, I ran inside the house, shouting for anyone who was home to come see my new car. Anna, Beth, Messer and Danny raced outside excitedly, their eyes popping at the sight of my new sports car. Each one of them hopped in for a ride, one at a time.

Dad and Carol came out to have a look at my new pride and joy. Even Dad admired Bennie, as he had always wanted a sports car, but he quickly changed his tone.

"I knew you wouldn't finish college," he said. "You're not going to amount to anything now. At least you had one year of majoring in fun and boys!" Then he and his superior attitude walked off.

I flipped him the bird behind his back, making Danny snicker, and then Anna and I jumped in my car and drove up Parleys Canyon to Park City in the slow lane at 40 mph. Fall's changing leaves had created a patchwork of reds, yellows and oranges across the mountains, and I tried to focus on all that autumnal beauty instead of my crumbling life. Beth had just gotten married, and now Anna was planning her own temple wedding, which she rambled on about the entire drive. Her fiancé, Mike, was a quiet and nerdy guy who sported a 1970s-style mustache and giant glasses. Anna was enamored with him, so I was happy for her.

"I had my temple interview with the bishop last night and got a recommend," she said. "I'm so excited! Mike has his interview tonight, then we're going to go buy garments and go out to dinner for our date night."

"What?" I asked over the noisy engine. She pouted.

"You weren't even listening to me, were you?"

"What do you think about my new car? Cool, huh?"

She didn't answer, crossing her arms.

We drove the rest of the way in silence. I was so racked with worry over the mounting pressures of adulthood that I barely noticed the brilliant foliage and pine trees in Park City. Even though I had a job and a car, I still needed an escape plan. I dreamt about traveling, moving into my own apartment and maybe even getting a dog. With both of my sisters dropping out of college after freshman year and marrying within 12 months of each other, it was only Messer, Danny and me at home. Leaving became even more urgent as Dad and Carol tried to impose their same high school rules on me. I had gotten my taste of freedom and knew I had to get out, but getting married as the way to do it was still the last thing on my mind.

I didn't have to gas up Bennie very often because I got about 60 miles to the gallon. When I did need to, I purposely avoided the Conoco station where Steve worked, as I had vowed never to date him again. One day, my ego got the best of me, so I pulled up to the pump to show off my cute car to him. Within seconds, Steve was there, filling me up with gas and conversation.

"Hey there," he beamed, "Long time, no see. You're not at Utah State anymore?"

"Nope, bought this hot rod instead," I replied. "Who needs a dance degree?" I noticed a large gash with staples on the right side of his head. "Hey, what'd ya do?" I asked, pointing at his shaved head. His filthy oil-covered hand immediately went to the injury.

"Sixty-seven staples and a metal plate in there," he said nonchalantly as his fingers ran over the metal.

"What happened?"

We stood at the gas pump for at least a half-hour as he recounted the horrific accident that had occurred a couple of months prior. He and a few of his friends had been drinking and jumped on their motorcycles. Turning a corner, he wrecked and hit the ground, smashing his helmet-less head. When an ambulance was called, he got aggressive with the EMTs and refused to go to the hospital, despite their wishes. When they persisted, he punched one of them in the face. The EMTs suspected he had a head injury since blood was coming out of his ears, but they couldn't convince Steve to go. His friends took him to their apartment to put him to bed to sober up.

"When I woke up the next morning, my roommate Mel said the bedsheets were covered in blood, so he and Joe dragged me out of bed, put me in the shower and drove my drunk ass to the hospital," he said. "I owe them my life!" He had been in a medically induced coma for a month, and when he woke up, he learned they had removed the temporal bone from the side of his skull and put in a metal plate.

"I want to take both Mel and Joe and their girlfriends out to dinner to pay them back for what they did," he said, finally. "Would you come with me?" His eyes pleaded with me and reluctant to refuse a date after listening to his horrific story, I nodded yes—I would have seemed like a cold-hearted bitch otherwise.

At dinner, I sat on the edge of my seat as I listened to his friends talk about their wild drunken night, which intrigued and distracted me from the fact that my new boyfriend had a hole the size of a golf ball in his head. He had lost his sense of smell and taste, but these were the only apparent residual symptoms, which all seemed minor compared to what the outcome of his terrible accident could've been.

He confessed that he had "gone off the deep end" since his mission by drinking and partying with his buddies, but since his accident, he had decided to clean up his act and get back to the church. He felt he had been given a second chance.

"With you, the tall, beautiful blonde of my dreams standing here," he said, "now I know it more than ever." I blushed. Steve seemed like a nice, decent guy and a returned missionary to boot—even if he was also a belligerent drunk who had crashed his bike and punched out an EMT. I didn't really know Steve or even particularly like him, but I remembered what he had said to me when I was still with Tex. If God had answered Steve's prayers that I was the *right one*, who was I to question it? He would be proud to take me to the temple to get hitched—just like my family wanted.

Even if I wasn't fully in love with him, maybe I could learn to fall in love with him—and if I couldn't, divorce was always an option, even if the church didn't approve of it. Besides, any of those scenarios would be better than living at home. My exit strategy was smacking me in the face. The way out was to tie the knot—a temple knot, no less. Finally, at barely 19, I took my turn in the engagement spotlight at the church.

Marrying young was the norm in our community, and every Sunday, young women clustered in a corner of the ward building admiring each other's new engagement rings. It was a rite of passage that every young woman looked forward to, and the sooner, the better. Who cared we were all marrying the first people we sneezed on or that we had hardly matured out of being silly, clueless teenagers? The prevalent thought was that if one didn't find a young man to marry by the age of 21, all the good ones would be gone. After that, the unwed girls would face a choice: going on a mission (which was basically admitting failure to find a husband) or becoming an old maid. I knew I was not missionary material, nor did I want to be an old maid.

Unexpectedly, my desire to get married and move in with a man I barely knew overwhelmed everything else in my life. I began imagining myself as Mrs. Steven Anderson and practiced my new signature for hours at a time. I dreamt about having children and being a mother, which I now believed to be one of the most important aspirations of my life. Still, these flights of fantasy were tempered with a suspicion that I was getting in over my head—that I was living up to everyone's expectations but mine. I did my best to push away any doubt, chalking it up to cold feet. I'd heard the many whisperings around the ward about girls who had broken off engagements, some even at the last minute, and I couldn't bear the gossip, scrutiny or shame of being added to that list. Unable to be completely honest with myself or Steve, I forged on with our plans—after all, it was what our parents, various church leaders and auxiliary groups had been driving us toward our entire lives. Next exit, Temple marriage!

Chapter Twenty
1979

*S*o, *this is what heaven must be like*, I thought as I stood shoulder to shoulder with my fellow Mormons. Hundreds of us filled the room, dressed in white and waiting for the ceremony to begin. It was the day before my wedding, and my stomach twisted itself in knots, partly in excitement and partly in terror. We all stood quietly on the thick white carpet, dwarfed by colossal crystal chandeliers. Waiting. Anticipating. I watched the others file in, jockeying for a spot as my nervous hands glided over the shellacked wood of the chair in front of me. The light blue velvet cushions and endless rows of movie theater–style seats seemed to go on for eternity.

Only an hour earlier, my parents, and Steve and I had entered through the imposing wrought-iron gates that guarded the Salt Lake City Temple. Near the granite spires towering above us, the angel Moroni, the otherworldly visitor who came to Joseph Smith as a boy, blew his golden trumpet against an ominous winter sky. Only pure and faithful church-attending Mormons were allowed inside, so I felt a deep sense of accomplishment as I pulled out my temple recommend, a laminated bi-fold card with a picture of Jesus on the front and my name and the bishop's signature on the back. I proudly displayed my celestial passport to the temple workers attending to everyone entering the mysterious castle-like structure.

It was my first time back in the temple since I'd been sealed to Dad and Carol and only my third time back overall, but it was proving to be a much bigger ordeal than my other two visits. Everybody entering carried little suitcases containing their ceremonial clothes, so the lobby looked more like an airport than the House of the Lord. I must have appeared terrified, as a matronly woman gently took hold of my elbow and guided me away from Steve.

"Come with me, darling," she whispered in my ear. "Don't be afraid."

With Carol on my opposite side, we walked silently through a dozen L-shaped white hallways, each one seeming a mile long. Earlier that day, I had been told explicitly by Carol to listen to the temple workers who would guide me through the entire endowment process, the sacred initiation into the temple. I looked to Carol for reassurance that I was behaving correctly, and her face beamed, shiny from the sheen of perspiration across her brow. My stomach clenched as we turned another corner and headed into the unknown, scurrying like mice in a maze.

When we finally reached the dressing room, the temple worker leaned in close to whisper in my ear. As she spoke, her fetid breath drifted into my nostrils.

"There is no talking in a normal voice allowed in the

temple, as to keep the spirit calm, peaceful and inviting for the Lord," she said. With that, she handed me a folded white cloth no bigger than a pillowcase. Carol and I joined the flock of women, skittish angels in various shapes and sizes dressed in white and walking around silently with eyes like deer in headlights and smiles plastered on their faces. Everyone kept their hands clasped together in front of their upper thighs. As we passed them, they would simply nod or whisper "Congratulations" or "Welcome." Finally, the time had come for me to don my temple garments, the part of the ceremony I had been dreading. The fact that frumpy, uncomfortable underwear would become a permanent fixture of my wardrobe from that day forward did not excite me in the least. Angel chaps seemed more suited for Grandma Dot and Carol, not a young bride-to-be.

Once I stepped into my private dressing room with the curtain drawn, I shook out the white cloth to find a hole in the middle of one small sheet.

"What the hell?" I said to myself a little too loudly. I poked my head outside of the light blue velvet curtains in search of Carol, or anyone who could tell me what I was supposed to do with it. When I couldn't see anyone close by, I retreated into my room. Clearing my throat, I whispered to the girl in the dressing room next to mine.

"Excuse me, what am I supposed to do with this white sheet they just handed me?" A confident voice came from the other side.

"Just slip your head through the hole and make sure you are completely naked underneath," she instructed.

"Okay, thanks," I replied, unable to hide the tremor in my voice.

Outside my dressing room, I joined a dozen other young girls who were all standing nervously in front of their own rooms. We looked like a KKK gathering I had recently seen on the nightly news. I shivered as the pristine white room felt cold, and I tried to rub away the goosebumps on my arms. A few minutes later, our temple worker reappeared and instructed us to follow her. Escorted in a single file, we went to yet another white room where we were told to take a seat on the cushioned benches. A homely female temple worker, who appeared to be wearing a wig, sat on a stool by a pretty ceramic basin and called us forward one at a time. To my chagrin, "Diana Rae Cannon" was the first name that rang through the air. I stood up with no idea of what to expect. She motioned for me to come close and I obeyed.

She reached underneath my sheet and placed her wet prodding hand between my legs, touching the holy water to my privates and my posture stiffened. My eyes went wide, I gulped and the room spun as she said something about blessing my womb for childbearing and becoming a priestess in the next life. Her hands moved from my groin to my breasts and the top of my head, and then it was done. I walked away with warm water running down my legs, feeling violated and confused. *I should have been warned about this!* I shouted in my head. *I would have never agreed to go through with all this bullshit if I had known what I was in for!*

Carol stood waiting for me in front of my dressing room, looking so elated that she momentarily derailed me from fully expressing what I was thinking.

"What was that all about?" I asked, my lip quivering. "That was disgusting!"

She tilted her head, confused that I couldn't understand the meaning and beauty of the ritual.

"That was the washing and anointing, honey," she said. Her weak attempt to sugarcoat my experience did not assuage my humiliation and anger in the least. "It's part of the endowment ceremony where they purify you. It's like another baptism." Her tone hinted at her frustration over my continued defiance.

I couldn't understand why Carol seemed so surprised by my reaction. No one had prepared me for such a perverted experience. All anyone had told me before going to the temple was that it was too sacred to talk about. I had tried to pump Beth and Anna for information and insight about what was going to happen, but all they could say was that it would be "very special" and I was "going to love it."

Well, I didn't love it—the ritual made absolutely no sense to me. The church constantly preached that we needed to remain pure, chaste and clean by abstaining from premarital sex so we would be worthy to go to the temple. I had fooled around innocently with my high school boyfriend Todd and had almost had sex with Tex at college, but I always stopped him just in time, following the church's rules. Steve and I had only ever made it to third base, which church authorities called "heavy petting." Again, we refrained from going all the way at my insistence. I wanted to remain as pure as possible. During my required temple interview three weeks before the wedding, I confessed to these transgressions and was told I was still worthy to receive a temple recommend and enter the House of the Lord. Steve, on the other hand, had had many other previous girl-friends, some of whom he'd had intercourse with, thus putting off our temple wedding date for six months to give him time to repent.

As I stood alone, fuming in the unflattering light of my dressing room, I wasn't sure whether to laugh or cry. It occurred to me that I had just let a complete stranger go to third base with me, and that was supposed to be different somehow? Because it was in a holy temple of God? Praise the Lord, and please pass the bullshit!

The time had come to put on the hideous holy temple garments, and I gazed at my pathetic sight in the mirror. At age 20, I still had the lean body of an athletic dancer, tall and svelte, but in my angel chaps, I suddenly felt 30 years older, fat and like I was the ugliest bride-to-be on the planet. I couldn't imagine spending my upcoming wedding night in such unattractive undies.

We had been told over and over that the temple garments, or "garments of the holy priesthood," as some church leaders called them, were to be worn day and night by all members of the church who had received their endowment. Garments for men and women were both one piece, always white with a slit in the crotch area. They covered the entire thigh, ending just above the knee; one could even opt for a longer pair that ended mid-shin. The capped sleeves covered the shoulders for women and up to mid-arm for men. Each of the sewn markings at the breasts, belly and knee had their own significance, which the temple workers explained. The reverse L-shape over the right breast symbolized the "square," the justness and fairness of our Heavenly Father. The V over the left breast signified the "compass" or "North Star," representing one's moral compass. The mark over the belly button represented "strength in the navel and

marrow in the bones," while the mark on the right knee signified "that every knee shall bend and every tongue confess
that Jesus is the Christ." All of these marks were sacred
symbols.

Finally, we were given our instructions: we were
required to keep our religious underwear covered with clothing, and our garments were never to be altered. Their
purpose was to serve as an armor of God against the evils of
the world and a reminder of the covenants made in temple
ceremonies. Since they were considered sacred, discussing
them or showing them in public was a sin—especially to non-
Mormons.

I was paralyzed by the image of myself in these dreadful
garments. *Do I really have to wear these every day for the rest
of my life?* I thought. *Even on my wedding night while
attempting to be sexy and desirable for my husband? What a
joke.* I tried to shake off these unnerving thoughts and started
getting dressed. I grabbed my white bra and tried to put it on
over the baggy garments as instructed by Carol, who was
now standing outside my dressing room like a police officer.
It looked hideous, and I missed my pretty pink lacy underwear that lay discarded in my little suitcase. My bra-over-the-
garment situation felt uncomfortable and ridiculous, so I
slipped my arms out and quickly put it on underneath,
covering it with the garments. At that exact moment, Carol
popped her head in to check on me and saw what I was
doing.

"Diana!" she said. "You know better. Your bra has to go
on top of the garments so you'll be fully protected."

"Protected from what?" I protested as I reluctantly made
the switch. Carol's stern face ended the discussion.

I swapped out the bra and slipped into the plain white, long-sleeved, high-collared dress, which draped to the floor and covered all my skin. All that was left showing were my face and hands, but oddly enough, I felt like an angel once my fully dressed reflection greeted me from the mirror.

Pushing aside the curtain, I stood before Carol, who reached for my hand, but before we could say a word the same temple worker who had rounded my bases and gotten to third appeared and escorted us to the expansive endowment room. My mind kept swirling. *How many girls had she violated today?* I thought. *Did she wash her hands? What kind of pervert would even want that job?*

I tried to catch my breath in the expansive endowment room. It had high-domed ceilings and massive columns with gold-plated details, and sheer scallop-shaped curtains framed the soaring arched windows where swaths of light shone through and filled the ethereal room. *So, this is what heaven is supposed to be like?* I thought. Standing there in my ill-fitting temple dress, I paused to take in the enormity of it all. *This is what all the hype and secrets were about?*

I felt like an imposter in the white-washed churchy scene, but the otherworldliness of the space still stirred my soul somehow. I remembered what I had been taught—that in the purity of the endowment room, one made promises to God to live up to the teachings and covenants of the gospel. In this very room, worthy members of the church received a gift of power through ordinances in the temple that gave them instruction and covenants (and for the men only, the gift of the holy priesthood needed to attain exaltation and salvation). I felt something, even though I didn't understand it.

I stood quietly, comforted by the lingering scent of Carol's sweet gardenia perfume, and scanned the room. It was divided into rows of seats for women on the left and men on the right, but I hadn't yet seen my husband-to-be since entering the temple. I wondered if he, too, had experienced the holy groping. Finally, I spotted Steve in the sea of men in white, about 50 yards away from me. The first thought that flashed through my mind was: *Shit, what am I doing?* And then: *Shit, I just swore in the endowment room.*

With our wedding scheduled for the next day, it seemed strange that Steve and I had to be separated during all of this. The only familiar faces were Carol, Debi and Anna, who all sat next to me regaled in funny white outfits of their own. Beth was absent because she had just given birth to twins a few days prior. It meant a lot to me that Debi had come all the way from Idaho, as she had two small kids and was pregnant with her third.

When the ceremony finally began, it involved a series of rituals with special handshakes and incantations along with endless standing and sitting. We repeated sacred refrains and made promises to slit our own throats and disembowel ourselves if we spoke of the ceremonies outside of the temple, which didn't seem very church-like to me. Everyone was instructed to extend their right thumb and pinky outward and drag their thumb across the throat to symbolize this dire warning. We also had to make a stabbing motion into our abdomen, symbolizing disembowelment. I felt a deep fear growing inside of me. *Does anyone else in this room think this is madness?* I thought. *Am I the only one?*

Next, we placed accessories on top of our heads and clothes like sheer white veils and green aprons to represent

Adam and Eve's fig leaf while I barely suppressed my giggles —with everyone lifting their veils up and down while reciting strange intonations, it felt like we were in a bizarre Disney castle with a bunch of wide-eyed fairies rather than in a sacred temple. The mental image was so distracting that I could barely pay attention to what was going on. *No wonder no one in the family had warned me about what goes on in here*, I thought. *They had to make their own promises to God, afraid for their lives. I'm going to tell Messer so she doesn't freak out like me. She's even more prudish than I am.*

A parade of about 12 men and women walked up the center aisle toward the semicircular wall that went from floor to ceiling and was half a football field long, covered by heavy theatrical blue-stage curtains with hundreds of scalloped folds. The group formed a prayer circle under the domed ceiling, painted to represent an ethereal sky blue. While chanting strange words, they raised their arms toward the ceiling then released them down to their sides, over and over. I couldn't understand a single word being said. *Are they speaking in tongues?* I wondered.

Next, the temple workers role-played the story of Adam and Eve in the Garden of Eden and the tale of the Earth's creation, which dragged on for an hour. Finally, I was ushered to the mysterious blue curtain, which parted with dramatic flair. Behind it was a sheer and shimmering white curtain, representing "the veil." I had always been taught that when we died, our spirits crossed through the veil and back into the spirit world. The whole purpose of the veil ritual was to reenact what would happen when faithful Mormons were resurrected and reunited with their loved ones after passing through to the other side. I couldn't control myself any longer and giggled at the absurdity of it all until Carol shot me a sharp look of disdain.

A strange man stood next to me, and after introducing himself as Brother Jorgenson, he held my left hand in a secret grip we had just been taught and then guided my right hand through a hole in the sheer white curtain, where my clammy hand met a bigger, limp hand on the other side. I strained to see who was behind the curtain, wondering if it was someone I knew, but couldn't make anything out. I felt the stranger press his right knee and inner thigh against mine. The man standing next to me whispered my new temple name in my ear. I would be called Miriam at the resurrection and throughout eternity. He gave me a wink, indicating I was doing all the right things and was ready to move forward.

I jumped when Brother Jorgenson pulled a wooden stick with a ball on the end out of his pocket and tapped it three times on something hard behind the curtain, letting the worker on the other side know we were ready.

"Who's there?" a man's voice echoed from the other side. All I could think of was the Tony Orlando and Dawn song "Knock Three Times," but I only wanted to knock "twice on the pipe" for "no." I peered down the row at the others standing at the veil. We looked like marionettes in a bizarre holy puppet show.

Shit, I've already forgotten my new name, I thought, racking my brain. I craned my neck and scouted the room for Steve, but my husband-to-be was nowhere in sight.

Mumbling something close enough to my new given name, I was gently pulled through a long slit in the curtain where I found myself in the celestial room, greeted by Dad,

Carol, Debi, Anna and Gloria, Steve's mom, who was teary-eyed with joy. Steve stood next to her wearing a wide toothy grin.

In that moment, the weird rituals faded out of mind, and I succumbed to the beauty and peaceful calm of the celestial room. Crystal chandeliers glistened above the Queen Anne–style furniture, all pristine chairs and couches that looked as if no one had ever sat in them. Murals of heavenly figures graced the ceilings, and our reflections reminded us that through faith we would go on and on for eternity.

Mormons believed in three heavenly kingdoms, and that once resurrected, all humans would stand before the Lord to be judged according to their desires and actions. Each person would be assigned an eternal dwelling place in a specific kingdom of glory. The three kingdoms were the celestial, terrestrial and telestial—the latter a word that Joseph Smith had coined himself. The celestial kingdom was the highest of all, reserved for near-perfect individuals who lived their entire lives so purely that they could bring their families into eternal life with them and live with Heavenly Father. The second highest was the terrestrial kingdom or middle ground, for somewhat religious people who lived respectably but were misguided by others into disbelief in the gospel. Finally, the telestial kingdom was the bottom of all the heavenly kingdoms and was described in scripture as a place for those who rejected the teachings of Christ. It included liars, sorcerers, adulterers and whoremongers, according to the Book of Mormon. Individuals who committed unpardonable sins were banished there, along with Satan. Stories of this dark place filled the nightmares of Mormon children.

As I stood and listened to the familiar explanations about

the kingdoms, something in my stomach dropped. The promises the temple workers were describing offered hope and happiness. Who wouldn't want to buy into the fact that when we died, we could be with all our loved ones in the afterlife? Perhaps in a place similar to, if not better, than the room we were standing in? Still, the more I listened, the more I realized how nearly impossible it seemed to get there. Maybe some of my family would achieve this exaltation like Debi, Beth or Anna, but what about Mom and Dad, or my brothers Linc and Tom? Would we not end up in different kingdoms? How would we ever all be together?

As I ran through scenarios in my mind, I realized that nearly all of them were pictures of my family broken apart—even in the afterlife. In a sea of hopeful, rosy faces all around me, I felt myself deflating. I was so confused—people I cared about were getting deeper and deeper into this religion, especially my oldest sisters. I didn't want to be isolated from everyone else and I didn't need to be different, but I just wasn't buying it. I tried to push my doubt aside, to pretend to be devoted and do what was expected of me, but I couldn't shake away a new thought that had entered my brain: I was just a garment-wearing pawn in the grand theatrics of this absurd religion.

As the ceremony ended, we walked out the wrought-iron gates in a bubble of exuberant family chatter, and something inside me changed. Everyone around me was buzzing with warmth and connection, but I couldn't feel any of it. The temple was suddenly not a place I wanted to spend time in anymore—even though I had to return the next day for the real thing.

On the morning of my wedding, I took a quick inventory

of my life. It was February 1, 1978, and at 20 years old, I was about to marry a man I didn't love. Outside of our Douglas Street home, a blizzard whited out the silent street. I slid across the sidewalk with a hand-me-down temple suitcase in my clutch and a Snickers bar in my coat pocket, slamming into the back door of the car. When I managed to get in and plop next to Messer and Danny, I felt Dad's impatient eyes on me. We only had 15 minutes to make it to the temple.

Upon our arrival, I realized that I had shut the bottom of my wedding dress in the door so it had been dragging along the snowy streets for miles. It looked as if I had pulled it out of a dumpster, which didn't seem like a good omen. I tried to wipe off the sleet, but eventually gave up and hurried inside.

The wedding service was short and sweet as we knelt across from each other at the altar. Most of our family, or at least the pure ones (and those who claimed to be) who held temple recommends, sat in seats that lined all four walls. Grandma Dot, Grampa Rex, Dad, Carol, Debi, Anna and Gloria all beamed as the temple worker announced that we were now husband and wife. Steve and I awkwardly kissed to seal the deal and I got a little giddy, caught up in the moment and excitement of playing house as Mrs. Steve Anderson with my sparkly ring on my finger.

Steve and I met outside of our dressing rooms, where he leaned in for a kiss.

"You look gorgeous," he gushed. After shyly thanking him, we joined hands and waltzed outside of the temple as husband and wife. We were greeted by the rest of the family, some of whom had been at the wedding and others who were either not old enough or not worthy enough to enter the temple. I ran straight to Messer first for moral support, and I sobbed as we held each other in a long embrace.

"I can't believe you're married now," she whispered in my ear. "How was the temple? Was it amazing?" She assumed I was sobbing tears of joy but soon realized differently as she held the tops of my arms, slowly pushing me away from her so she could see my expression.

"It was crazy and not at all what I expected," I said, not hiding my fear and shock. "I need to tell you about it." She handed me a tissue.

"You're getting mascara all over your face," she replied. "What happened in there? Are you okay?" I wanted to tell her everything, but only 24 hours earlier, the temple workers had made me take a vow to slit my throat if I did. My new mother-in-law, Gloria, found me and offered a warm embrace. Gloria had been an inactive Mormon for many years, but obtained her temple recommend in time for our wedding. She and Steve's dad had divorced several years prior, and I knew his dad had been in the military and had an affair with a younger female officer. Both he and his new wife and daughter had promised to come to the wedding as well. Steve had three full siblings, one sister and two brothers, and a half sister, which amounted to a relatively small family for Mormons.

"I'm so happy to have another daughter," Gloria said, embracing me. Short and heavyset with stylish short brown hair and heavy-rimmed glasses, Gloria was as sweet as a garden of roses. We had gotten very close during the engagement, and she was eager to step in as my surrogate mother, which I was glad to accept.

The reception center I had chosen on the East Bench of

Salt Lake had a beautiful winter backdrop with a white sleigh, snow-covered trees and plaster of Paris deer with faux fur. As the Cannons formed their line, Carol spotted my mother Joyce in the crowd and invited her to join us. She came over and gave me a hug but seemed uncomfortable.

I barely spoke another word to her that entire evening; frankly, she felt like a stranger to me. Mom had attended Anna's nuptials just a few months before mine, but it was the same thing—not much interaction or emotion. Beth was still harboring resentment that Mom didn't attend hers. Mormon wedding receptions were the last place on earth to spend quality time with guests. Rather than grand affairs with mingling, dancing and fine dining, they were fairly low-key with minimal food and extremely long reception lines. Mine was especially lengthy as I didn't want to leave anyone out, which meant Mom, Dad, Carol, seven bridesmaids, a maid of honor and a flower girl who were standing beside me waiting to accept congratulations from the guests. After everything was over, the wedding party was corralled, seated at a small table and served a typical Mormon menu of a small ham sandwich, a tiny cup of nuts and an eclair, paired with either red or green punch.

Later that evening, I was finally alone with my husband in a fancy hotel room in downtown Salt Lake City, and I wasn't sure what to do with myself. As I stared out the window at the city lights, it felt like I was in a soap opera. Unlike my husband, I had done nothing to prepare for this moment. Meanwhile, Steve ordered chilled nonalcoholic sparkling grape juice and chocolates to infuse some romance and my immaturity took over.

"Excuse me while I slip into something more comfortable," I purred as I sashayed across the floor, unbuttoning my dress like I had seen the women do on *All My Children*. I was trying my best, but I was not excited for the evening. Even so, I was well aware of my obligations as a new bride and wife. My mind rushed with questions about how to behave, what to do with my garments, if sex hurt and if Steve even knew what to do. *I've only been on birth control for a couple of weeks*, I thought anxiously. *Is that long enough? God, I pray that I don't get pregnant.*

After we did the deed, Steve was asleep in minutes as I lay on our king-sized bed feeling alone and scared. After listening to my husband snoring and feeling forlorn in the dark, I quietly got up and removed my nightgown, replacing it with my bulky new underwear. *Might as well be a strait-jacket*, I thought.

Chapter Twenty-One
1979–1985

With our lackluster first night as newlyweds behind us, Steve and I boarded a plane to have our honeymoon in Orlando, Florida. More than the wedding, I was excited for our honeymoon trip to Disney World that Steve had planned, which was the perfect Mormon version of a romantic destination: another picture-perfect magical kingdom full of fantasy. Steve and I both still loved amusement park rides and cartoon characters, we hadn't traveled much, so Florida seemed exotic. Upon arrival, I immediately fell in love with the palm trees and tropical air.

With the slight February chill in the air, wearing garments every day didn't seem so bad—especially because all our fellow Disney fans were wearing long pants too, so we didn't feel out of place. Along with eating endless amounts of junk food, Steve and I rode every roller coaster we could, and it proved to be the best part of the honeymoon. At the top of the Ferris wheel, Steve leaned in and kissed me.

"Just look at that view," he said, sweeping his arm

panoramically. "I'm so excited about our future together. Maybe we should move here!" I nodded in agreement, trying to picture the fairy tale he was describing. Just then, a marching band came in to view with Mickey and Minnie dancing in line with the band. We waved and hollered at them, and Minnie looked up and waved back to all of us at the top but tripped over Mickey. Everyone around us laughed.

"I can't believe we're married now," I said. Steve leaned in and kissed me again and, in spite of myself, I was happy.

When we returned from Florida, our small one-bedroom apartment in Murray, Utah, with cottage cheese ceilings and ugly beige carpet, felt like a far cry from sunny Orlando and spic-and-span Disney World. Luckily, six months later, we bought a brand-new, split-level house with a single carport in Sandy, Utah at the base of the Wasatch Mountains—but as far South as we were, the entire place felt as foreign to me as Las Vegas. Sequestered in a new development of tract homes, isolated from my old world in Salt Lake City, we were suddenly homeowners in the suburbs with a high-interest mortgage and a $500-a-month house payment. Still, it was starting to feel like we had achieved the American Dream, even if we had to pretend to be grownups and play house. It was becoming clear that it was breeding time in Mormonland, so the pressure was on. Debi and Beth had three children each, and Anna had just gotten pregnant with her first. Naturally, we tried to start a family as well, now that we had tied the knot and I was a fertile 20-year-old Mormon housewife.

All the fun of being newlyweds faded quickly since Steve and I weren't getting the hang of being husband and wife as I hoped we might. We argued a lot and Steve always had to have the last word; though I disagreed with him and had plenty of thoughts of my own I wanted to get out, I couldn't find the strength to defend myself and would clam up. No matter how strong of an opinion I had to share, it didn't matter—I couldn't speak up, and Steve wouldn't really hear me when I did anyway.

We found ourselves in counseling only six short months after the wedding, during which our therapist told us we had serious communication issues. It seemed like we might actually face our problems head-on until Steve accused the therapist of siding with me and refused to go back. We only made it through two tense sessions until Steve called "bullshit" on the whole thing.

To get involved in our church, I met the new bishop in our ward, who was a handsome Hispanic man (which was unusual for white-bread town of Sandy). I found him to be charismatic and charming, and even had a little crush on him despite the fact he was married and had six children. Steve and I received an invitation in the mail for a meeting at his house, calling on all newly married couples in the ward to attend, so I was eager to go.

On a Wednesday evening, we gathered in his freshly carpeted basement, where he and his wife served cupcakes and punch. Ten couples sat on the floor encircling Bishop Gomez since they had no furniture yet. He boasted that his beautiful wife had the shapeliest legs he had ever seen, parading her in front of us so we could verify it for ourselves. She shyly walked a circle in front of everyone, hiking up her dress ever so slightly so we could have a peek. She did have great legs, but the whole thing felt inappropriate.

The next item on the evening agenda was the church's position on multiplying and replenishing the world. Bishop Gomez preached that it was our responsibility to get busy and start bringing God's children to Earth.

"There are already spirit children who have chosen you as parents," he explained." They are just waiting to be born!" His last lesson, however, was the toughest to swallow. According to Bishop Gomez, the church leaders had sent a letter to all the bishops insisting they talk to their congregations about the church's opposition to oral sex. Until that point, I had been buying into his charm and everything he said, but suddenly, I was lost. He stood stiffly in the middle of the circle as he read the recent edict from the church's first presidency.

"Oral sex is forbidden, even among married couples," he said. "It's unnatural, impure and unholy and will keep you from obtaining a temple recommend." I appeared to be the only one who didn't know the details of oral sex, but I was certainly aware that the atmosphere in the room changed from one of friendly spiritual conversation to awkward, uncomfortable silence. People started to get antsy, shifting around on the carpet and clearing their throats. Several couples even offered excuses to leave.

Steve and I never talked about oral sex before that night, let alone practiced it. We were both too naïve and embarrassed to broach the subject, though now there was a looming threat tied to this devious activity. That night was also the last time we saw Bishop Gomez in our neighborhood —one week later, he left his wife and six children for another man and moved to San Francisco. I wanted to approach the bishop's wife and offer my support and sympathy, but she stopped coming to church and moved from the area within a few weeks as well. It was all too much to fathom for our pure Mormon minds.

What was more unexpected was the following year, Bishop Gomez returned to church with his lover, despite the rumors that he'd been excommunicated. It was our monthly fast and testimony meeting, when the church was open to anyone who wanted to testify before the entire congregation. "Open to anyone" typically meant faithful church members who were in good standing, but that wasn't stopping Bishop Gomez from making his way up to the front to get in line to speak. The ward members couldn't hide their curiosity and discomfort, whispering and craning to get a good look at the bishop's young, handsome lover. Finally, Bishop Gomez stood confidently at the pulpit.

"I am here to ask for your forgiveness," he said. "I am an imperfect man. I have deceived my congregation and abandoned you, for which I am profoundly sorry. I hope you'll find it in your hearts to forgive me and become an advocate for acceptance of homosexuality." I couldn't believe what I was hearing—and from a glance at the faces around me, neither could anyone else. Finally, Bishop Gomez became so emotional that he couldn't finish his thoughts and walked away from the pulpit to sit next to his lover. As soon as he had sat down, the service continued as if nothing had even happened, though there were plenty of stares and hushed conversations to go around.

Steve and I talked all the way on our walk home, both surprised and impressed by the bishop's courage to face his old friends and neighbors after leaving the church. It seemed particularly strange that he was asking for reacceptance, since the church's position was that being gay was a sin and a curse, and that gay people had absolutely no place there. I liked Bishop Gomez, and I couldn't understand the church's unforgiving stance. I didn't know any other gay people (at least, I didn't think I knew of any), but I couldn't imagine turning my back on someone just because they were attracted to the same sex.

I felt the same way later that year when the church made an announcement to all its members worldwide. In June 1978, just four months after Steve and I had gotten married, President Spencer W. Kimball announced that he and the church's 12 apostles had received a revelation from God that they should reverse their policy and allow Black people to receive the priesthood and temple ordinances. Parts of the community took it like a bombshell, and much like the incident with Bishop Gomez, it was like some hidden part of the church's belief system that I'd inherited had been pushed uncomfortably into the light. It was great the church was changing its stance now, but why had it had any other stance in the first place?

As previously disenfranchised communities were trying to integrate into new and expanded roles in the church, I also tried to fill my expanded role of wife, sister and daughter in a way my family could be proud of. Like everyone else, I wanted to earn my spot in the celestial kingdom.

I had sure come a long way from the thieving, lying, smoking bad kid I once was, and I was proud that I had left that world behind. Still, this new world was boring, and I was restless. Most of the couples in our ward were around our age or slightly older, but everyone looked the same and dressed the same. The houses looked the same, and everyone had a bunch of kids. I found myself gravitating toward my non-Mormon neighbors, Carly and Tom, for some excitement. We became close enough that when Steve was at work, I would sneak over to drink coffee with her and gossip about our Diet Coke–binging neighbors. It helped that Carly and Tom's kids were around the same age as ours, and they got along fabulously, so we all quickly became best friends.

Steve and I did our best to be good community members, diving right into newlywed life and making close friends in our Sandy neighborhood and at church. While we weren't much good at married life, we were professionals at getting pregnant—it seemed like all we had to do was wash our angel chaps together and boom. It was all still a world away from having good sex, but I was a fertile baby-making machine who craved motherhood, even if I was ill-prepared for the task like my mother had been.

Steve and I had been married for a year when Messer got engaged at 18 years old. She had met her fiancé, Stan Casto, in church. When he'd first asked her out, she wasn't interested given their five-year age gap; instead, she lined him up with her best friend. When that was a miserable failure, Stan went back to pursuing Messer. Despite Stan not being a returned missionary, he was still a recent convert to the church and had been pursuing a medical degree, so Carol and Dad considered it only a small ding on the potential celestial partner checklist and gave Messer their blessing. Everyone in the Cannon family was going gaga over Stan. When I first met him, though, I thought he was a giant asshole.

"I love your sister," he declared. "Everything about her is perfect except her nose." I was just glad Messer hadn't overheard his condescending comment, which pissed me off right out of the gate. I was protective of her, but there was absolutely nothing wrong with her cute little button nose. Six months later, Stan proposed to Messer on the sidewalk right outside of Dad and Carol's house. As far as she knew, they were just going on a date, but as they headed to Stan's car, he dropped to one knee and said, "Let's get married, Lisser." To my dismay, she accepted without hesitation.

Because I was 21 and sporting a seven-months-pregnant belly, Carol tried to convince Messer I shouldn't stand in her line as a bridesmaid since I looked like a "beached whale," but Messer refused to exclude me. When the day came, I donned my light blue floral dress (without the belt) and stood proudly with all the other bridesmaids who had cinched waists and non-swollen feet. I was just happy to be a part of my little sister's wedding; neither one of us would have had it any other way. The newlyweds weren't able to pull off a honeymoon because Stan was set to graduate in June, so he whisked her off to Fort Lauderdale, Florida, where they stayed in his parents' three-bedroom condominium for a month. When they returned, it wasn't long before everyone had enough of Stan's inflated ego and cutting remarks, but we put up with him for Messer's sake.

In the summer of 1980, my first child, Stephanie, so-named because it was the feminine version of Steven, was born—and she was adorable, smart and precocious from day one. I loved being a mommy to my blue-eyed angel, partly because it gave me a distraction from the realities of my marriage, though it didn't last for long. Though I believed Steve loved me, the simmering tension between us was transforming into explosive fights. After a particularly intense shouting match with him, I burned rubber down the road with six-month-old Stephanie on my lap, which reminded me of Carol's many dramatic departures from Dad.

The only person I felt I could go to as I fled was Messer, who had just moved into a large Tudor-style home in Murray. Now a practicing family physician, Stan proved to be even more of an arrogant jerk, but he had a soft side and tried to be sympathetic when I was in trouble. As fervent churchgoers, both Stan and Messer convinced me to return home to Steve as "my duty." Stan gave me a priesthood blessing, asking the Lord to guide me so I would continue to stay committed. He also gave me a lecture about the temple vows I had made to Steve and to God for time and eternity.

"It is your obligation to make it work," he said sternly. Feeling hopeless and having nowhere else to go, I relented and returned home a couple of days later to continue with my depressing home life. The only things keeping me committed were my daughter and family—I especially wanted Grandma Dot and Gramps to be proud of me.

Each Sunday, the entire family still met at Grandma Dot and Gramps's house. I looked forward to these routine visits; taking Stephanie into the warmth of Grandma Dot's home and where we would most likely bump into Dad, Carol, MaryAnn, Garn, Sammie and Linda kept me going. Unfortunately, Gramps had become ill and passed away rather suddenly in 1981, leaving Grandma widowed once again. She'd been handling his death with quiet dignity, explaining that they had just been earthly companions. She loved him, but they were both sealed to their original temple spouses who had already passed. My heart ached when I realized Stephanie would one day grow up and not remember him.

Two-and-a-half years after Stephanie was born, I had my second child, Scott, which Steve and I planned to be our last. Scott was a dream baby, happy and complacent, and between him and Stephanie, my heart swelled with an intense love I had never experienced before. Steve was also exceedingly pleased to have a son and adored our kids just as much as I did—even if his love for being a father wasn't improving our relationship.

Steve had worked as an auto mechanic his whole life, and while talented when it came to solving mechanical problems, he was not good at dealing with customers and had several aggressive encounters. Eventually, he got fired after a blowout with the station owner's son. Rather than making a big deal out of losing his job, Steve reframed the situation.

"I'm never going to work for anyone else again," he said. "I want to be my own boss." He managed to buy a struggling neighborhood gas station a little further east in the upscale Harvard-Yale neighborhood, but he had major shortcomings as a businessman that doomed it to failure. I bailed him out of tax troubles a couple of times, giving him $2,000 from the savings Grandma Dot had given me as a gift and later by selling my beloved Karmann Ghia for $1,000. He thought I didn't know about the money he secretly borrowed from his poor mother, Gloria. Even though we were always broke, Steve would still show up with a new television or a car out of the blue. One day, he came home with a slightly used black Buick Riviera with a red crushed velvet interior.

"Where did you get this?" I asked, knowing we couldn't afford it.

"On trade for services!" he replied. Nine months later, it was repossessed.

Life carried on, I walked around in a fog. I did my best to stay out of Steve's path and got through each day by focusing on the kids. I fantasized about being married to Tex or my high school boyfriend Todd, both of whom were long gone and already starting families of their own. In so many ways, I was daydreaming about an escape from Steve.

In the summer of 1984, my ward leaders asked me to attend girls' camp as a counselor (a church-sponsored five-day camp program for the young women in each ward). That entire year, I had been a teacher to these young ladies but never felt comfortable with such a leadership role. I knew I wasn't mature enough, and at 24, I still felt more like a teen than a role model. I happily accepted the invitation, however, since it was an opportunity to escape from daily life. One night at the camp, we were all sitting around a campfire and staring at the flames flickering against the black starry sky. For whatever reason, it was the exact moment when I knew my marriage to Steve was over. That night, while trying to sleep on a cot in a tent with 15 fidgeting teenagers, I silently rehearsed what I would say.

I grabbed Bishop Cowen by the elbow the following morning, walking him away from the tent area and asking if we could talk.

"I've decided to divorce Steve and I thought you should know," I said calmly. "We fight all the time, and I don't love him."

Bishop Cowen was a young bald-headed man with a raging superiority complex, and he immediately started lecturing me on the consequences of breaking my temple vows, reminding me how serious it was in the eyes of the church. I let him ramble on but tuned him out, uninterested in what he had to say. I had already decided. He said he would pray for us to do the right thing, but his words felt hollow to me.

That Saturday I came home dirty, tired and resolved. Above all, I was excited to see the kids. I had never been away from them for a five-day stretch before and missed them terribly. Steve's mom had come to help out while I was gone, but she left shortly after I returned home. After taking a cool shower to combat the summer heat, I went into the living room to soak up some swamp cooler air, collapsing onto the silk floral couch Steve's mom had given us. The kids piled on me like puppies as I tried to recap the week's events to Steve. We played with the kids until bedtime. Once Steve and I were alone, I finally mustered up the courage to break the news.

"While I was at camp, I had time to think about our marriage and what I want," I said, walking into the living room where Steve sat on the couch with the TV blaring and his hand in a bowl of potato chips. The light from the TV colored his face in a haunting blue.

"I'm tired and I want to watch this show," he replied without emotion or bothering to look up. "Let's talk about this later."

I stomped across the room and yanked the TV plug out of the wall, irate that he would try, once again, to dismiss and ignore me.

"I'm going to take this goddamn box and throw it out the window," I threatened, fully ready for a confrontation. The room went dark, but I could still hear him chomping on a mouthful of chips. He put the bowl on the cushion and washed the chips down with a swig of Coke.

"Shit, do we have to do this now?"

"Yes, we're doing this now," I snapped, busying myself by turning on lamps, picking up toys and straightening magazines on the table as I talked. "I'm not happy. I think we should separate for a while, but I'm not leaving this time. I need you to move out of the house immediately."

Not wanting to look at his face, I continued into the kitchen and stood at the sink, pretending to wipe it down. I felt him enter the room—he was a big man, and when he was angry, he seemed bigger. I turned to face him, but since I was afraid of becoming cornered, I tried to get past him and back into the living room.

"What the hell are you talking about?" he shouted, breathing erratically. "What happened at camp to bring all this on? I'm not going anywhere!"

"Be quiet, you're going to wake the kids up! Please just leave," I begged. "I've made my decision. I want a divorce. All we do is fight, and I'm tired of it. I'm tired of your lazy ass sitting here watching TV while I do all the work."

"What are you talking about, Diana? Are you crazy? I'm not going anywhere. And I don't really give a shit what you're tired of." Steve returned to the couch and sunk back in, reclaiming his territory.

I moved to the top of the stairs and watched him incredulously. "If you turn on that fucking TV again, I'm gonna lose it," I said, pointing at the front door. "Go pack a bag and get your ass out of here. Tonight!"

Steve jumped out of his seat and charged at me, coming within two inches of my face. "You've lost your fucking mind!" he screamed, spitting chips everywhere.

"If I had a gun in my hand, I would shoot you in the

face," I spat back. He turned and walked down the hall to our bedroom. Within 15 minutes, he drove out of our driveway and into the dark.

All I had wanted for years was for him to be gone, and now the house was eerily silent in his absence. I plopped myself down on the couch, with so many emotions swirling through my head. Kicking the empty bowl off the cushion, I curled up into a ball and sobbed at the thought of having to explain Steve's absence to the kids.

Six weeks later, I discovered I was pregnant again. Before I'd told him to leave, I already knew that I was done with our marriage, but I was too weak to say so or turn him down. A few weeks before our big fight, I had let him climb on top of me, crying and biting my arm while he finished the deed. I had fully inherited my mother's penchant for hard marriages and easy pregnancies, which was not necessarily a winning combination.

In the spring of 1985, on the exact day Steve and I received notice that our divorce was finalized, I gave birth to our third child, Haley. As difficult as the situation was, and as many times as I wished I hadn't gotten pregnant, Haley was an angel. Her presence was an immediate lifesaver after the sadness and disappointment we felt from Steve being gone. Stephanie and Scott snuggled her every chance they could. She left me no time to feel sorry for myself as a 27-year-old single mom living in the most conservative, family-focused state in the union.

As tired and deflated as I was, I was ferocious in my love for my children. It made me think of my mom, who had abandoned six kids of her own when things had gotten too difficult—one of whom had only been a toddler at the time.

Watching Stephanie, Scott and Haley together was putting things in a new perspective. Sure, it was unclear how I would afford my rent or groceries and I was teetering on the edge of a mental crisis—but I would *never* leave my kids. I couldn't fathom it.

Excerpt from Joyce Cannon's Journals

ADVENTURES ON A PSYCH WARD
1964

I don't remember how many times I vacationed at the LDS Hospital psych ward, but I think it was four or five. At each visit they ejected me after two months, though I begged them to let me stay and offered to scrub floors and clean toilets. They said after two months they'd have to transfer me to the real looney bin down in Provo. I couldn't face that.

Nearly all the therapy that took place was done by the patients in formal or informal therapy groups. Being listened to and accepted, even after you confess your deepest, most secret sins, is powerful medicine.

I met interesting, neurotic, dysfunctional, goofy people, and with few exceptions came to love them.

In those days, I smoked two to three packs a day, and since we had a lot of free time on our hands, we often played cards.

And of course, when playing cards, I smoked incessantly, as did several others.

One of my favorite fellow patients was Jewel, who was in a wheelchair with a diagnosis of hysterical paralysis. She blithely informed anyone who was interested that her doctor said there was nothing wrong with her legs, she just couldn't deal with her sexuality. Damn! Why didn't I think of that?

Since depression was a common problem, conversations often revolved around suicide: who had attempted what, why it hadn't worked and what we planned to try next time. During one of these conversations, a nurse I'd never seen before and never saw again added her viewpoint on the subject saying, "If I ever really want to kill myself I know how to do it so it can't be undone—just drink melted lead." Now there's a solution none of us had ever considered, and I'm sure each of us filed it away for future reference (hoping we'd never get quite that desperate).

Speaking of desperate, finally one night I'd had all I could take. I locked myself in Ted's den, grabbed his .22 revolver and put a bullet in the cylinder. As he kicked the door down I put the gun to my head and pulled the trigger. There was a click and nothing happened. I went into shock and Ted was enraged. I remember being on the floor with him kicking me. I didn't know revolvers revolved before they fired.

Back I went to the psych ward, but this time, I had no hope of therapy making anything better. I remember lying in my bed for hours trying to will myself to die. I realized how little Ted or I were able to think about the kids.

FURTHER ADVENTURES ON THE PSYCH WARD
1965

For years I'd heard horror stories about psychiatric facilities that did shock treatments, and during my stay on the LDS Hospital psych ward, I had occasionally seen people who wandered around zombie-like in their nightgowns. It was common knowledge they'd had shock treatments. Nevertheless, when Dr. B. said he thought shock treatments might help my depression since nothing else seemed to work, I agreed to try it. I was in so much emotional pain by then I would have tried anything that had any chance at all of helping. And maybe, if I were lucky, it would kill me and I wouldn't have to do it myself. Hey, it was worth a try.

One of the side effects of shock treatments (I thought of it at the time as a fringe benefit) is a period of memory loss, which may or may not be permanent. The idea is during the series of six treatments (one every other day), your brain gets scrambled and rewired so you can find healthier ways to deal with your life.

My memory of that period and for a while after is still fuzzy. After I got out of the psych ward, my mother took me and Melissa, who was still a toddler, to stay with them in Phoenix for a period of time— I don't remember how long we were there, and I don't remember going home and resuming my life. What I do remember is that finally, at long last, I started to get angry.

The rewiring had apparently unlocked the door to the cellar where I'd been stuffing rage all my life, since it had never been safe to express it. I remember wishing for a padded room where I could lock the door on the inside and throw the granddaddy of all temper tantrums—just kick the crap out of that room and then throw myself on the floor and kick and scream like a two-year-old until I was exhausted or the anger was gone, whichever came first.

Since I didn't have access to a padded room, I just went around being irritable all the time. One day, Ted asked, "What happened to you? You used to be a nice person." By this he meant I had been a compliant doormat and he wanted me to continue being one. I just got madder and madder, which made him madder and madder.

When Dr. B told me he thought the prognosis for our marriage was "poor" and the prognosis for me, outside of marriage and without my kids was "guarded," what little hope I'd managed to hold onto evaporated. And just when I thought things couldn't get worse, they did.

One day, Ted informed me there was a benevolent plot afoot. He thought he was being considered for some illustrious position as ambassador to somewhere. A position for which only he was uniquely qualified and for which he was being tested to see whether he was worthy. He thought there was a mind-reading device in the earpiece of his glasses and "they" knew his every thought. He was convinced the kids and I had tiny microphones in our ears and were receiving instructions about what to say and do. He also thought he was receiving messages over the radio and television, and when he had questions for "them," he sat by the front window and watched the cars going past. Each color meant something different and presumably he got his answers.

As a result of this "testing process," Ted was on his best behavior and treated me and the kids better than he ever had.

The kids loved it. It was a mixed blessing for me since I was a virtual prisoner in the house.

DESPERATION & DEPRESSION
APRIL 1966

Ted's dad was diagnosed with cancer of the pancreas in spring of 1966 and died within a couple of months. It was shortly after this that Ted became psychotic. I don't remember how I was able to talk Ted into seeing a therapist, but he finally went to a psychiatrist (Dr. C.) and was put on a strong medication. I think it was Thorazine. He was even hospitalized for a while on my psych ward. It felt strange to go there as a visitor.

During this time, I was barely putting one foot in front of the other and waiting for Ted to get well enough to take care of the kids so I could kill myself. Once again, the promise of suicide kept me moving through the nearly intolerable days.

When Ted finally stopped being delusional, he became more abusive than he had been before the psychotic episode. He was verbally and physically abusive with the kids, and when I tried to intervene, he looked at me like he wanted to kill me and followed me around the house saying cruel hurtful things until I hid in the bathroom with the door locked and sobbed until I was exhausted.

The last couple of years before I left Salt Lake were spent struggling to keep putting one foot in front of the other. What little hope I had was that therapy would somehow make a difference—would change me into someone who could cope with her life, but toward the end of that time, and especially when Dr. B. said the only way I could help Ted was to stay sick myself and allow him to work out his problems through me, I knew I had nothing left to hope for.

I was reaching the end of my ability to keep myself alive for one more day for the sake of my kids, which is what had kept me going for this long.

I could see no good options. If I took the kids and left Ted, I had no way to support us, and if I stayed, it was just a matter of time until I had to commit suicide. There was simply no way for it to work out well for the kids.

HOSPITAL HIJINKS
July–September 1966

I first met Lynn when she was working as a volunteer in Occupational Therapy. She helped me with a couple of craft projects I reluctantly allowed myself to be coerced into doing. Then one day, she was admitted as a patient and attached herself to me like a barnacle.

They had a hard time diagnosing her problem. She kept passing out. Her neurosurgeon said it was a psychiatric problem and her psychiatrist (my Dr. B.) thought it was organic. But there she was, swooning all over the psych ward. When she passed out, they put her in a wheelchair and took her to bed, but she wouldn't settle down until they found me to come sit by her bed and hold her hand while she recovered.

From the beginning, she had a talent for getting into trouble and seemed to enjoy doing it. She said she had a devil (named Irving) living in her head, and I almost came to believe it. No matter what she did, it was always Irving's fault. The devil made her do it. I'd never known anyone so bold and adventurous or so intent on getting her own way (except, perhaps, my mother).

One day, she hugged me and said she loved me. I said, "Yeah, I love you too."

"No," she replied, "I don't mean I love you like a friend. I'm in love with you."

"No you're not," I responded, "you just like me a lot." I had no such feelings for her and no experience of anyone who did.

One evening after dinner, when I was in my bed trying to die, a nurse came in and insisted I come out to the day room where another patient's roommate was playing her guitar and singing. I reluctantly dragged myself to where the performance was happening, and the first song she sang was "Born to Lose." It felt like the story of my life, and I sobbed all the way through. After that, she sang some happier songs and even got some of us to sing along. I was surprised and shocked when I began to have sexual feelings for her.

The next morning when Dr. B. made his daily rounds, I told him about my reaction to this boyishly dressed woman. He asked, "Do you think she's a lesbian?"

Shocked, I said, "Oh no, she's just masculine." I was convinced that no one I knew could possibly be "one of those."

He said not to worry about it, nearly everyone has those feelings at least once in their lives and it doesn't mean a thing. Whew! What a relief. I didn't need one more thing to feel bad about.

Lynn figured out some seemingly innocent code words to be used when other people were around. The one that comes to mind is "chum." When she called me that, I was supposed to know it was an endearment like "sweetheart" or "lover." I dealt with all this in the same way I had dealt with insoluble problems all my life: denial. I thought she'd get over it.

When her roommate was discharged, Lynn wanted me to move in with her, so we went to the nurses' station and made the request without thinking too much about it. I had often switched rooms in the past when someone I knew and liked was readmitted. I was surprised and puzzled when they said they'd have to think about it, then kept putting it off day after day and having meetings to discuss it.

They finally solved the problem by discharging me and keeping Lynn. I visited her several times, and she called me at home, often while Ted was there, and wanted to talk for long periods of time. Ted didn't like the way my voice sounded when I talked to her and started to get seriously annoyed when she called.

I fell into my familiar role of trying to keep everyone happy while feeling like the rope in a tug-of-war.

Apparently, having had sexual feelings for the psych-ward singer opened a door. I had more-than-friendly feelings for Lynn and was scared to death by them.

Ted was becoming angrier than I had ever seen him, and I was more and more frightened by the potential for violence I saw in his eyes. If I were going to die, I wanted it to be on my own terms.

∼

OCTOBER 1966

Lynn called one night after I had taken two sleeping pills and crashed. She said Ron (her husband) had issued an ultimatum that she never see me again or that she leave him and their three kids. She wanted me to run away with her.

I said, "I can't go with you, I don't have any work skills and couldn't pay my way."

She said, "That's okay, I'll support us."

To which I responded, "But I hate housekeeping. I don't want to keep house for a man or a woman."

Lynn said, "I'll take care of everything, just come with me."

My brain was in a stupor, and I told her I couldn't think right then and that she should call me in the morning.

When she called the next morning, I gathered up all my courage and said, "Yes." She had made me an offer I couldn't refuse. My suitcase was only partially unpacked from my last visit to the psych ward, and I repacked with as much clothing as it would hold.

When I finally left, it was with the hope that Dot would take care of the kids, and if I could manage to stay alive and get myself together, I might one day be able to help my kids. I knew I would be of no use to them if I were dead.

Leaving my kids was the hardest decision I ever made. In retrospect, I feel it was the best one for all of us, but I hope I never have to make a harder one.

On the afternoon of October 7, 1966, Lynn and I left nine children and two husbands and headed west into the unknown.

Chapter Twenty-Two
1985

On October 16, 1985, two bombs exploded in Salt Lake City. Stockbroker Steven Christensen, 31, found a box with his name on it when he arrived at his downtown office that morning. Soon after, Katherine Sheets, 50, picked up a newspaper resting on a box in her driveway. Both of the boxes exploded, and Steven and Katherine were both killed. Katherine had been the spouse of the intended target, J. Gary Sheets.

Mr. Sheets and Mr. Christensen had been associates in a financial firm, and police suspected the bombings were tied to the company's collapse—but when a third bomb went off the following day and seriously injured a rare document dealer named Mark Hofmann, who sold items to the Mormon Church, the story took a wild turn. The story of these high-profile murders shifted from being about a business dispute to being about a forger who was in over his head. The news made national headlines and was just the sort of excitement my father needed to boost his career.

My dad had just been re-elected as Salt Lake's county attorney and had been praised for the prosecution of several high-profile cases. His team convicted Ervil LeBaron, a polygamist murderer and conspirator whose case had consumed the community and become the top story on the nightly news. Building and prosecuting the case against Mark Hofmann made my dad something of a local hero, and it was dumping more fuel on the already raging fire of his ego and narcissism.

All the hoopla was boosting his and Carol's moods, but behind closed doors, things continued falling apart. It was becoming more and more difficult to hide the fact that Dad's successes triggered his mental illness, and his co-workers had taken note and were reporting his increasingly erratic behavior.

Meanwhile, my entire fertile family was actively multiplying and replenishing the Earth with more of God's children. Debi, a happy homemaker with five boys, lived in Soda Springs, Idaho. Anna and Beth continued to pop out babies, and Messer was pregnant with her first as well. She and Stan were building another big house not far from mine, on their way to a picture-perfect Mormon family life of their own—at least, from the outside looking in.

Pam had recently re-entered the family picture when she returned to Salt Lake with hopes to reclaim her young daughter, Amber. Alcohol and drugs had taken over Pam's life, and a year prior, she had dropped her three-month-old baby girl on her head when going down a flight of stairs after a booze-fueled party. The state threatened to take Amber away, so Carol and Dad stepped in, and Pam moved to California to live with friends and escape the responsibility of motherhood. Carol and Dad raised Amber as their own and had just started with the adoption process when Pam showed up 18 months later, penniless and reeking of Jack Daniel's, to reclaim her daughter.

Pam, who was neither clean nor sober at the time, didn't have anywhere to stay, so I offered her a temporary bed in my house. With our two babies and two toddlers, life was filled with endless hours of diaper changes and meal preparation. Pam was perpetually tired, so many of these responsibilities fell on me while she napped or sat outside on the back porch and smoked copious amounts of cigarettes.

The household was frenetic and noisy, but now and then, we found a moment to talk.

"Where are Linc and Tip these days? Pam asked me, nervously tapping a pack of Virginia Slims on my kitchen table. "Last I heard, Linc was in the Army." I snickered at the name Tip, explaining that he'd changed his name to Tom long ago, but just thinking of my brothers made a lump form in my throat. They both seemed like strangers to me.

"Well, Linc was stationed in Germany with the Army and decided to stay and work there," I said. "Dad says he's been leading kayaking trips and teaching skiing, and apparently met and married a Scottish girl named Rosie. We haven't met her yet, but we heard they had a traditional Scottish wedding with kilts and bagpipes."

"No way," she replied, twirling her unlit cigarette. "Didn't they invite anyone to the wedding?"

"Nope. We all sorta lost touch," I explained, wiping the counter off with a lime green sponge.

"Will you stop cleaning for a minute?" Pam said impatiently. "Jesus, you're making me nervous, Carol Jr." She slid her chair out and opened the sliding glass door to the back-yard so she could light up. Because she was barely leaning outside, her smoke was drifting back into the house. She had a wistful look in her eyes like she was supposed to be some-where else. I could relate to the feeling. I updated her on Tom, who was living with his girlfriend and playing in a band, and Mark, who was rumored to be living with a woman in Austin, Texas.

As I watched Pam, I realized just how old she looked. Heavy smoking had grayed her complexion, and hard times had hollowed her eyes, but I rather enjoyed the smell of her second-hand smoke, despite having been a regular church-goer and Word of Wisdom follower for the past six years (except for the occasional sip at my neighbors' house, that is).

"Do you think your mom is a lesbian?" she asked without warning. I could feel her gaze on the side of my head but was reluctant to make eye contact, shocked by her brazen ques-tion. I rubbed my head with both hands.

"Maybe," I said finally. "I dunno. Why, do you know something I don't?" Pam was worldlier and much more expe-rienced than I was, having grown up outside my Mormon bubble.

"No, I've just been curious," she replied. "I was nosing through Mom's photo albums the other day and saw a recent picture of her—she just looks different. And her friend looks totally butch."

"When Mom and Mart came to visit me at Utah State back in 1977, I sort of wondered if she was gay, but all my friends were there and I didn't want to bring it up with anyone, so I ignored my instinct. What's *butch*, anyway?" Pam laughed at my ignorance.

"You are such a dork. You really don't know? It's when a woman looks and acts masculine, like a man."

"Ew," I said. "Well, I guess there's only one way to find out if it's true. Let's ask Carol, she'll know."

We piled in the car and headed over to Carol's house, finding her baking chocolate cookies in her frilly pearl white apron in the kitchen as we entered. Before she could greet us I blurted out, "Is Mom gay?"

Stephanie broke loose from my hand and found some toys in the living room. Suddenly, I wished I had waited to see if Dad was within earshot, worried my inquiry would anger him. Talking about Mom remained an unspoken taboo, and despite being an adult, I was still scared of his wrath. Thankfully, there was no sign of my father.

"Yes, she is," Carol replied. Pam and I shot each other an incredulous look.

"Remember Lynn?" she continued. "She was the woman your mom met at the hospital back in 1966 and the two of them ran away together. Your dad and I have known since then." I took a deep breath. "No! I didn't know any of this," I replied, exasperated. It had been 19 years since Mom left, and I was just now learning about Lynn and that she was a lesbian.

"Hmm," I said. "I thought so." I didn't want to come off as dramatic, uncool and naïve to Pam.

Back home, I called each of my three sisters and told them what I'd learned about Mom. No one could believe I had the audacity to come right out and ask Carol, but more importantly, we all had to live with the shocking knowledge that our mother was a lesbian. We were all a little disturbed by the sexual aspect of being gay, but at the same time, we all laughed and joked that if we'd had to be married to Ted Cannon, we'd be gay, too.

As soon as I got off the phone, I thought about calling Mom, but decided against it. I didn't know what to say to her, so I went on for years wondering what her life was like as a lesbian. I wanted to be open-minded about homosexuality, but I was well aware of the church's strong opposition to it as sinful behavior. I didn't really believe my mom was evil (nor was Bishop Gomez, for that matter). It all seemed confusing. Even though I wanted to be accepting, it seemed I was willing to accept anyone being gay—except for my mom.

After Pam moved into her own apartment a few weeks later, things calmed down. It thrilled me to have my space back, and life seemed easier without her drama. Even though I had to apply for state and church welfare programs and stand in the free cheese line for food to supplement our meals, I was content to be making it on my own. I bought clothes for the kids and myself at our church's distribution center called the DI, which stood for Deseret Industries. It was the church's non-profit retail store. To shop there, all that was required of me was to attend church and pay tithing, which amounted to 10 percent of my meager gross income.

Unsurprisingly, Steve proved to be hit or miss when it came to child support, and eventually, he stopped paying altogether. After several months of non-payment, I garnished his wages through the court system, and he was ordered to pay $55 per child per month, plus back support. He paid for a few months before quitting his job. At that point, I realized I needed to go back to school, get an education and find a career that would enable me to support my children on my own. Relying on Steve or depending on government and church handouts weren't strategies I could live with.

After applying to the University of Utah as a non-traditional student, I was accepted and granted financial aid. To my relief, the State of Utah paid for day care. The experience wouldn't be easy, especially for my sweet children, but I knew I didn't have a choice.

Chapter Twenty-Three
1985-1988

Divorced only 10 months and with three mouths to feed, I sat in the lobby of the State of Utah's Division of Oil, Gas and Mining at the Triad Center downtown, applying for a secretarial position. I waited on the gray leather couch in my favorite floral dress, feigning confidence with my proper posture and calm exterior, with the aromatic smell of forbidden coffee wafting through the air. I was nervous as hell. *I need this job*, I thought.

After what seemed like forever, a friendly executive assistant named Audrey appeared. She looked about seven years older than me and a million times more sophisticated with her A-line bob and designer business suit. She interviewed me in the conference room, and when one of her co-workers popped his head into the room, interrupting our conversation, she told him to "fuck off." *I like this woman*, I thought as I suppressed a snort of laughter. The next morning, I received the call that the job was mine. A miracle!

A week after I started working, my new boss Ken began

overtly flirting with me at the front desk, and I was more than happy to flirt back. *He's handsome and charming*, I thought, *but holy shit—he's my boss!* I was flattered that he seemed interested in me, a low-level, divorced secretary on welfare with three children. It turned out he knew everything about me from my resume and was responsible for my getting hired. Apparently, he had gone into Audrey's office before she interviewed me and said, "Hire that one," while pointing at me (which Audrey told me later). There had clearly been much more qualified applicants, but Ken had a plan, miracles aside.

Things moved rather quickly between Ken and me. He was in the middle of a divorce and had been separated for about a year, sharing custody of their four-year-old daughter, Nealy. After work, he would take me to the most expensive restaurants downtown. I felt guilty going out because it meant the kids had to stay at day care even longer, but Ken was more than willing to pay for the overtime for a chance to be alone with me. Slowly, I began breaking the Word of Wisdom as I enjoyed forbidden pleasures like chardonnay with dinner and cafe au lait afterwards. Ken, a non-Mormon, had significant experience in the realms of cocktails, fine wine and gourmet dining, which made him even more attractive to me. In contrast, I was a naïve, garment-wearing Mormon woman, and Ken took pleasure in corrupting my devout and prudish ways. He wasn't just not Mormon—he hated the religion and made no bones about his opinion of Joseph Smith "the con-man."

For the first time in many years, I finally had a sexual urge, and Ken and I didn't waste much time before diving into bed. Before that could happen, I knew I needed to ditch my garments and swap them out for something that wouldn't embarrass me or require explanation. I wasn't sure if Ken had ever seen the funny underwear, but I wasn't about to have him see me wearing them the first time we had sex. I gathered up all my angel chaps and disposed of them in the manner approved by the church, which meant cutting out the markings over the breasts, the belly and the right knee. I burned them in the fireplace and tossed the bulk of the material in the trash can. I didn't feel the least bit ashamed to change to normal civilian underwear; in fact, it felt divine. I never got used to those ugly, hot, bunched-up, ridiculous garments anyway.

People were talking about us in our tight-knit neighborhood, so I got a call from the bishop wanting me to come in and meet with him. In his office, I confessed to having broken my temple covenants, which was code for "I am having sex." He pushed his chair back and took off his glasses, loosening his tie.

"Tell me in detail about your sexual encounters with Ken," he said studiously. I blushed, answering that I would rather not discuss it, but he continued to pry. I'd had enough —more than enough, actually.

"This is bullshit!" I raged at him. "I don't have to tell you anything. All you need to know is that I am a divorced woman, falling in love and having sex with my boyfriend."

The bishop nervously cleared his throat as he leaned in closer to me.

"I need to know because you made certain promises in the temple when you married Steve," he said calmly. "I want to be sure that you know that there are procedures and consequences for breaking temple covenants. We will actually need to hold a church court. Your membership is on the line."

His words infuriated me. Hell, I didn't care about losing my membership. All I could focus on was the absurdity of the situation.

"You should be ashamed of yourselves as church leaders for encouraging young people to enter the temple without any preparation and make promises they can't keep," I blurted. "It should be illegal for anyone under the age of 25 to make outrageous commitments that they are supposed to live up to for eternity."

The force of my words made him jerk back, and for the first time during the interrogation, he was speechless. I stood up and headed for the exit. Pausing, I turned and added, "And let me know when my court date is." I slammed the door behind me for added effect.

Once I got to my car, I stopped to take a breath, still trembling. Despite the rush of emotions, it felt glorious and freeing to speak my mind. Twenty-five years of pent-up frustration, hypocrisy, judgment and feeling unworthy had suddenly and unexpectedly come to an end. The wine bottle had been uncorked, the coffee beans spilled and the angel chaps had sprouted wings and flown away—and I was done taking anyone's shit.

A month later, I showed up for my assigned court date, where I found Bishop Calloway surrounded by a team of pale-faced young counselors determined to set me straight. Seething, I sat there for 10 minutes as they probed me once again for details about my sex life, but I held my ground. Their inquiries were perverse to me, and I certainly was not going to let them humiliate me for their own twisted satisfaction. I was at the end of my rope.

"Just let me know what you all decide about my status," I said, standing up. "I won't be coming back to another kangaroo court." As I started to leave, Bishop Calloway held up his hand.

"Sister Anderson," he called out, "we need you to know that we love you and we are still praying for you. Know that the Lord still wants you to wear your garments and pay your tithing so you can continue to receive the blessings of the church." *I've had enough "blessings" to last me a lifetime, thank you very much,* I thought, shutting the door behind me and not looking back.

When I got home, Ken was waiting for me. He had offered to watch the children and already had them tucked in for the night. Once I calmed down, I felt victorious as I shared the details of the scene with him. He laughed at my descriptions of those pasty-faced, dough-headed idiots.

"Man, that took balls," he said. "Good for you." We celebrated with my first taste of champagne, accompanied by one of Ken's funny toasts: "Friends may come, and friends may go; and friends may peter out, you know. But we'll be friends through thick or thin, peter out, or peter in."

I never told anyone in my family about being dis-fellowshipped from the church, and luckily, they didn't bother to ask. Everyone was too focused on their own life sagas. My family's perpetual chaos continued to let me get away with almost anything, and while Beth and Anna cornered me several times concerned about my salvation, something bigger always came up. This time, it was my dad's turn to step into the spotlight, but not in the way he was used to.

Ted Cannon went from being our city's hero in 1986 to the city's great embarrassment in 1987. The media began blasting rumors that Dad had sexually assaulted two of his secretaries, which launched a federal investigation. The allegations came at the height of his career when he was considering another term and an eventual run for a seat on the federal bench. The investigation dominated the news for months, all while Dad kept claiming he was innocent and the target of personal vendettas against him. He said it was all to sabotage his career and keep him from being re-elected.

He had many supporters, especially us kids and everyone in our ward—but then, a grand jury indicted him on a misdemeanor of criminal libel for defaming a local reporter. He pled no contest to the other charges of sexual assault, misuse of public funds and official misconduct. The sexual harassment charges were eventually settled out of court and the city paid his secretary $68,000 (she wrote a scandalous tell-all article for *Redbook* Magazine in 1990).

A horrified Grandma Dot was convinced my father was being wrongfully persecuted by the media. Since Gramps had been gone for years, she had ample time on her hands. She spent many hours neurotically clipping and saving articles printed about him in the *Deseret News*, the newspaper owned by the church and favored by faithful Mormons. She and Aunt MaryAnn even made several scrapbooks based on the fiasco, as Mormon women did for any occasion or event that could be cut, glued and assembled into a book. As we walked in the door for our weekly Sunday visit, she'd hug Dad and scorn the wicked people who were doing this to him.

"Those Damnacrats," she would say, shaking her fist in

the air. We all thought it was funny, as "Damnacrat" was the worst swear word we'd ever heard her utter, but both she and Aunt MaryAnn were adamant he was innocent.

Sitting in the courtroom as the judge read Dad's sentence out loud, a court psychologist diagnosed him with bipolar disorder and ordered him to stay on medication for two years following his 30-day sentence. Even with this news of bipolar disorder, Dad dismissed the diagnosis by saying he had a unique type of bipolar, which meant he was in constant mania and this "unique form" did not respond to treatment. But he had no choice—for at least for two years, he had to stay on the meds and provide proof of compliance through regularly scheduled blood tests. It was the first time that it truly hit me that Dad had a mental illness.

For Dad and Carol's marriage, the scandal was the straw that broke the camel's back. Danny, who had just graduated from high school, didn't waste a second getting the hell out of the house, ditching any plans to be a missionary. Instead, he moved to Los Angeles to attend art school. Luckily for him, he had a very different college experience from the rest of us, fully financially supported by his wealthy father. He was accepted to Otis Parson, a well-known private school, and flourished as an artist.

Finally free from the responsibility of raising kids and unable to withstand the public humiliation associated with the fall of the house of Cannons, Carol hit the road and moved into a place in Murray. Jilted twice, my father stewed in his hatred of women. Their divorce went forward while he carried out his sentence in jail. But even behind bars, he fed his narcissistic nature. He said he felt like a "celebrity" while he was in the slammer and was helping the other inmates with their legal problems. He journaled manically while he was locked up, claiming that the entire prison experience wasn't that bad, and that he even made some friends.

Visiting my dad in jail was unsettling. He started asking for contraband and raged against Carol until the guards threatened him. Finally, before we were about to leave, he leaned over to me.

"Take this," he whispered across the table, sliding a book toward me. "Keep it for me until I get out. I'm not supposed to have it in here." His handwriting on the front of the hardbound red book read *Jail Journal*. I waited until I was home to crack the book open and read:

T. CANNON
COALVILLE, UTAH
SUMMIT COUNTY JAIL
CELL # 233
AUG. 12-SEPT. 5, 1987

25 days (5 days off for good time) on a 30-day sentence, imposed as a condition of probation by Judge X (who is neither Honorable nor judicious let alone judicial. He is really just a twerp.)

The whole sorry saga—two bitch wives. Two broken hearts. Carol and her lousy stinking MC (Mormon Church) guilt. Blasted hopes and expectations—reputation destroyed (tho now rehabilitating by all accounts on the basis of "Poor Old Cannon—he done some; but the consequences are too much" —a sort of sympathy/forgiveness "rehabilitation" if you can call it that. I suppose shortly now some well-meaning asshole

will tell me "You paid for your crimes—you just need to make
a new life from here." I PAID ALL RIGHT, for non-crimes
that I never fucking did anyway.

If I want vengeance that's neither surprising nor inappropri-
ate. I just wish I knew a way to get it! I don't give a fuck for
all this turn the other cheek, learn your lesson crap—never
have. I want a piece back—and by God, if there's any right,
justice or equity I should have it! Anyways, when I get outta
here, there's still a bunch of goddamn shit awaiting. And
there's that most contemptible despicable fuck bitch Carol
still out there to nag my ass forever just because she still lives.
The asshole. The phony—the fucking quitter.

I need a haircut.

Despite attending almost every one of Dad's trials, I was
still convinced that Dad was mostly innocent, even after he
was locked up (though I wondered if he was guilty when it
came to the sexual harassment charges). Still, his disjointed,
disturbing journal made me question everything, and I was
suddenly certain the court-ordered medication was a good
call.

Outside in the real world, our family was surrounded by
people who felt the state had unjustly accused my dad.
Many Republicans argued that Ted Cannon was being
framed and railroaded, and even Ken was impressed by Dad,
rather liking the attention he received from dating the well-
known Republican's daughter.

"The mining community needs good Republicans in
office," he would say. Ken thought my dad was brilliant,

interesting and funny. He couldn't understand my fear of him—but then again, Ken didn't know the half of it.

I never could be honest with Ken about how I truly felt about my dad and his craziness, especially since he was constantly singing Dad's praises. Ken couldn't get over the fact that my dad had an IQ of 192. While there was no doubt my father was a genius with his photographic memory and extreme creativity—he could rattle off poems, whip up a sketch of just about anything from memory and create elaborate and exact army battle scenes from the French Revolution with figurines—he was a *mad* genius. No one in my family could figure out why, if he was so damn smart, he made such a mess of things in his life. I respected Ken's opinion and wanted him to not only fall in love with me but with my family too, so I didn't elaborate on Dad's idiosyncrasies. The more Ken became enamored with Dad, the more I bought into the idea that perhaps my dad was a misjudged badass, and the deeper I fell for Ken.

Two years later, when things quieted down and Dad had been out of jail for more than a year and a half, Ken and I got married in a beautiful garden setting at a lovely house in The Avenues. Ken had insisted that a judge marry us in a civil ceremony with our four kids as part of the wedding celebration. It was a day of delicious food and dancing, and we even served champagne to the great disapproval of my family. Still, I didn't care; I was determined to reveal the truth about my lifestyle with Ken and to blend our families in a way he and I saw fit.

Ken encouraged me to continue my education and gave me the opportunity to go to school full-time so I could earn my bachelor's degree at the University of Utah's physical therapy school. Not long after, Grandma Dot fell ill and was placed in a nursing home. It was devastating for our family—especially Dad, who had been struggling since he got out of jail. He visited her daily and sat for hours by her bedside.

A distraught Beth visited daily too. Despite being overwhelmed with school and family, I went to see her fairly often. Sitting by her bedside one day, I held her tiny hand.

"I'm so proud of you honey," Grandma Dot said weakly, barely uttering the words. "I hope you're happy."

"I've never been so happy," I told her. And it was the truth.

It was gut-wrenching losing Grandma, as she had been my lifeline for so long. We considered her our own personal angel who kept watch over us, even as we got older, but even more difficult to deal with than my own sadness was my acute awareness of Dad's heartbreak. He had clung to her tightly because she was really all he had left. Now that she was gone, I worried about what would happen to him.

After Grandma Dot's funeral, we drove in the procession to the cemetery where she would rest in peace right next to Grandpa Ted. When Beth saw Grandma's casket hovering over the deep hole, she fell to her knees and sobbed, her entire body shaking, and I knelt beside her.

"Losing Grandma is going to unravel my world," she choked out. "She's the only person who truly loves us, and now she's gone. I don't know how to live without her." I put my arm around her waist and helped her up.

"We have each other, Beth." Even I couldn't deny the hurt. Losing Grandma Dot was like losing our mother all over again.

Two years into our marriage, we moved to Salina in

Central Utah when Ken was promoted to general manager of Utah's largest underground coal mine. Ken was thrilled, but it meant I was going to have a long commute to school in Salt Lake—143 miles to be exact. Relocating right in the middle of an already tough program was hard enough, let alone the transitioning to small-town life. In the beginning, I found Salina to be a sad and desolate desert community. Horses, cows and chickens had replaced the vibrant big city residents I was used to.

They say humans can adapt to most anything, and the longer we lived in Salina, the more I supposed it was true. Over the course of the next six years, my life became filled with 4H, camping trips and watching the girls barrel race in the local rodeo. Ken taught Scott how to hunt and fish, and I was thrilled we had all bonded as a family. We all dove in and tried to adapt the best we could, eventually enjoying small-town life for what it was. While I ached for cultured city life, long bike rides helped me grow to appreciate the beauty of the countryside. Ken had given me the gift of a solid, loving family, which pushed away the haunting memories of my broken past. At least until my father came to visit.

Chapter Twenty-Four
1994

As the kids grew, the routines of small-town life took hold of our family. Stephanie, now 14 and in junior high, had landed the lead role in *Lil' Abner* and invited my father to attend. Grandpa Ted, as the kids called him, had phoned a couple of nights earlier to accept her invitation, announcing his plan to drive to Salina with my brother Tom. That last detail came as a complete surprise to me because I hadn't seen Tom for four years.

Tom had apparently become close to my dad, and the two of them had even started an online business together. Behind their decision to visit us, Dad mentioned there was a Scottish Festival nearby, and that he and Tom had rented a booth to sell their hand-drawn pictures of Scottish castles. Their plan was to come see the play the night before the festival and asked if they could spend the night at our house.

Naturally, I said yes—but then I immediately regretted it. I was anxious about the idea of having the two of them in my home.

The kids had suffered the wrath of my cleaning frenzies before and knew how mad I got if they didn't help, and preparing the house for Tom and my dad was no exception. After we were all exhausted getting the house ready, my father and Tom pulled up to the front curb in Dad's beat-up Mazda sports car, a mid-life crisis purchase after his divorce from Carol in 1986.

"Shit," I said a little too loudly.

"What's wrong, Mommy?" my youngest asked as she jumped into my arms. Haley was a momma's girl who still loved to be held, even at nine years old, and the other kids teased her about being spoiled.

"Nothing sweets, I just stubbed my toe," I said. The doorbell rang twice followed by three loud knocks. "Shit," I said again, turning to the door. Haley squealed, jumped out of my arms, ran to the door in a flash and threw it open. I mustered up a huge fake smile.

"Hi, how was the drive?" I asked, trying to be polite. Dank cigarette smoke wafted into my nostrils as Dad and Tom walked in and we all exchanged brief and awkward hugs. Dad looked like he hadn't seen a barber in months. His sandy red hair had now turned pure white and hung well over his ears, greasy and unkempt. He was wearing torn-up beige shorts and a ragged black T-shirt lined with sweat marks.

Tom was still wearing his hair long, just as he did when he was a teen. He was slouched and so damn skinny, his jeans barely hung on his hips. His eyes bulged as if he was in a perpetual stage of panic, and chain-smoking had shaded his teeth an unsightly brown. *Even though he smells like an ashtray,* I thought, *at least he looks relatively clean.*

He was standing awkwardly at the front door with his hands deep in his pockets. He seemed nervous in his own skin, which was an effect Dad had on all of us. In honor of Tom's visit, I had a big pot of spaghetti waiting, his favorite meal.

Later that night, Stephanie performed her part in the play to perfection, beaming as she locked eyes with me and the rest of the family in attendance in the middle-school auditorium. We celebrated by having dessert at the famous Mom's Café, where Dad must have eaten three scones, each one the size of a dinner plate and slathered with a fake honey butter that came out of a tube. He did this while talking non-stop, not even taking a breath or bothering to wipe the mess off his face. The kids watched him with wide eyes and gaping mouths.

Back at home, Haley slept with Stephanie in the basement in her newly decorated room with frilly floral curtains and perfectly matching wallpaper. When I tucked her in, she was still grumpy that Grandpa Ted would occupy her bed. *Who could blame her?* I shuddered at the thought.

Trudging back up the stairs, I could hear Dad, Tom and Ken in a boisterous conversation in the kitchen. Ken pulled out a chair for me to join them before I could excuse myself and made his way to the cupboard, dusting off four highball glasses and pouring too much Crown Royal into each one.

"What are you guys talking about?" I asked.

"Tom has a gig at Hog Wallow in Salt Lake," Dad proudly announced.

"So you're still playing in a band?" I asked, genuinely interested.

"Yeah, we're getting a few gigs around town. Local pubs

and bars. We're in high demand right now," he replied, showing some enthusiasm at long last.

"Rock, right?" I asked. "That's so cool! I'll have to come hear you play sometime. What's the name of your band?"

"Loose Cannons." Dad held up his glass for another toast.

"Here's to all of us loose Cannons!" Dad said with spit flying from his mouth. We all laughed as the irony of the name sunk in. After a few more drinks, Dad looked at me from over the top of his glasses.

"Is there somewhere private where we could go to talk?" he asked. "I have some things to tell you." I felt the blood drain from my face,

"Uh, not really," I said. "What do you have to tell me?" Ken picked up his glass and stood up, chomping on some cashews in his mouth.

"Well, it's time for me to tip over in the fart sack!" Everyone laughed, and I couldn't help but snort, too, even though I'd heard this Ken-ism a million times. Tom followed suit, excusing himself and climbing into his own "fart sack" on the couch, leaving Dad and me alone.

Dad took several long draws on his cigarette, which bothered me because we didn't allow smoking in the house. Too afraid to set boundaries with him, I kept quiet as I gazed down at my half-empty glass. At the top of his third drink, he was clearly more relaxed but still smoking incessantly. He motioned for me to come closer as he sat at the head of the table, so I moved to take a seat next to him. He looked me in the eye.

"You know I love you, right?" he said. "As far as I am concerned, what I am about to say doesn't change anything."

Oh, my God, what skeleton is he going to drag out of the closet now? I thought. *That he has to go to prison again? That he molested me as a child?* My heart was racing.

"You need to know I'm not your biological father," he said finally. I was stunned stupid and couldn't get any words out. My mind had conjured up many awful things he *might* reveal, but I hadn't prepared for this one.

"Wait, what?" I mumbled, feeling shattered. "You mean I'm not a Cannon? Who is my father, then?" Tears welled in both of our eyes as I watched my drunk dad try to put out his cigarette in his empty whiskey glass and miss, tapping the burning red cherry end onto my brand-new kitchen table. Still paralyzed by the news, I sat there and watched as the varnish melted away, eating into the wood underneath, leaving a perfectly round black hole in the table that might as well have been my heart. My dad paused for a moment before continuing.

"The same goes for Messer, too."

Excerpt from Joyce Cannon's Journals

AFFAIRES DE LA COEUR
1957

In the early years of our marriage, I was usually either pregnant or nursing a baby and we couldn't afford sitters, so dealing with the advances of other men didn't get serious until Ted started working for Shell Oil Co. Shortly after he was hired, we were invited to a Halloween costume party at the home of one of the engineers. Ted designed my costume as a French Apache dancer with a tight striped T-shirt and short black skirt with a slit up the side. Fishnet stockings, stiletto heels, a beret and a dagger in my belt completed the outfit. The party was in a beautiful home with a huge basement, which is where the festivities were held. I was a great hit with the men, especially the two named Stan. One of them, while we were dancing, kept moaning in my ear, "Oh, you woman." The other wanted me to meet him outside at his car.

Once again, I asked Ted to dance with me so I could

avoid these guys. He gave me a stern lecture about not acting like a prude and embarrassing him in front of his friends.

As this happened again and again with different men at different times and places, I finally decided to relax and enjoy the attention I was getting. Ted became the sole arbiter of what I wore and even began designing dresses for me to make, since Sears and JC Penney didn't have the kind of clothes he wanted me to wear.

His favorite was a black corduroy dress that could be worn with a blouse under it for family dinners or without the blouse, in which case I wore what felt like a corset underneath that caused my breasts to bulge out the top of the dress. By the time we went anywhere, I looked and felt like the town hooker. I had long since given up the hope that Ted or any other man would ever see me as anything other than a desirable receptacle for his manhood.

Somehow, we survived, and as the twins got older and gained weight, they didn't need to be fed so often. We resumed a social life, and we often partied with the same neighbors I used to have coffee with and their husbands—some of whom worked with Ted.

One of the couples lived across the street. Betty was a housewife and Dick an insurance adjuster. There came a time when I would have coffee with Betty in the morning and sex with Dick in the evening when Ted was out of town, after the kids were in bed. Try as I might, I can't remember how this got started. I kept it a secret from Ted but didn't think he'd care even if he knew. I did know, however, that Betty would care, yet I continued to do it.

Then one night at a party with the Shell Oil people, I was dancing with a fellow named Rob, and he whispered, "Oh, how I could love you." He'd said the magic words, and it was the beginning of a tangled web of deception wherein I was juggling three men and four kids.

It was a great relief when we heard we were being transferred 50 miles south to Farmington, New Mexico, but my relief was short-lived. Rob had been transferred too, and he ended up living on the street behind us. Our backyards overlapped, and since the yards all had cyclone fencing, there was no privacy, no barrier between us.

~

BABY MELISSA
BORN MAY 13, 1961
SALT LAKE CITY, UTAH
A STREET AND 6TH AVE

After living in Salt Lake for a bit, out of the blue, I got a call from Rob. He was an assistant to the big mucky-muck of Shell Oil in Farmington and had somehow finagled a trip to Salt Lake on company time. As it turned out, he managed it quite often—and, of course, I got pregnant again.

Now, I was really in a pickle. The only two men I was having sex with both had vasectomies—and there wasn't going to be any star rising in the east. I told Ted I thought I was pregnant and that he'd better have his vasectomy checked because if it was intact, then I must have a tumor. My plan was that if he got it checked and it was indeed working, I would have to kill myself. Not much of a plan considering I had five and a half kids to raise, but I couldn't see many options, and suicide was always my backup plan.

Ted preferred to live in denial and refused to get his vasectomy checked out.

The next time Rob came to visit, I told him I was pregnant and didn't want to have sex with him anymore. He forced himself on me and not wanting to hurt the baby or wake the kids, I submitted. When he was leaving the house, I told him that if he ever came back I would call the police. I didn't realize it was rape until many years later.

Melissa was born on May 13, 1961. Fortunately for all of us, she was an angelic baby. She was born sweet and remains so to this day.

Part Three
Loose Cannons

Chapter Twenty-Five
1994

The morning after my dad's drunken revelations, I told Ken about what had happened.

"If I'm not a Cannon, who am I?" I asked him. We were raised with the belief that we were a kind of Mormon royalty. Grandma Dot and Dad both told stories of George Q. Cannon as an apostle to Brigham Young, that we were good, tough pioneer stock. The Cannon name in Utah was almost as prevalent as Young or Smith. George Q. even made it into the local school system, with his picture appearing in seventh-grade Utah history textbooks. The photo and historical account revealed that he was sent to prison for polygamy, so in the picture, he sat right in the middle of several other convicts in their black and white striped jumpsuits. My grandparents and father seemed to feel that because of that history, we were better than everyone else. For my father, his sacrifice of going to jail was like the sacrifice Jesus made, made for the good of the family. *So, I'm not a first-class citizen now*, I thought. *I'm a who-the-hell-knows? How am I going to tell Messer?*

I finally emerged from my bedroom to find Dad and Tom ready to head out the door. They looked ridiculous in their worn-out Scottish attire, and I was in no mood to share in their excitement. Just as Dad started making lewd comments about not wearing any underwear under his kilt, I interrupted.

"I'm going to drive to Salt Lake tonight to tell Messer," I said. "I think we should break the news together."

"Aren't you coming to the festival?" Tom asked.

"No, I've got things I need to do here." I averted my eyes from Dad, who looked like a lunatic in his kilt with his pale freckled legs exposed. I silently hoped no one in Richfield would make the connection between us. They said their goodbyes, and as they shut the door, I caught a glimpse of Dad's face, and it looked as if he had been crying. A lump formed in my throat, but just then, Haley came bursting in the room in a fury.

"Mommy, come and look at this. It's so gross..."

Shuffling into her tidy room, I noticed the bed covers had been pushed to the side, exposing brown skid marks on her favorite sheets. Haley was going into a full-blown temper tantrum.

"This is so disgusting!" she shouted. A half-asleep Stephanie walked in, curious about the noise, and saw the unsightly damage, too.

"He is never sleeping in my bed!" she said, as Ken and Scott appeared, too.

"God, now that's shit-the-bed drunk!" my tactful husband blurted. He jabbed Scott in the ribs, and they roared with laughter, which made Haley start wailing. Still numb, I disappeared into the kitchen and grabbed a garbage bag and a pair of dishwashing gloves. As I stuffed her soiled sheets into the bag, I promised to buy Haley a new set. Finally, the boys flipped the mattress over.

"Jesus Christ," Ken said. "What a pig!"

When Dad and Tom returned from Richfield to pick up their bags, they were both in a foul mood. They had only sold one of their Scottish castles the entire day and were complaining about the heat when they came through the door. They changed from kilts to shorts, then quickly said their goodbyes. Soon after they were gone, I jumped in my car and hightailed it to my sister's.

Despite having been there several times, I still couldn't get over the size of Messer's new abode. She and Stan had built several homes together, each one bigger than the last —and their latest was massive. No one in the family cared much for Stan's holier-than-thou attitude, and this new McMansion in Murray had only made his ego swell even more. He and my father were constantly intellectually sparring, and I had little tolerance for it—especially that night.

Dad pulled up and met me at the front door. Once we were inside, we pulled Messer into their formal front room, a shrine-like space decorated with statues of Jesus and pictures of the temple, reserved for family prayer and sessions with church leaders. I sat next to Messer on the plaid couch as Dad told her his news and she burst into tears, making all of us cry. I had never seen my father break down and sob so intensely before.

"I am still your father," he said, choking out the words.

"As far as I am concerned, you are every bit my daughters, no matter what."

"We feel the same, Dad," I said, echoing his sentiments. I was overwhelmed by his honesty and felt a deeper love for him. Even though he knew all along that Messer and I were not his own flesh and blood, he had kept on raising us. It was giving me a newfound respect for him.

When Dad finally stood to leave, we waved him off and then grabbed Messer's car keys.

"It's time to go to bed!" Stan blurted as we slammed the door behind us. We drove into town despite his protests, talking about Dad returning to his sad little smoke-filled apartment in Salt Lake, stuffed to the brim with old newspapers and empty food containers. His hoarding tendencies had worsened with no wife to clean up after him, and it was depressing to think of him all alone. He'd seemed truly undone by sharing the news with us.

We ended up at the tacky Village Inn on State Street, where Messer drank copious Diet Cokes and I downed coffee—for some reason the Word of Wisdom forbade hot caffeinated drinks, but cold ones were just fine, so diet soft drinks were the chosen vice of Mormons across the state. Even Carol would pop open her first Diet Pepsi right after breakfast and refill her glass throughout the day.

In the dim unflattering light of this coffee shop, we wondered if in his mania, Dad was just making everything up. But then it hit us: having this knowledge he had shared with us explained so much. We had always been so much closer to one another than anyone else, and we'd been told repeatedly that we didn't look like the others in the family as the only two blondes. Dad's news was just one more thing that bonded us. After talking it through, we agreed to take a trip to confront Mom and validate Dad's story.

Ten days later, we took Delta Flight 1845 to Reno. I hadn't been back since my brief visit with Ken, and Messer had never gone to see Mom. When we arrived, we found her excited to show us around town, but we had other things on our minds.

Standing in her living room, Messer blurted, "We need to ask you something." The minute the words escaped Messer's lips, Mom's face blanched. Her look told us that she knew exactly what we were about to confront her with.

"Dad came to Salina last week and told us he isn't our biological father," I stuttered. "And that you guys were swingers and had affairs. Dad's so manic right now that we figured he might be delusional and making it up, so we wanted to hear it from you—is it true?"

We left out the details because we wanted to hear her version to see if both stories matched up. And they did. It was as if she and Dad had talked about it five minutes before we got there. Messer and I both sat there stunned, and the tears flowed again.

"Why did you leave Messer and me there with him?" I asked, the anger rising in my voice. "He wasn't even our dad. Do you have any idea what he did to us?" At this, Mom started crying.

"I was either going to kill myself or leave," she said. "I was afraid he'd come after me if I took any of you along—plus, I had no way to support you. I could barely take care of myself. I'm so sorry. I wish I could have done better." She nervously wadded up a bunch of tissues, tearing them into tiny pieces as she spoke.

"Were you ever going to tell us?" Messer asked.

"I was waiting for the right time," she said, "but it never seemed right. I honestly don't know if I ever would have." The three of us stood up and got into a tight circle in her tiny living room and hugged.

"Poor us," I finally said, which made Mom laugh.

"Yes, poor us!" she repeated.

For the next two days, Messer and I hunkered down in Mom's trailer, talking about things we should've discussed a long time ago. She even dragged out a few pictures of our real dad, Rob Hoesley, describing him as an outgoing, charming guy.

"He was the first man I felt loved me for more than my body," she said. "He was athletic and bald with big ears. He looked a little like the actor, Telly Savalas, who played *Kojak* in the '70s. Do you remember him?" We both nodded yes, trying to absorb all this information.

"Did he know he was our dad?" I asked.

"And what about his wife, did she know?" Messer added.

"He knew because I told him, but he said nothing to his wife," Mom said, dropping a heaping teaspoon of Coffee Mate into her mug.

"Does he have kids? Are you still in contact with him? Do you know where he lives?" It was impossible not to bombard her with questions.

"I haven't seen him since I left Salt Lake," she said. "He could be anywhere. But truthfully, girls, besides Dick, Rob was the only man I slept with at that time—and Dick was sterile."

That night, I couldn't sleep. My mind was still spinning from all the things that Mom had told us. It was true—I really wasn't a Cannon. On top of that, I couldn't imagine my parents couple swapping. Images of suburban cocktail-infused gatherings, where '70s-style swingers dumped their keys into a large bowl and then went home with whoever they drew out, swam through my head. All of it was nothing like the straight-laced Mormon culture of the 1950s.

As I struggled to come to terms with this new information, I read up on the history of swinging. As I learned, it turned out that "swinging" had actually evolved out of World War II in the 1940s, originating with fighter pilots making death pacts with one another. These pilots had the highest fatality rate in war, and they believed that sharing their wives created a bond between families, so if something happened to one of them, a buddy might step in and watch out for the other's wife. World War II had happened only a few years before my parents were married, and this naughty notion of swinging was still on many people's minds, including theirs.

I discovered that a great deal of white middle-class people were churchgoers by day and wife swappers by night, but swinging also led to dysfunctional relationships, jealousy, marital affairs and all kinds of other trouble—especially for couples who were not particularly happy before these new amorous entanglements. From what my mom had told us, it all sounded a lot like my parents. Combining swinging with my mother's repressed, subservient housewife with the unstable, "lord and master" mindset of my father was a perfect storm.

On the flight home, Messer and I talked about what Mom's life must be like compared to ours. She lived alone (as far as we knew) in a double-wide trailer, and her house was unnervingly quiet. We never got around to asking her about her job, her love life or anything for that matter. We resolved we would go back again soon to get to know her better when life settled down.

"I still can't believe Dad isn't our dad," I sighed, tossing a handful of peanuts into my mouth.

"And we'll never meet our real dad," added Messer. "Thank God we have each other," She said, grabbing my hand.

When I returned to Salina, I didn't have the energy to deal with these newfound family secrets. My parents had been swingers, for God's sake—my dad wasn't my dad, and Mom was a lesbian. I did what I had always done and buried it in my head, deep in the dysfunctional family file. I welcomed the distraction of PT school and forged ahead, graduating with honors. To my surprise, Mom came to my graduation on that beautiful spring day. There was a sea of graduates with their families, mine included, all converging on the lawn outside when I spotted her.

She beamed as she introduced us to her new partner.

"Everyone, this is Norma," she announced with a hint of girlish excitement. We all shook hands and said our slightly sheepish hellos. Mom handed me a small wrapped gift and pulled me in for an awkwardly long hug as Haley hung on my leg. Stephanie, Scott and Nealy fidgeted by my side, all dressed up in their nicest clothes.

"I think you may have had the best family turnout of the whole event," Ken said. His mother Gladys came as did his siblings and their spouses; most of my side of the family had come as well, including Tom, Linc, Debi, Mark and Pam. Dad and Carol hadn't made the trip, which I assumed was because they had somehow found out that Mom and Norma were coming.

I had received an award for academic excellence that came with a sizable check, and everyone kept congratulating me for it. I had certainly come a long way from my remedial math classes and failing Latin back in high school, much to my and everyone else's surprise.

Ken had booked a hotel suite at the Little America downtown to host my graduation party, and once we were there, I finally had a few minutes alone with Mom and Norma. The more obviously masculine of the two, Norma sported a white butch haircut and khaki pants with a tucked-in plaid short-sleeved shirt while Mom wore a pastel blouse and a short but feminine haircut. I opened their gift, which was a beautiful watch with hand-painted beads from a recent trip they had taken to Central America. I hugged Norma, thanking her for the gift and for coming. It was strange of Mom to introduce Norma to us this way, but I still quite liked her.

After graduating, I was hired by a small, well-established clinic to work as a physical therapist in Richfield, a one-drag town 18 miles south of Salina and only slightly bigger. After a couple of years, I worked with the clinic to start a pilot outpatient practice in Salina, so I could be closer to home. Ken's job was very demanding; he was always working. As the general manager of the town's biggest employer, he had a major presence in the community and was a bit of a local celebrity. I tried my best to adapt to our new life in a small town, but nicknames like "City Slicker" seemed to follow me around. When I needed to get away from it all, I went on bike rides, usually by myself (which in turn earned me another nickname: "Sprocket Head").

Even cycling was considered a city thing, as no one in our small town could comprehend riding a bike for exercise. I was also the only person in town who refused to wear Wrangler jeans or get my hair done at the local beauty parlor. Part of me was bound and determined not to look like the Salina girls at the Dairy Freeze, so I resolved to hold on to my urban roots and not become a country bumpkin and remained loyal to my city hairdresser and Nordstrom.

A few months after Dad broke the shattering news to us, Messer and I hired a private detective to chase down his story of our alleged father, Rob Hoesley. Once I'd graduated and accomplished some of my educational goals, I allowed myself to dig up some of the buried memories that had been stuffed away for so long. I felt sad or angry most of the time but didn't understand why—but when I would try to talk to Ken about it, he didn't want to hear it.

"Mom used to lock us in our bedrooms, sometimes for days at a time, while she was off having coffee with her friends," I would tell him. "We were so hungry, we'd—" But Ken would put up his hand to stop me.

"I can't hear this," he would say. "It hurts me deep into my nuts." He'd then bend forward and grab himself with authentic physical pain. Ken had come from a stable, loving family and simply couldn't comprehend the nightmare of my past, nor did he want to discuss it. Instead, he put all his energy into his job and became so wrapped up with work that it dominated our conversations and social life. After five years of marriage, it felt like we barely spoke of anything important. Meanwhile, my past kept coming up and invading my day-to-day life and emotions.

I finally decided my depression was getting serious enough that I needed a therapist, and found one who favored a cognitive therapy model, which was a completely different approach than I was used to. In one of our early sessions, he presented a diagram of my family matrix before explaining that in many dysfunctional family systems, family members tend to adopt many of the same archetypal roles. In my family, he explained, I had been the scapegoat.

"The reason you were so much more severely abused by your father than the other girls was because you were the first bastard daughter to join the family," the therapist said. "Basically, you bore the brunt of your father's pent-up frustration."

His words shattered me. The diagram hadn't made sense at first, but now the deeper pattern was revealing itself: when Mom had abandoned us, Dad had been so angry at her and at women in general that he needed an outlet for that anger; in other words, he needed someone he could take it out on. There were only two women close enough to him to be potential targets. The first was Messer, who was spared because she was the youngest, our family's sweet little baby. With no other convenient candidates, the only one left to absorb that anger was me.

I felt tears form in my eyes looking at the family matrix with lines leading to me, my dad's cruelty now seeming inevitable as it was plotted out in front of me. The anger that anyone could expect a little girl to bear so much made my cheeks burn, though as the therapist continued to explain, these dynamics were often unconscious, even if they took familiar forms. Though I was still furious, I was beginning to understand my dad's perspective. What I hadn't taken into account before was how badly he must've been hurting, too. My therapist moved shortly after this session, and I didn't try to find a replacement.

One afternoon, I received an excited voicemail from Messer: "The private detective sent me a list of Hoesleys—call me!" Within a couple of days, we were sitting at her granite kitchen counter, the smell of baking chocolate chip cookies wafting in the air. Messer slid a folder containing a small stack of continuous feed printer paper toward me. While Messer's kids attended school and Stan was somewhere in his scrubs, we dove into our own investigative work. It was exciting, but we weren't sure what we would do if the correct name turned up.

We eventually contacted Jean Hoesley, Rob's only daughter and our suspected stepsister. She cut us off before we could even get started with our inquiries, announcing that her father had passed and not to call back. Undeterred, we got busy writing her a letter, not knowing if we would ever hear back from her.

1996

Dear Jean —

Our names are Diana Cannon May and Melissa Cannon
We have an incredible story to share with you. We hope
that as you read this letter, you will try to understand
our reasons for sharing it with you.

Our father is Ted Cannon. He and your father
were friends and worked together at Shell Oil in
Farmington New Mexico.

Two years ago in March of 1994, our father
revealed to us that we are not his biological
children. As you can imagine this came as quite a
shock to us. It had never occured to Diana at
35yrs. old and Melissa at 32yrs. old that something
like this might be true. We went through all
the emotions: denial, sadness, anger, and finally
acceptance. After the initial shock of being told
this, a million questions flooded our minds. We
wanted them answered. Our father did the best he
could to answer our questions but we were still
left with alot of them unanswered. We felt that
the only other person that could answer our
questions was our mother. Now, our parents
have been divorced for about 30 years. After
the divorce, our father married our mother's
sister. We, two boys and four girls were
raised by them, not to mention the four kids
our aunt brought to the marriage.

As the truth about my past continued to unravel, I stuck
with counseling, but Ken refused to join me. He started
working even longer hours and detached himself from me
and our now-teenaged kids. He couldn't be bothered with
their teen drama and stopped attending their school and
extracurricular functions. It confused me, and I grew even
angrier because I desperately needed his emotional support.

He couldn't understand why I couldn't just enjoy the life we had together and set aside the past.

One evening, Ken came home from work to the local missionaries at our door. Haley had recently expressed an interest in learning more about the Mormon Church, and we had spent the last hour in a discussion with the elders.

"Hi boys! Don't leave—stay for a beer," he joked. The goal was to make them feel awkward, since naturally, beer was taboo.

"No thanks, Brother May," one of them replied. "We've got another appointment." Eventually, they would slowly back away, slightly terrified of Ken's gregariousness and sinful offers.

When the elders took their leave, Ken slammed the door and turned to me with lips pursed, briskly adjusting his ball cap by the bill.

"I am not their fucking brother," he said angrily. His irritation at all things Mormon hadn't lessened over the years. He came close to me, poking my sternum with his index finger. "If you ever think of going back to *that church* and wearing those Jesus Jumpers, that will be the end of our marriage, you hear me?" As he stormed into the kitchen for a beer, Haley and I shared a look, rolling our eyes. He was never scary—just full of hot air.

At times, especially if we were fighting, Ken dug up my past, throwing the idea that I was going to end up just like my mother and run, leaving him for another man—or even a woman—in my face.

"I'm just waiting for you to snap," he said.

"Me too," I replied—but suddenly, it was no longer a

joke. My past kept resurfacing and. almost a year after sending our letter to Jean, Messer and I got a reply.

Jan 6

Dear Diana & Melissa,

As I feel you are convinced my Father is your biological parent, I will share his medical history with you. He died in 1979 at age 64 of cardio respiratory failure due to atherosclerosis, coronary, severe. a contributing factor was emphysema (he was a fairly heavy smoker from an early age). He suffered from gout & also had a disease called Reiters Syndrome, which can be genetically passed on.

You are correct in this... my beautiful mother is frail in every respect, & struggling. She loved & understood my Father. Any disturbance to her small world would be devastating.

For the time being, I would appreciate it if this is our only contact.

Sincerely,
Jean.

But that closed door reopened the following year, when we both received a postcard from Jean from San Diego, granting us permission to visit and meet each other, as her mother had recently passed. Messer's eldest daughter had an upcoming soccer competition in San Diego, so she made plans to meet Jean on her own while she was there. I wanted to join her, but couldn't afford the trip; Steph's horse had become ill with colic, and the vet bill used up our small reserve.

The two of them had a brief lunch at a deli, and Messer was not overwhelmingly convinced that Jean was related to us. She felt I looked more like Jean than her.

"Did you take a picture of her?" I asked when she returned.

"No, it was really weird," she said. "She wasn't all that friendly with me, so I didn't dare ask. The only thing that stood out to me was her ears. They're way bigger than yours, and they stuck out from her hair." She giggled. "She's even shorter than me, maybe five-foot-two, so I dunno. It was strange for both of us. She said she has no other brothers or sisters, and she never got married and has no children of her own."

"Oh man, I wish I could've gone with you," I said. "Let's go again, together, so I can see for myself." I had every intention of doing just that, but somehow, the years passed, and all we did was exchange the occasional Christmas card.

I didn't fully understand the effect that finding Jean and knowing Ted Cannon really wasn't my father had on me, all I knew was that a giant hole had opened inside me. I tried to fill it with anything and everything: obsessive biking, exercise, trips to Salt Lake, spending money, drinking, eating and anything else to distract me. Unfortunately, nothing I could think of could help me feel complete—so I had to move on to the unthinkable.

Chapter Twenty-Six
2001

On an Indian summer night in 2001, I took the first steps to betraying my husband. The sunset had cast a golden light across the fields and the fermented smell of silage and fresh-cut hay filled the air. After receiving a message on my pager, I left my sleeping husband and met Ben on Main Street, following him to his family's farm three miles out of town. Sporting a summer tan and feeling lean and strong from obsessively riding my bike, I drove my red Ford Bronco down the dark, rutted country lane, my stomach somersaulting all the way.

When he kissed me for the first time that night, I thought I might melt. He held my face in his powerful hands and gently placed his lips on mine. I stepped away, flushed, feeling every cell in my body vibrate. I had stepped over the edge into infidelity.

Our unexpected romance had started innocently when Ben joined the biking group I'd started a few years earlier. Ken would occasionally come along on shorter rides, but mostly he opted out when our group of seven pedaled mega distances. Ben was openly flirtatious in the absence of my husband, and I relished the attention, but I also played it cool, knowing it was inappropriate and dangerous. I took measures to never ride with Ben alone—I certainly didn't want to be the topic of conversation around town, as I had a reputation to uphold as the mine manager's wife, too. With the local paper desperate for any story (you could only read so much about the school's lunch menu or which citizen had been found drunk on the street), avoiding the gossip spotlight was paramount.

Standing six feet three inches tall with a tan face and lean athletic build, Ben was a true Salina redneck with his Western boots, Wranglers and penchant for strong cologne. My heart raced at the excitement of our new and forbidden romance. A few weeks after our first kiss, we met at the rodeo grounds and had sex under the stars, surrounded by sage-brush. I tried to ignore the thorns jabbing into my bare skin, along with the stabbing sense of shame I felt in my heart. I knew the affair was destructive but couldn't help myself.

As time passed, Ken started coming home less and working more. His relationship with my children grew distant, and his daughter Nealy hardly ever visited. On several occasions, Ken point-blank asked me if I was having an affair. Of course, I lied, thinking I was protecting every-one, including my kids—I even lied to my own therapist as I didn't trust anyone in my small town, but eventually, the deceit led to panic attacks where I'd wake up in a full-blown sweat in the middle of the night, convinced I was having a heart attack.

I decided to move back to Salt Lake. I needed to leave my

shame behind and avoid the inevitable verbal lynching from the town's busybodies. I didn't waste any time packing my bags after Ken reluctantly agreed to a divorce.

"Are you really going to tear our family apart after 16 years?" he asked, looking deeply into my eyes. He had aged well, still handsome, but he looked tired and defeated. His hair was graying around his face, and the circles around his eyes had darkened.

"You're the one that forced my hand to leave," I replied defensively. "You act like you want nothing to do with me. All you do is work and when I try to talk to you, you won't listen—and I hate this godforsaken town!"

His voice fell as he said, "At least I didn't cheat on you."

I was still in denial that he had any evidence of my infidelity, but I didn't refute it, either. I kept my mouth shut and finished loading my stuff. As I backed out of our long driveway in my rented U-Haul, Ken stood near the garage. He watched me pull away from our life together as I'd done with Steve years earlier. My plan was to head north and get settled and then come back for Haley. Stephanie and Scott already lived on their own away from Salina.

I looked back one last time. Ken, slightly slumped, started crying as one hand came out of a jean pocket to wave goodbye. I wept all the way to Salt Lake, barely able to see the road through my tears. At one point, I pulled over and heaved at the realization of what I had just done. I had worked so hard at making myself believe everything was his fault, and I had barely felt sympathy for him until that moment. Was I fated to follow in the well-worn tracks my parents had laid down many years before?

Ken was fair about the divorce, and we split with little

drama. He even helped me find my new house. No one in the Cannon family really asked about the details behind our divorce, and if the subject came up, I simply lied, offering that we'd grown apart and I hated Salina. Messer, sworn to secrecy, was the only person I had confided in, but I had a hard time admitting the details of my torrid affair and subsequent collapse of my marriage. She just listened, never uttering a negative word, but I was sure that despite loving me unconditionally, she thought I was going straight to hell for my transgressions. Neither Dad nor Carol had any room to talk or judge me, so they didn't. All Dad said was, "He was a good egg. I'll miss that guy."

The affair with Ben carried on for a while, with both of us pretending that we could date now that we were divorced. Meanwhile, I pulled myself up "by the bootstraps," as my dad liked to say, as a career woman with a great job and the sole owner of a 2,500-square-foot townhouse in Murray where I lived with my 16-year-old daughter Haley. But our relationship felt strained. Angry with me for jerking her out of high school during her junior year, Haley barely spoke to me for months. In Salina, she had been a cheerleader and a member of the competitive dance team, popular with swarms of friends. Having been recently baptized by the Mormon Church, she had strong connections with her peers in her Salina ward. I had pulled the rug out from under her during the prime of her life with no honest explanation and enrolled her into the nearest high school, where she felt lost and alone. Now a small fish in a big pond, she was having a hard time adjusting. Haley was depressed and mostly sat around the house moping, eating and watching TV.

"I hate you. You ruined my life!" was how most of our conversations started and ended.

Now 18, Scott moved to St. George with a few friends. Although legally (and from all outward appearances) he was an adult, I knew better. To me, he was still a little blond boy, his nose and cheeks spotted with mild acne and freckles. Just a few months after settling into the desert town, he got pulled over in the middle of the night and got a ticket for driving under the influence. His truck was impounded, and he spent the night in the drunk tank. I got a collect call from the purgatory jail the next morning.

"Mom," he sobbed. "You *have* to come get me. It's scary in here."

"Were you drunk when they pulled you over?" I asked, already knowing the answer.

"Yes," he replied. "But I—"

"I'm sorry you're scared, honey," I replied, cutting him off, "but I won't come get you. You'll be released soon and I'll be there." Our conversation was timed, and it ended when I heard the dial tone. I slumped to the floor and sobbed. I had wanted to rescue him, but he needed a wake-up call. It was one of the hardest things I'd ever had to do.

I waited for three long days before the call came to finally get him, and Stephanie offered to ride with me on the four-hour drive south. She had recently graduated summa cum laude from a two-year local college with plans to transfer to the University of Utah to go to dental school. As the oldest and most responsible, Stephanie had assumed a motherly role in our family. I kept waiting for her to admonish me for falling short, but instead, she held her tongue and only said, "Poor Scott." After we picked up a

mostly sullen and quiet Scott, we drove him and his belongings back to Salt Lake in silence.

As time passed, my self-esteem plummeted, and shame
and guilt got the best of me. I felt like a complete failure as a
wife and mother, and there was a nagging voice in my head
that I couldn't turn off. *The only reason your life is such a
mess is because you have abandoned God and His church*, it
said. I was so depressed that I figured the only hope for me
was to take another shot at Mormonism.

Though I had been away from it for 16 years, and had
long since been disfellowshipped, I was reaching for something, any connection in my new upside-down reality. I had
screwed things up enough for myself and everyone I loved
during my disconnected time with the church, and despite
still holding misgivings, I felt it was time to face my
punishment.

Looking for forgiveness, but not yet ready to be honest
about my issues, I occasionally went to church on Sundays
with Haley, and we found some solace and happiness there. I
took from it what I needed, which was to feel loved and
accepted. It felt nice to attend a new ward where no one
knew our history.

Feeling abandoned and alone on so many fronts, I
reached out to my mother for help for the first time. She
offered to pay for a therapist, knowing I was barely making
ends meet as a single mom, and she even suggested flying to
Salt Lake for a joint therapy session. I had stopped going to
therapy after my therapist moved out of Richfield and didn't
seek out another one as I was preoccupied with my reloca-
tion to Salt Lake. I wasn't necessarily thrilled to go back, I
accepted her offer, both surprised by her generosity and

encouraged that we might finally build a relationship. After some research, I found a family therapist named Dr. Graham, who accepted my insurance, and made an appointment with him to see what he was like. I had seen him only twice before I asked him if my mother could join us in a session.

My mother arrived on a Tuesday, rented a car and made it just in time for our 50-minute session. Much to Dr. Graham's and my surprise, she talked endlessly about herself the entire time. When I finally got a word in about my issues and sorrow, I broke down. Mom sat stone-faced, waiting for her turn to talk again. At that point, she dropped the bomb that her father had molested her as a baby. She had even written a poem about it, which she brought out during our session and read with great command:

The Beginning: Even when I was two I knew my mother was the boss in our family, so when my father stuck his penis in my mouth and I couldn't breathe, my two-year-old mind thought he was killing me, and my mother must have told him to do it. I thought it was because I was bad and now they had a new baby who was good and they didn't want me anymore. Daddy got really mad when I threw up all over his brown pants and the floor of my bedroom.

Obviously I didn't die, but I was left with the bone-deep conviction that my continued existence was dependent upon being very quiet and doing everything my parents wanted me to. Life seemed precarious, and the slightest transgression felt like a life and death issue.

One would think from this, I would have become a passive compliant child—and I tried, I really tried. But I seemed, even then, to have had a strong rebellious streak that

throughout my life has gotten me into all sorts of trouble. And
surviving made me strong.

She read it like she'd rehearsed it a hundred times, her
deep voice raspy and crackly as if she was getting over a cold.
Once she finished, the room was deathly quiet except for the
sound of her soft whimpers. When I finally looked up from
my lap, I realized I had shredded the tissue I was holding.
Dr. Graham cleared his throat.

"Joyce, thank you for sharing your experience and
poem," he said. "But can you tell Diana how it makes you
feel to see her in so much pain over your abandonment of her
and the family?" Mom looked up with a blank stare.

"Diana just told you how sad and depressed she is, and
she wants to understand why you abandoned her and the
family. I believe she feels the past may be contributing to her
unhappiness and inability to form healthy relationships with
men," he explained in a calm voice. Mom couldn't quite pull
herself together to answer his questions.

Our time was soon up, and we walked out of Dr.
Graham's office into the bright light of that summer day.

"I have to leave if I'm going to make my flight," my mom
quickly announced, giving me a perfunctory hug and
walking to her car before I could ask her to stay or explain
herself. As I watched her car pull away, I was completely
undone. What she had said in the therapist's office was
shocking and horrible, but I was furious she had come so far
just to talk about herself.

On the advice of Dr. Graham, I finally got up the nerve
to write a letter to my mother. Even if I had no intention of
ever sending it, I had to get my feelings down. Later that
afternoon while Haley was at work, I changed into sweat-

pants, pulled my wavy shoulder-length hair into a ponytail and climbed on top of my neatly made bed. With the television muted, I started to write:

July 22, 2002

Dear Mom,

First, I want to thank you for your willingness to (at the last minute) fly to Salt Lake to help me with my therapy and to listen. I wonder if you feel like not much was accomplished. At least it was a start. I have done a great deal of thinking and processing since you left, so the trip you made was worth it, for me anyway.

You say you are "okay" with me expressing my feelings (thank God, I have some), but I know this must be difficult for you to hear. I already told you, my first instinct has been to apologize for the way I feel. I've done enough of that, and I am not apologizing this time. I want to and need to feel these things and express them to you. Someday, if and when I am ready, I would like to share all of this with Dad. I have bottled all this up for so many years, I'm sure I don't yet understand the magnitude.

Truth is, I've known I have had some deep-rooted problems stemming from childhood, but I have no real memories, so I couldn't begin to understand them. I thought I was making up crazy thoughts in my head, which made me even crazier. You've told me over the years that you've done and continue to do "your work" and are in "a good place" to be able to deal with what I want to say to you. I hope so! But, I disagree with you that you are "better."

You say that you were "sick" when you left. Undoubtedly! But this is how I see it—there are no good excuses for why you left. But, you did! You had to have been in such a horrible state of mind that you didn't feel you had a choice. God help you!

You left six, innocent, helpless children with a very sick man, who after you left continued and increased the abuse! What angers me the most, is that you were, and still are, so wrapped up in yourself and in your pain that you didn't and still don't give a rat's ass about any of us. It feels like you left and you never looked back! Maybe you did from a distance, or you might have heard from family members how we were, but the fact is, we weren't okay. Nobody protected us or nurtured us. That was your job! Mothers protect their babies! What's worse is you still don't get it. You only think about yourself and that's it.

Perfect examples:

1. You show up four years later, take us to lunch and leave, abandoning us again!

2. You return every one to two years, get what you need out of the trip and leave. Abandoned again.

3. You only offer help from a safe distance by sending money, the occasional call, financing therapy, etc. That's bullshit!

I'll never forget when you asked the four of us girls: "Do you kids know what it's like to really love your children?" What? Are you fucking crazy? Yes, by some small miracle we know! No thanks to the worst example of parenting ever! And, if you really loved us or cared about us, you would have come back. You would've been there for us through good and bad times. If you really mean that you love us, prove it! Sell your

*house and move to Salt Lake where your entire family lives.
Be here, be present!*

*When I was young, I remember begging you to move out
here several times, especially when Carol and Dad divorced,
and when our kids were little and when we needed you the
most—through divorces, financial trouble, health trouble and
simply to share life. You missed out on everything, and you
still miss out. Selfish! Again, God help you!*

*I am just happy I will never have to live with what you
live with every day. I still don't think your pain is about abandoning your children, I think it's more about you, and your
childhood issues you've never resolved.*

*I refuse to take that kind of legacy and dysfunction
another generation further. I will resolve my feelings and
issues, and work on getting healthier, even if it takes a lifetime. I am working on forgiving myself, too.*

*Now, I need to decide what kind of relationship I want to
have with you. It will never be normal, I understand that
much. I am so done with superficial garbage! I am hurt, angry
and sad about the choices you made, which severely impacted
all our lives. I don't think you have a fucking clue as to the
damage you have caused. You still can't see past your own
pain to see or feel any of ours.*

*In therapy last week, you were the most emotional when
you talked about your issues with your mom and dad, and
showed very little emotion when I was finally able to express
my feelings to you, face-to-face. I finally broke down sobbing,
and you remained stoic. That was supposed to be my session,
not yours. That's messed up!*

*You are still a very sick woman and I feel sorry for you!
You must be deluded to think you are okay—I don't think you*

are! I know all of us kids are not. I do, however, have a desire to get better. To be there for my kids, and for their kids and my great-grandkids. Really be there!

No, I am not coming to visit this fall to put together a goddamn puzzle, play cards or look at fucking photo albums. I can't pretend everything is rosy anymore, I just can't do it!

I don't need you or Dad now. You weren't there when I did and you're not here now. I need to learn to live my life without parents.

Your very hurt and damaged daughter,
Diana

Once finished, I held it up proudly and wiped the tears and mascara off my face with my sleeve. I felt 50 pounds lighter, sprung off the bed and hid the letter in the middle of my *Gray's Anatomy* textbook, where I thought it would stay forever. I ended up sending the letter on my birthday, August 20, fueled by the frustration that I hadn't received a call or birthday card from either her or my father. It was a relief when I dropped the letter off in my mailbox, but the next month proved agonizing as I waited for a reply. Finally, an envelope with a Reno return address appeared in my mailbox:

September 12, 2002

Dear Diana,

I keep re-reading your letter and all I can think of to say is "mea culpa." I have gone back and looked hard at how things were on Second Avenue before I left and realize that even when I was there physically, I wasn't really there. Things were awful before I left, and I was a grownup (?). I can only try to imagine how dreadful they were for you kids afterwards.

I get it that you want me to hear and understand your pain and the effect my and your dad's mental illness had, and continue to have, on your life. I get it. I wish I could go back and do it better, be a better person, a healthier person, the kind of mother you needed and deserved. If I could, I would. But I cannot. And the painful truth is nothing I do now can make it better back then. I can never provide now the nurturing parent you needed when you were small.

I apologize abjectly for my part in your pain, and for the continuing problems it has caused in your life. I am so sorry. So dreadfully sorry.

I'd like to know how you're doing with this, and to be helpful in any way I can, but I'm going to assume that if you want to talk to me you'll either write further or phone (and I'll call you right back). You be the one to make contact. Next time I come to Salt Lake, you get to be the one to decide if you'd like to see me.

I love you and hope you will be able to forgive me for being such a damaged, and damaging, mother.

Chapter Twenty-Seven
2002-2003

My religious life and relationship with the Mormon Church had been like a carousel ride—a lot of jumping on and off after spinning in circles. I couldn't help but notice all the *other* riders seemed happy and were having a good time. Maybe *I* was the problem? Maybe I just needed to stay on the painted horse long enough to feel a bit of the magic everyone else seemed to be enjoying? Or at the very least, learn to be happy riding the undulating seats to nowhere and letting the lively carnival music wash over me. Finally, tired of being miserable and watching from the sideline, I jumped back on and took a spot next to a single church-on-every-Sunday Mormon fellow. *Maybe he's exactly what I need to be happy?* My faithful family members were more than thrilled with my renewed interest in the church and I felt excited to be dating again. And, by God, I was not going to fuck—I mean *fudge*—it up.

Conner, who was an angel-chap-wearing Mormon, announced on our first date that he was a high priest. I didn't know exactly what that meant other than I was supposed to be impressed. I went home and immediately called Messer.

"What the heck is a high priest?"

After a pregnant pause, she said, "It's usually a title held by someone in the bishopric or stake presidency. Why?" She started to giggle because I was the last person on earth she expected to be asking this. I told her about my date with Conner.

"Is he a bishop or something?" she asked, her pitch rising.

"No, he didn't even go on a mission," I replied.

"That's weird. I wonder how he became a high priest then."

"I dunno." I wanted to change the topic because I didn't care what his position was in the church, but she cross-examined me further.

"What ward is he in? Did he say how long he had been a high priest?"

"I don't know that much about him yet, other than he's a lawyer from Provo. He's been divorced for over a year and has four children. They're all raised except one teenage boy who lives with his ex-wife. He's super shy and says things like 'gee willikers' and 'jumping Jehoshaphat.'"

Messer snorted with laughter, making me laugh, too.

"I'll ask Stan when he gets home about being a high priest," Messer said, chuckling again as we hung up.

That night I lay in bed, unable to sleep. *Conner is dreamy*, I thought—*all six feet five inches of him.* He was my type: thin with an athletic build and a chiseled face. I even liked his super short, missionary haircut. His nerdy, shy demeanor intrigued me, and his sparkling clean vocabulary was a stark contrast to the many years of redneck language in coal mining country. As we spent more time together, Conner discovered the real me and blushed and laughed at my cursing. He even started using a few swear words, but they felt forced. Much to my surprise, he drank coffee, beer and wine with me. I wasn't sure if he had indulged before meeting me or not, but I had my doubts. He knew next to nothing about finely brewed or fermented drinks, so I took it upon myself to educate him. He mostly just followed my lead when it came to ordering and exploring some of the fun things in life.

One night, while we were out to dinner at an Indian restaurant, our conversation turned to why each of us had gotten divorced. He got tears in his eyes as he described his 30-year loveless marriage.

"We was never in love and hadn't been intimate for eight years," he said, taking a big gulp of cold beer and wiping his eyes with his napkin. "Right before we split up, things was gettin' pretty bad. I hurt my dang back in the garden and couldn't barely move. One morning, she put her foot in the small of my back and kicked me as hard as she could, and I fell out of bed onto the floor. 'Oh my heck, whaddya do that for?' I asked her. She told me to get my lazy ass out of bed and get to work. That was the last straw. I crawled to my closet, got dressed and left. We was only 18 when she got pregnant, and our bishop told us we *had* to get married, that I had tarnished her to the point no one would ever want her again. She's been pissed off ever since. And I was pissed, 'cuz I didn't get to go on a mission."

I was hooked by his story, and I believed it and felt sorry for him. Then it occurred to me. "Wait, you haven't had sex for eight years?" I asked. He shook his bowed head. "Why did you live like that for so long?"

He rambled on, making his ex-wife out to be a crazed woman and himself a saint for putting up with her. But when he spoke of his kids, his voice softened as he explained how he'd stayed for them. I got the sense they were all very close and that his kids were sweet angels, but it turned out quite the opposite was true.

Conner's children were ill-mannered and icy cold in the beginning, and they made absolutely no effort to welcome me. In fact, some were downright rude, which seemed out of character since they were all extremely embedded in the church culture of politeness. Their entire lives were focused on missions, temple weddings, baby blessings and church callings. *Maybe that's why they don't approve of me,* I thought. *Maybe they're worried we're not good enough for their churchy family.*

My youngest daughter Haley had recently turned 17, and the week before meeting Conner, I caught her sneaking out one night to visit her boyfriend Monty. My son Scott had a steady job at Big O Tires as a mechanic making decent money, but he also liked to drink heavily and experiment with drugs with his apartment mates. My oldest daughter Stephanie was an honor student, but she was no stranger to the party scene (as evidenced by the booze bottles, full ashtrays and empty beer cans I would find scattered about when I visited her apartment). Clearly, the Word of Wisdom had not taken root in my family.

Because Conner's kids were ultra-Mormon, they were focused on missions, marriage and church and mostly just kept their distance from us. They never said anything outright about me or my kids, but when I tried to organize family dinners on Sundays, they rarely attended. When they did, they often segregated themselves from my children and their conversations revolved around church callings. Conner even made me hide the coffee pot or any evidence of alcohol in the fridge before they came over.

Our families couldn't have been more different, but none of it seemed to derail Conner's opinion of me. After only a few months of dating, he proposed to me on a hilltop overlooking the Provo Temple. On that chilly September evening, as the sun had just disappeared behind the Great Salt Lake, he slipped the emerald-cut sapphire onto my finger.

I took a deep breath and said, "Yes." It felt like a good decision—that this time, I was going to get it right. Stan and Messer generously offered their ostentatious colonial-style estate and manicured backyard in Murray as a wedding venue, and we had a simple ceremony in April of 2003.

Mom and Norma, who were now 10 years strong in their relationship, flew in for the event, explaining that it would be their last trip to Salt Lake because traveling was becoming too difficult at their age. Mom refused to wear a dress, but she looked nice in a floral blouse with a bow at the neck. I breathed a sigh of relief when Norma arrived in a navy leisure pantsuit, because her usual attire was a baggy T-shirt with a wild animal graphic on the front and no bra to wrangle her giant breasts.

Beth and Anna came in full support, but none of my brothers showed up. I purposely didn't invite Dad, not wanting another scene like the one at Messer's son's wedding, where his pants fell off as he walked up the aisle to his seat.

For about 10 years, Carol had missed numerous important family events, including my graduation from the University of Utah and many family reunions. After she and Dad had divorced, Carol moved to Idaho a few blocks from her daughter Debi, who had become her caretaker. Because Carol was struggling with an addiction to pain pills, it was a grueling full-time job; Debi would often find her passed out in her home, sometimes for two days at a time.

Debi often called me to vent about having to take care of Carol, as she had seven kids of her own, but none of us truly understood the severity of the problem. In desperate need of a break, Debi begged her husband to drive Carol the 175 miles to our wedding. I was happy she had come and even happier to see that having Mom and Carol in the same room hadn't caused any chaos.

For the first years of our marriage, Conner and I focused on building a new life together as our children forged paths of their own. Haley and Monty married exactly one year after she graduated high school and moved into a duplex in Sugar House. I gave up my successful PT career in Salt Lake to run the assisted living center in Lehi that Conner owned, and we pooled our resources to contribute equal amounts for a down payment on a house in the quiet Mormon neighborhood of Alpine, nicknamed Happy Valley. I was grateful that my kids were grown and that I had a career and a new man. Besides, it was the nicest home I had ever owned and the first place that didn't require endless cleaning or painting to feel livable.

As I immersed myself in my new job at the facility, I

grew to love it. I'd always had a soft spot for elderly people, but it had only developed over my years as a physical therapist.

Conner and I both put in endless hours at work and played hard on the weekends—camping, boating, hiking, biking and snowmobiling. We tried to include all the kids on most of these trips, but a chilliness remained within his family, and I never felt comfortable with them.

In the middle of the night in May of 2006, we received the dreaded phone call. Connor's mother, Mabel, was 98 years old and had passed away in the care center Conner owned. We had just seen her the day before and knew the end was near, but there was no way to prepare Conner for when the call actually came. We got up and got dressed to be there to say our goodbyes.

It was becoming clear that Mabel's death had triggered something inside Conner: he was changing in front of my eyes. Earlier in our relationship, he had always seemed fairly close to his siblings—not real close, but polite and cordial. Now, all at once, he seemed to be in constant intense arguments with them. Even though he was the youngest, he was in charge of the family estate and began arranging meetings. At first, I was invited, but the tension in those meetings was so thick that they were too awful to endure, so I sat out. I had become close with his older brother and wife, and I could tell they were mad at Conner after one of their meetings about a week after Mabel had been buried. They had been yelling so loud behind a closed door that I knew they were fighting about the division of the estate, though I wasn't sure about the specifics. When they all emerged from the office an hour later, they were all red-faced. After it was over, I tried to talk to him about what had happened, but he just shut down and wouldn't talk to me.

As he grieved, I wanted to comfort him and to understand what he was going through, but he would literally turn his back to me, either walking away from me or rolling over if we were in bed. I thought he might just need time to process things, but things only got worse and worse. Over the course of a year, we grew further and further apart, and Conner grew angrier.

I was standing at the sink one day washing dishes when Conner entered, ranting about his mother's estate and threatening to sue his brothers and sister.

"Why can't them bastards just trust me and be happy with what they get!" he shouted. As he was storming around and shouting behind me, Mabel's face popped into my head almost like an intrusive thought. The volume of Conner's voice seemed to turn down as her voice took its place in my head. I remembered a moment from shortly after Conner and I had gotten married. Mabel had come to visit us as newlyweds, and she and I had been alone together in the kitchen, with Conner out in the yard somewhere. *He'll make a wonderful husband,* she said, both of us standing by the sink. *Just be careful not to make him mad, because he's got an awful temper!* We had both laughed and I'd taken it as a joke, though now I wondered if it had been a warning.

"I think our problem is you!" Conner shouted with an accusatory finger, the kitchen now swimming back into focus as Mabel's words echoed in my mind. "You're losing your testimony of the church! You just need to read the scriptures and quit swearing and drinking coffee." It was coming out of nowhere. I had already given up my occasional glasses of wine with dinner and margaritas (my favorite) with girl-friends, since we were now going to church regularly to assuage his guilt. His behavior and allegations made no sense to me. How was *I* the problem when I had been following his wishes and adhering to the Word of Wisdom?

Having grown up under the dreaded shadow of my dad, I was beginning to see shades of his words and behavior in Conner, and it made me uneasy. I wondered if I was becoming the scapegoat again.

Concerned about Conner's increasingly unstable state of mind, I suggested we start going to couples' counseling to work on our relationship. Though he resisted at first, he eventually relented under the condition that we see Dr. Miller, a therapist he knew and that he'd seen in the past. Once we agreed, I made us an appointment to see her the following week.

On the day of our session, I was relieved that Dr. Miller was quiet, soft-spoken and seemed like she truly wanted to help. I felt comfortable with her, which gave me some hope—maybe there was a chance that counseling would help us through this rough patch after all.

To begin our counseling regimen, Dr. Miller asked to see us separately to see what we wanted to talk about together. In my individual session with her, she asked about my past experiences with my family.

"Oh, I don't think we have enough time to get into all that," I joked, remembering the grueling experiences I'd already had with Dr. Graham. I was eager to keep things as limited to Conner and I as I could and to steer away from anything that might open up even more wounds.

I was encouraged by our initial meetings with Dr. Miller.

It felt like we were starting on a healthy track to work on our marriage until one Sunday, when Conner went into another one of his tirades.

"Have you bought a house behind my back?" he shouted, his most bizarre accusation yet.

"What?" I asked, bewildered. "What are you talking about?"

"Don't lie to me!" he said, his voice rising and chest pumping in and out. "We're done with these counseling sessions—we're going back to temple and that's it!" His paranoia had taken over to the point that I didn't even recognize him anymore. I didn't want to stop going to counseling, but I couldn't upset him any more than I already had—even though I hadn't even done anything wrong. I didn't know what to do.

I was desperate to make my third marriage work, so after several bishop interviews and acquiring our temple recommend cards, Conner and I agreed to enter the temple together as a couple—truthfully, my biggest hesitation was having to wear those goddamn garments again.

In a panic, I called Messer to ask if she would go with me to buy new garments and join Conner and I in the temple. She agreed, knowing I needed moral support. Thankfully, since Conner and I weren't getting sealed to one another, I did not have to go through the awful washing and anointing ritual again, even if I did have to go through the procession of so many other ceremonial rituals to be re-admitted to the temple.

As much as I wanted to be a faithful churchgoer once again, I could hardly pretend to buy into any of the doctrine anymore, no matter how hard I willed myself to. *Just stay the course,* I kept repeating to myself. *It's going to make you happy eventually.* In truth, the ceremonies felt just as strange and nonsensical as they had more than 20 years ago—perhaps even more so.

As our ceremony was nearing its end, the only redeeming moment was seeing my cute little sister after someone pulled me through the veil into the celestial room. I was overcome with emotion.

"See, Di, this is what heaven is going to be like!" she said as we sat and held hands. "I'm so happy we'll be together in the next life."

She wept as she said it. I wished I could believe her.

Chapter Twenty-Eight
2007

One afternoon, a slight-framed gentleman in his early 40s walked into my office on a sales call, asking if I would like to place an ad in a community magazine for our senior facility. I barely took the time to look up at him from my computer screen as I replied.

"No thank you, I'm not interested," I said, doing my best to conceal my irritation at the interruption. A No Soliciting sign was clearly visible at the entrance of the facility. Rather than retreat, the gentleman surprised me by taking a step forward and sticking his hand out.

"My name is Pete," he said with bravado, revealing his big white teeth. He left me no choice but to stand and take his hand.

"Hi, Pete, I'm Diana. Could you please just leave your business card?" With unfailing persistence, he pressed on while pulling something from his briefcase.

"Conner and Sheila sent me here to talk to you about placing an ad in this magazine." There was an immediacy to what he was saying, and the way he spoke and looked at me made me uneasy. *Conner and Sheila?* I thought. *Who the hell is Sheila?* The salesman obviously picked up on my uncertainty as he placed the magazine down and glanced at the door.

"Maybe I should stop back again in a week or two once you've discussed this with your husband," Pete said with a smile, heading toward the door.

"How do you know my husband?" I asked. He paused, his fingers on the doorknob. "Conner, Sheila and I all attend an early-morning spinning class together. Conner mentioned I should come see you about the ad." He turned the knob and opened the door. "I know you're busy, so take a look and I hope to hear from you. Have a great day, Diana." Alarm bells were sounding in my head. *Spin class with Sheila? Why's he going to the gym with the woman he works with?*

Conner and I had been going to the gym together most mornings for three years until one day, he announced that he liked the spin class in Lehi, just south of Alpine, better. I wasn't willing to make the drive, but he made the switch. I walked across the hall to my assistant Mona's office. The always-cheerful Mona looked up, peering over reading glasses perched on the tip of her bulbous nose. Chubby, barely five feet tall and with curly ashen hair framing her round face and cheeks, she reminded me of a cute little gnome.

"What's up?" she asked, snacking on a handful of pretzels.

"I'm not sure," I muttered slowly. My legs felt weak, and my stomach was turning. I had no idea why I was having such a physical response to what the salesman had said, but

I couldn't ignore it. Sheila worked as a receptionist at Conner's law firm, which handled our assisted living business's legal paperwork. Nine months prior, Conner had mentioned hiring a new receptionist, but he hadn't said much about her, and I hadn't asked. When I spoke with Sheila on the phone, she seemed pleasant enough. When I pictured her in my mind, I envisioned a middle-aged frumpy Mormon woman—just like the other women in his office.

"Have you ever met Sheila from Conner's office in person?" I asked Mona.

"Not yet," she replied, crunching away. She paused, tilting her head with a questioning look. "Why?"

"I'm going to lunch," I replied, breezing out of her office. "Be back in about an hour." Mona followed me into the hall. "You okay?"

"I smell a rat," I mumbled, quickly gathering my purse.

I drove straight to Conner's office in Provo for a surprise lunch visit. Rather than entering through the front door with the other clients, I parked in the back. Stepping out of my SUV with a fast-food bag in hand, I broke into a sweat in the 100-plus degree heat. With a deep breath, I turned the scorching metal door handle and opened the employee door. Straight ahead, a brunette in her mid-30s swiveled in her chair to face me. She immediately jumped up, pulling her short and extremely tight skirt down to cover her upper thighs.

Fuck! I thought. *I should have known—that's no frumpy Mormon assistant.* She was the opposite of what I'd imagined. The ends of her hair were dry and frizzy, and her bangs were teased and sprayed up into a perfect round roll. A heavy dose of blue eyeshadow and frosted pink lips completed the trashy small-town ensemble.

She knew who I was because she awkwardly glanced at Conner's office while forcing a quiver of a smile. I took three confident steps toward her, placed a giant fake grin on my face and held out my hand.

"You must be Sheila," I announced. "I can't believe we haven't met yet." She stuck out a clammy, limp hand, which I grabbed and shook a little too firmly.

"I uh," she began, but then Conner appeared in the doorway, looking as if he might vomit. Still cheery, I pivoted to him.

"Hi, honey!" I said. "I had a crazy idea to surprise you with your favorite burritos for lunch." As I turned to head for his office, I caught the two of them exchanging nervous looks. I handed him the greasy sack, but he didn't accept it.

"I have clients all day," he said, scratching his neck in irritation. "I really don't have time for lunch, Diana." His voice cracked as he said, "You should have checked with me first." Conner's giant protruding Adam's apple bobbed up and down as he attempted to swallow his panic. I dropped the burrito on his desk with a thud.

"Okay," I said, forcing a smile. "I guess we can try for lunch another time." With that, I flew out the back door, trying not to faint. I wiped a steady stream of tears on the ride back to work, beating myself up for my stupidity.

Mona found me in my office a few minutes later with puffy red eyes.

"Oh my God, what happened?" she asked with concern.

"He's fucking her," I said.

Something inside me was shutting down. The pain,

anger, fear and betrayal were all fading away, replaced by a
need to get even. I was determined to become a calculating
femme fatale in a detective movie. Everything I felt would
have to wait; what was most important was that I get orga-
nized and put a plan in place. First, I had to keep my knowledge of the affair to myself. After that, I needed a strategy to
catch them red-handed—but I wouldn't be able to do it
alone.

Not knowing who else to reach out to, I called Stephanie
and Haley, sobbing about my cheating husband. Haley had
recently divorced Monty and Stephanie had her hands full
with the stresses of taking care of two toddlers at home.
Though my daughters may not have been the wisest co-
conspirators for me to choose, the circumstances of our lives
had aligned in a way that none of us had expected. As such,
and without getting too far ahead of ourselves, we banded
together to follow Conner around for a week or so—just out
of curiosity, and to see what might happen.

We called our newly conceived PI work Operation Bust-
A-Ho. Whenever we met up, I'd hop in one of my girls' cars
so as to not be spotted, and we would follow Conner from
work, hoping to catch him on the way to see Sheila. Instead,
we ended up following him to the gym, to the store and to
the care center, where he often visited his mom.

After our unsuccessful first attempts, I started feeling
guilty for involving my daughters in my drama and hired a
professional private detective to find proof of Conner's affair.
Within two weeks, I had the evidence I'd been looking for.
The photographs the PI took proved beyond a doubt that
Conner had been having an affair with Sheila but also that
he'd been meeting other women for dates and bike rides.

Even with the evidence in hand, I knew I had to be patient. I resolved to keep playing the part of happy, oblivious house-wife, never giving him even a hint of what I was up to. I had him by the balls, but I wanted to put even more of a squeeze on him.

On the eve of his annual hunting trip, I stole Conner's keys and made a copy. After he took off, I dressed in all black and put a headlamp on my bike, riding 19 miles to his office. In fewer than 60 minutes, I made hundreds of copies of documents from his work computer. As a final flourish, before I turned off the Xerox machine, I photocopied my middle finger and carefully positioned the black and white image on his desk. I couldn't help but smile the entire way home.

I got no sleep that night. Buzzing with adrenaline, I stayed up reading through his business papers. He had lied to me from the very beginning about his divorce timeline, and it was no wonder his kids hated me—to them, I was the "other woman" who broke up their family. On top of that, I discovered a plethora of other incriminating evidence, such as financial cover-ups, family business scams and incrimi-nating personal letters. I hid the evidence, along with the stolen keys.

When Conner came home from hunting with no kill, I wondered where he'd really been. But more importantly, it was time to drop the bomb.

"I know you're having an affair with Sheila," I said calmly, sitting at the foot of our king-sized bed. "Do you love her?" He abruptly stopped changing his clothes.

"I am *not!*" he exclaimed, buckling his belt. "Don't be ridiculous, Diana."

For a good 15 minutes, he nervously paced the floor, denying the affair. I slowly divulged tidbits of information, like the fact I had hired a detective, just to make him sweat. I kept the incriminating paperwork to myself, for the time being.

"I want a divorce," I declared with conviction.

"Please, we can work this out?" he begged. "I don't love her!"

"Go to hell," I replied. With that, I stood up and walked out, slamming the door behind me.

With my revenge plan now fully executed, all the emotions I'd repressed were coming back to the surface, and I felt like a dam ready to burst. I needed someone to talk to—and preferably a professional rather than someone else in my family. Even though Conner and I had stopped seeing her together, I decided to make another appointment with Dr. Miller on my own.

On the day of our session, I was eager to get into all the details of what had happened in the past weeks but was surprised to see Dr. Miller's calm demeanor had disappeared, replaced now with total urgency. As I entered her office, she shut the door behind me, and I had barely sat down when she started speaking in a direct tone.

"I could lose my license for telling you this, but you need to get out of your marriage," she said sternly. "You are going to get hurt." I was about to tell her that our divorce was already underway, but she cut me off.

"I'm not sure what Conner's capable of, but he scares me," she said, "and I don't want to see you on *Dateline*." I had already decided that I wanted to leave Conner, but what Dr. Miller was saying was something entirely different. The risk wasn't just that I would be in an unhappy marriage for the rest of my life if I didn't leave. In her professional opinion, the real risk was that I might be killed.

When our session was over, I rushed to have the locks changed on the house and continued with the divorce paperwork. *You're almost out*, I thought feverishly. *Pay attention and see this through.*

I hired the best and most expensive goddamn divorce attorney in Salt Lake—a real shark compared to the minnows he had retained. To my relief, I had the advantage, and I was able to play Conner like a fiddle. Since he was afraid that I had too much incriminating evidence against him, he accepted most of my demands regarding the settlement, and things moved forward relatively quickly. Whenever I felt my sadness creeping up, I reminded myself to focus on getting even—even if it felt like I might fall apart at any moment.

I had recently pulled up to Sheila's house and laid on the horn, disrupting the quiet of her tight-knit Mormon neighborhood. Her oldest teen son came out of the house and stood on the lawn, blinking at me.

"*Do you know your whore of a mother is fucking my husband?!*" I yelled at him, loud enough for the entire world to hear. As the divorce was being finalized, so was the reality that I was on my third failed marriage. I had somehow managed to hold on to my sanity my entire life, even if only by a tiny thread, but now, I was going into an emotional tailspin. I had kept the house and won a victorious settlement, but I couldn't feel anything. I went dark, wallowing in self-pity and despair as my children and Messer watching helplessly by my side as I fell apart.

Why is this time so different? I wondered, racking my

brain. *Why am I so depressed when I should be glad to be done with the crazy bastard?* I didn't love him anymore; in fact, I *hated* him more than I had ever hated anyone in my life. So what was it?

While riding my bike through the beautiful Hobble Creek Canyon, the aroma and colors of pines and maple trees led to a moment of utter clarity, and the a-ha moment finally came. *Karma,* I thought, the weight of the word nearly tipping me over into oncoming traffic. *This is what karma feels like.*

Chapter Twenty-Nine
2008–2009

After deli sandwiches and ice cream one afternoon, Beth, Messer and I strolled through our childhood neighborhood in the lower Avenues. We walked for over an hour until we reached our old house on Second Avenue.

"That's where Anna and I used to sneak out the window and sit on that flat part of the roof and smoke," Beth said, pointing up at the second floor.

"Oh yeah, I remember that!" I said, though staring at my 51-year-old older sister in her mom jeans, I couldn't believe that a cigarette had ever touched her pious lips.

"You smoked?" Messer asked incredulously. I chuckled, "You did too, sis! You were too little to remember, but Beth and Anna were cigarette-smoking, foul-mouthed little thieves until they turned churchy!" I teased. "We all were."

"Very funny, Diana," Beth snarled.

We stared at the gabled house, now painted a cheery bright yellow. After a moment, a middle-aged woman opened the front door to see who was gawking at her property.

"I hope we're not bothering you," I said, stepping forward. "This was our family home, and we were just reminiscing."

"Would you like to come inside?" she asked with a warm smile.

Walking inside sent a flood of visceral emotions through my body. I felt a flood of energy from years past as we slowly followed the woman into the front hall. She graciously let us wander on our own, excusing herself to her computer. Beth and Messer stood in the foyer where we used to jump into the dirty clothes pile, and I closed my eyes, trying to envision my younger self racing through the halls.

Something lured me upstairs. With my first step, the wood creaked under my weight as it had done all those years back. Fear was coursing through my veins, making me want to retreat, but I kept climbing, counted each step as I had done as a child—13 in all. At the top, I turned and entered Dad's old office, feeling tears in my eyes at all the bad energy I sensed around me.

What's wrong with me? I thought. Overly anxious and barely able to breathe, I rushed down the stairs and fled out the front door for fresh air. Beth and Messer joined me on the front lawn, where I was gasping for air.

"Are you okay, Diana?" Beth asked as she stroked my arm.

"What is it?" Messer asked.

"Something bad happened in the office upstairs," I said. "I don't know what it was. Do you guys remember anything?" They both shook their heads no.

A couple of months later, we were on a plane. Normally, we would be giddy with excitement to be together for a weekend, but this time the mood was somber. We were well aware that our trip was primarily a recon mission. When the flight attendant came, Messer, Beth and Anna ordered tomato juice. Exhausted from both my divorce and working full-time, I ordered a Bloody Mary, which the others eyed with silent disdain. When we touched down, Mom and Norma picked us up at the airport with smiling faces and detailed our weekend plans to us on the drive home: buffet dinners at the casinos, new shows, walks along the Truckee River and jigsaw puzzling.

After we got back and ate lunch, we settled in on the comfy couches in the living room, with Mom and Norma sitting next to each other and all the girls squeezed together opposite them. I took a breath—it was time to do what we came here to do.

"I had the weirdest reaction when I went into Dad's study," I explained. I had a sick feeling that something bad had happened in there, but none of us remembered anything. All that came to mind was playing with Dad's mercury.

"Yeah, something happened to Diana when she went in there," Anna said. "She ran out of the house, and we all thought she was going to be sick. It was crazy. Do you know what happened?"

Mom nodded with wide eyes.

"Well, I can certainly tell you what triggered that," she said, her face now ghostly white. "I tried to shoot myself in that room." We all simultaneously gasped at this.

"Oh, Bless your heart," Anna said. It was her go-to phrase in situations like this one.

"Your dad kept a loaded .22 in his desk drawer, and when I ran out of the dining room one night, I knew I had to do it," Mom said. "I had it to my head and was pulling the trigger. It didn't fire, so I pulled the trigger again. I was playing Russian roulette but didn't realize it. I didn't know shit about guns." At this, Norma reached over to rub Mom's back, and she started to cry.

"By the third click, your dad had made it up the stairs, knocked me to the ground and wrestled the gun out of my hand," Mom continued. "He was so pissed off that he stood there kicking me over and over again, like he was beating a dog. At the time, I wished he would have just killed me. He grabbed the gun and unloaded it as I lay there whimpering. There was only one bullet, and it was in the next chamber."

We all sat stunned. Before her words could even register, she got up and excused herself. Norma was never one for idle chatter so we all just sat silently, munching peanut M&Ms.

We went to bed early that night after a quick bowl of soup, too exhausted to continue our probe. As we all lay only two feet apart from each other on air-filled mattresses pretending to be asleep, the enormity of what had just happened finally began to sink in.

"What if Mom had really killed herself that night, guys?" I said quietly, sitting up on my mattress. Now that I'd broken the silence, Anna, Beth and Messer all shot up, too.

"Things would be so different now," Messer whispered.

We kept talking in hushed tones all night because Mom's room was right across the hall. I didn't dare say it out loud, but as I lay back down, I thought: *Maybe it would have been better if she had ended it all that night. It would've spared us all 42 years of wondering why she didn't love us enough to stick around.* The gun never fired, but we were all left with our respective holes—still, I felt guilty for thinking such horrible thoughts.

"I'm glad she's here," I whispered finally. "I have to know what her life was like without us."

Over coffee and hot chocolate the next morning, we all awkwardly tried to initiate lighter conversation. Mom hadn't come to the kitchen yet, so we were sitting at the table with Norma, who had emerged in her underwear with her hair sticking straight up. As if on cue, the wall clock started chirping so loud I about jumped out of my skin.

"Ah, that's the red-winged blackbird," Norma proudly announced. "We saw that bird last time we were in Salt Lake. They're beautiful." We all smiled and nodded, some of us kicking each other under the table. I was surprised to register a quiet gratitude for Mom and Norma's passion for birding. *Whatever breaks the silence in here,* I thought.

Just then Mom appeared, and it looked as if she had been awake for hours. She was showered, dressed and toting a big binder, which she placed on the end of the table before sitting down. We all eyed it while she poured herself a cup of coffee.

As she returned with a steaming cup, she rubbed the front of her binder.

"I'm taking a poetry class," she said brightly. "I'm compiling all of my writing into a book, and it's almost finished! I'd love for you girls to read it if you're interested."

We all nodded and smiled politely, with more barely concealed kicks under the table.

"Maybe next time we come down," I said. "I don't know about y'all, but I'm spent."

Chapter Thirty
June 2009

After flying home from Reno, my dad called all four of us girls in a panic.

"My apartment management is performing random inspections for the so-called well-being and safety of the residents," he said, "and I've gotten just a little behind on the housekeeping."

Ted Cannon, once a well-respected community member residing in a high-rent prestigious neighborhood, was now living in government housing in downtown Salt Lake. Our house had often been filthy when we were kids, but when we showed up to help him prepare for his apartment inspection armed with our arsenal of buckets, sprays, rags and feather dusters, it was clear he had taken living in squalor to a whole new level.

"Sorry for the mess, girlers," he said. "I just haven't had the energy to lift a damn finger. Lemme give you a quick tour!" The haze of smoke that was spilling out from behind him was so thick we could barely see into the one-bedroom apartment as we followed him inside, heroically trying to hide our disbelief and disgust. His apartment was dark and dreary, and the tub-shower combo in the bathroom was filled from floor to ceiling with putrid garbage bags and loose trash. The fact that his tub had become a dumpster also meant months of no bathing. A foul odor emanated from his body, and his legs were red and swollen. Upon closer look, I saw a clear fluid dripping from his calves to his purple puffy feet.

While Dad described his "eclectic" taste in design, it became increasingly difficult to hide our growing nausea. I pulled my sweater up over my nose in a vain attempt to filter out the smells as my flight-or-fight response kicked in, but Dad had been so volatile lately that I was scared to leave my sisters alone with him. I inhaled as much of my perfume from my sweater as I possibly could.

To my horror, as soon as Beth spotted Dad's antique queen bed that he had been sleeping in since he was a child, she said, "Oh, I love that bed. If you ever decide to get rid of it, I want it."

Appalled by the globs of gum lining the headboard and his soiled sheets, my thoughts turned to a can of gasoline and a match. *I would burn everything in this damn apartment if I could,* I thought. Worst of all, however, was the kitchen. Dad sauntered into the tiny L-shaped space, but quickly disappeared behind stacks of pizza boxes, Chinese takeout and other containers clumsily stacked to the ceiling and filling the air with their putrid stink.

"Well, we better get to it if we're going to get done here," I said in an effort to cut the tour short and get down to business. Dad came out from behind the boxes with a tumbler of booze in one hand and a lit cigar in the other.

"Okay, I'll let you girls get to work," he said. "Don't want to be in your way." With that, he trudged through the apartment kicking boxes out of the way to clear a path and sat down in front of his computer. I was boiling inside, but I wasn't surprised. He hadn't lifted a finger to clean before we got there, and he obviously had no intention of doing so now.

"Crazy fucking bastard," I cursed to Messer under my breath as we scrubbed the linoleum. Messer and I hastily opted to clean the kitchen, leaving Beth and Anna with the equally gruesome task of the bathroom. The madder I got, the faster I worked. I wished I had a jar of menthol like I had seen those forensics teams use when investigating a week-old murder scene on TV. We hauled out 35 bags of garbage to the communal dumpster that day and scrubbed every counter and floor—all the while gagging and doing our best not to lose our lunch.

There was a dense layer of hair covering Dad's matted down carpet. He had no pets, so it perplexed me that thick white hair was everywhere; either he was shedding profusely or cutting it and leaving a trail from where it fell from grooming that day. No vacuum could suck the greasy rat's nest off the floor, but we made a pass at it and then got the hell out of there. Dad mustered up a drunken "thank you" before we left.

"I'm never doing that again," I told my sisters as we walked out of the decaying building. "I don't care if he loses his apartment and ends up living on the streets, I'm not going in there again! And I'm burning all my clothes the second I walk in the door!"

Despite claiming I would never return, I still got sucked in one last time by Beth—I relented for her, not for Dad.

Since we had done such a fantastic job cleaning his place, Dad asked us if we would come every other week. Beth and Messer agreed; Anna and I opted out. On one of the scheduled cleaning days, Beth called to ask if I could take Messer's place since she was out of town. After bitching about it for a few minutes on the phone, I agreed to go.

When Dad answered the door, he wore only a filthy white sheet draped around his waist. Shirtless and pale as a corpse, he waved us in with a burning cigar in hand and an oxygen tube under his nose. When the sheet fell away exposing his flaccid penis, he merely said, "Oops, sorry, girlers."

Beth and I quickly looked away, "Sheesh, Dad, what are you doing?" Beth asked.

I hurried past Dad, mumbling, "God, I wish you still wore garments!" I was glad I had worn scrubs purchased at the DI thrift store when I brushed past his large naked body. Dad had put on a lot of weight in the last few months, tipping the scale at 300 pounds. We had grown accustomed to his odor, but this time it seemed to have gotten worse. As he took a big draw on his cigar, I noticed the grayish-blue pallor of his face—a sure-fire sign of his bodily decay.

I wanted nothing more than to leave, but I knew Beth wouldn't join me, and I couldn't leave her there alone. With no other option available, I got busy dusting the living room, where a thin layer of ash covered every surface. He had left his computer screen on, revealing a disturbing image of a naked woman on a porn site.

"Dad, you know you're not supposed to have the oxygen tank in here while you're smoking, right?" I asked, turning away from the lurid image on the screen. "You're gonna blow the place up."

"Yeah, yeah," he said. "But if it was going to happen, it would've by now." Dad sat at his computer and started rambling about someone he had met over the internet who lived in the Philippines. "Her name is Minnie, and she's my sexy little darlin'. She's young, but she sure seems interested in your good ol' Dad. Guess I haven't lost all my sex appeal after all. I wrote her a poem. Can I read it to you, girlers?" There was nothing we wanted to hear less.

"How old is she?" I asked, trying to derail the poetry session.

"She's 23, but she's very mature for her age. I'm thinking if I could move someplace warm to live out the rest of my life that would make me happy. Plus, I could live like a king on my pension in the Philippines." *He can't be serious*, I thought to myself. Dad plucked a few pages from the printer and, standing there half-naked in a bedsheet, he began reading his poem with great bravado, as if he were performing for a large audience:

MINNIE

Remarkable girl is my Minnie Garcia
She is here for a while and then types "okkk cya"
Bee-like, she is very industrious
Wanting to see can we fix it to be "us."
On the go all the time
A'hunting computrious
To see who to get to know
'N' maybe give a Café show :-)

Showed interest by mouse click
Took shot at old Cannon looked some old stick
Calling self Tiger Ted and blowing own horn
Risk-taking Minnie had no idea he loved porn!

No shy one my Minnie an' knows what she wants
@ JC locked on him
And went for his pants
Threw cute hook in the water
Caught glum old fish
Look out Min who go for, you may get your wish!
Wasn't even a battle
So much did he want to jump into her saddle
To ride her furiously and put her up wet
That did it, he's a goner, the hook was well set.

Minnie soon showed how much she is sweets
Had him dying to hit the proverbial sheets
Implied she was up for it
He dreamed of her tit
He near fainted from pleasure
(dumb Tiger thot he was taking HER measure!)

"Haha silly Tiger,
Min loves ya," relax and be coddled
Love her back for you need her like babe needs his bottle.
Tho' he still flips around some, the ludicrous guy
Is in love to the teeth and not a bit shy

Clinging years' customed loneness, squawking unbelief

Tiger deep in his heart thanks God for relief...
His Minnie.

Old b/f unfaithful
Saddened her first
Then Min showed true colors and axed "How duz he durst
Treat me, Me the Minnie, thataway?" She almost had cursed!
Made her mad like a hornet
Almost blew blast like a cornet!
Sure, she's got temper
In IM I've seen it
Big type for excitement
On Mike she might scream it!

"Okay, I get it, Dad!" I shouted. I had to stop him before I lost it. There were still four pages to go, and I couldn't stand to hear any more. Thankfully, he got the message but continued reading silently until the end.

A heavy melancholy hit me on the drive back home as I realized I was grieving the loss of my father even before he was dead. He had stopped taking his court-ordered medication several years ago, and his mania had increasingly gotten worse. Sadness gripped me as I stood half naked in my garage after tossing my scrubs into the garbage. I collapsed to the ground, tipping over the shelf of garden tools. *I wish he would just die*, I thought, crying a river of tears. It was the last time I saw my father.

Over the course of the next year, Dad completely unraveled both mentally and physically. His apartment fell into such disarray that the horrific stench seeping into the hallway caused the neighbors to file official complaints.

When confronted, Dad threatened his neighbors with a lawsuit and brandished his antique shotgun.

Uncle Garn, Beth, Anna, Messer and I got together and decided it was time to write a letter to propose that he check himself into a nursing home. His cellulitis had gotten so debilitating that he had ended up in the ER several times with terrible skin infections. Since he'd left it untreated for so long, the infection had traveled to his genitals, enlarging his scrotum to the size of soccer balls. His doctors put him on antibiotics, demanding that he be admitted to the hospital and get educated on avoiding further complications and how to take better care of his cellulite. Each time, a couple of hours into his hospital stay, he'd feel a little better and leave against medical advice. "I can't sit around here anymore. I need to get home and pack for my trip overseas!" he would rant. "Once I get down to sea level in a warm, humid climate, I'll get better. You'll see."

After running the grammar and spell-check hundreds of times, in fear of his wrath over dangling participles or typos, we agreed it was a well-composed email. Ironically, despite our father's slovenly lifestyle and erratic behavior, it was still very important to us not to make any errors. Having grown up with a copy-editing father who red-lined even our Post-It notes, we knew the letter had to be perfect. When we hit send, delivering the email from a made-up and thus untraceable address, we hoped he would realize that we truly wanted to help, that the letter had been written out of love and concern for him.

Much to our dismay, Dad flipped out—and once again, I was the scapegoat who took the brunt of the blame. Dad was convinced I had orchestrated the plan since I worked in health care and had run an assisted living center. He wrote all of us a scathing email with most of his wrath directed at me. He wrote that the egregious attack on his person was instigated by "church-lady" Diana: *This is the worst, most God-awful idea! Shipping me off to a decrepit old-folks home is a life sentence, worse than prison or a trip back to the psych ward.*

Ted Cannon had no intention of abandoning his sordid one-room kingdom unless it was on his terms, and I was finally smart enough to steer clear of his apartment and wrath.

When Dad finally left his apartment, he went out kicking and screaming escorted by four Salt Lake City police officers, only to later find another run-down duplex rental not far from the apartment he'd been evicted from, where Beth and Messer kept cleaning, cooking and obsessively worrying that he would become homeless if they abandoned him. After watching my dad's explosive eviction on the evening news later that night, I made another appointment with Dr. Graham in Salt Lake City.

Though Dr. Miller helped me through what she considered a near-death situation with Conner, I couldn't keep seeing her because I'd moved back to Salt Lake. Instead, I'd continued going to therapy on and off with Dr. Graham again. Whenever I felt like I'd stabilized, I would stop making regular appointments—but situations like my dad's eviction kept leading me back into her office. In our latest session, I was busy explaining all the ins and outs of my dad's situation, how he'd coerced us into cleaning his nightmarish apartment and had never even said thank you when Dr. Graham stopped me.

"Diana, I want you to think about something for a minute," he said calmly. "Do you think you will ever have the relationship you want to have with your parents?" I told him that I didn't, and he nodded. "So, if that's the case, do you think you stand to benefit from holding on to your expectation that your father might act differently one day?" I opened my mouth to say something in response, but I couldn't find the words. Instead, my lips just started trembling.

"I commend you for your strength and I frankly find it somewhat miraculous that you haven't become a textbook victim in adulthood yourself," Dr. Graham continued, "but I'd like you to consider that it's up to you to determine what kind of relationship you want with your parents, if you want one at all. It's perfectly okay for you to work on your own happiness and disconnect from your parents."

As I walked out of his office, his words repeated in my head over and over. *Holy shit,* I thought. *I can divorce my parents, too?* I buckled myself into the driver's seat of my car and sat in the quiet with my thoughts for a good 30 minutes. *I can't help or save my father,* I thought finally. *It's too late, and he's too far gone.* I put the keys in the ignition slowly and brought the car to life, still moving slowly. *But it's not too late for me and my kids.*

Chapter Thirty-One
2008–2009

"She kicked me out, Mom," Scott slurred. My entire family had learned a long time before not to talk to Scott on the phone after 6 pm, as he would most likely be drunk—but this situation called for breaking the rule. "I'm such an idiot," he continued, sobbing brokenly on the other end as my heart broke for him. "I don't know what to do." I turned off my TV and sat cross-legged on the floor.

"Try to calm down, honey," I said gently. "Tell me what happened." As he explained, the fight between him and his wife Brandy had started over whose responsibility it was to keep up with which chores around the house. Between the important details, Scott couldn't stop wailing. "My wife, my job, my home," he said. " I'm about to lose everything! I need help, Mom." I felt his pain but wasn't sure what to do with it —so many of these situations had happened in the past, and it wasn't entirely clear from his explanation how this one was different. Still, it certainly seemed to be.

After telling Scott to go to sleep and call me in the morning, I told him I would book him a room in an extended-stay hotel near me for a couple of nights so we could figure out our next steps. After we got off the phone, he called me and said that he hadn't slept at all but had driven to the hotel already. I cringed that he had driven to the hotel drunk but was still relieved that he had called—and that he'd made it there safely. It was clear this was not a standard episode with Scott; things were getting out of control, and my mind was going into rescue mode. Scott had gone on benders before, but this couldn't continue. Things had to change, and he had asked for my help.

I got zero sleep that night as I googled everything I could on the topic of alcohol and drug detox and rehab, sorting through pages and pages of ads that all seemed to say the same things while obscuring the real information—like whether any of the programs were actually effective or not, whether any of them could actually help my son. After hours of searching, I found a 30-day rehabilitation program in Sandy, Utah that seemed like the best option available. I knew that Scott would refuse to do a 12-step program based on past conversations we'd had, and his very vocal disbelief in any Higher Power. Fortunately, the program I'd found was spiritually based, but didn't require AA—and with a sizable chunk of the money I had saved up, I was able to pay for it.

After a few days of discussion, Scott agreed to go to the program. So I picked him up and drove him to the facility, which would be his temporary new home as he detoxed and started his journey of rehabilitation. While we waited in the lobby for his assigned counselor, incense and yoga music filled the air, making us both more comfortable immediately. I could see Scott was relaxing, too.

"I love the smell of incense," he said.

"Me too," I returned, rubbing his back. "I hope you take advantage of all of the programs they have to offer here, honey." Finally, his counselor emerged and introduced himself as Matt, welcoming us both with a hug.

"He's in good hands here," Matt said reassuringly. When it was time to say goodbye, Scott gave me a long hug.

"Thank you, Mom," he said through sobs. "I love you."

As I left Scott in my rearview mirror, I gripped the wheel and tried to focus on the road rather than my thoughts. *It's a good program*, I thought, nodding to myself. *He's in a good place where he can finally take some responsibility for his own actions and his life. It's all up to him now.* Though the anxiety that the program might not help or that Scott would try to leave were still swimming around inside me, I tried to put them out of my mind, let the program take its course and get back to my life while waiting for him to come out of the program and help him plan his next steps. When I got home, however, I got a phone call from the counselors at the facility.

"Part of Scott's program are regular, weekly family therapy sessions," the counselor said. "We have him scheduled on Friday at 4 pm, so we look forward to seeing you then." This was news to me.

"Wait, sorry," I started, "I just dropped Scott off—I thought the program was 30 days long?"

"That's correct, ma'am," the therapist continued, "but a *required* part of that program is that Scott's family members attend group therapy with him as well—all immediate family." It seemed that there was no way around it, so I tried to figure out the logistics of getting time off work and coordinating Stephanie and Haley's schedules so we could support Scott. Though I understood that it was valuable for us to support Scott, it confused me that we were *required* to attend —after all, most of the recovery work was his responsibility, not ours.

When Friday came, Stephanie, Haley and I hugged Scott and took our seats in a crowded room with the other families in treatment. Finally, the counselor leading the group started to speak.

"I'm grateful to all of the family members here today to support their children in recovery," he said. "For others, I want to clear up one common misconception about addiction, recovery and why you're here." After saying those words, he paused for a moment to give the room a chance to prepare themselves.

"The common view of addiction is that it's a character defect or a sign of weakness," he said, "but science tells us that's not true. Addiction is not an individual failing. Addiction is a disease—and it's also a *family* disease. Recovery from addiction is very difficult on its own, but without the cooperation and support of the family of origin, it can be nearly impossible." It was clear that a lot of the room—myself included—wasn't ready to hear those words and everything they implied, but the counselor wasn't flinching. "You being here is an incredible first sign of support, but if you find yourself wondering why you need to be here or what part you play in any of this, please remember what I just said."

After his grim introduction, the counselor led the group in a discussion, with different families working out their issues in public view of the others. At first, nobody seemed to want to talk—but then came the accusations, from parents and children alike. Some parents talked about how much their children's actions had hurt their family, while others talked about the anger and pain their parents had never acknowledged. Finally, it was time to break into smaller groups to talk directly to our own family members. *What a relief*, I thought. Scott had been on a bad path, but we still had a relationship. We could talk to one another, and whatever we had to say couldn't be as gut-wrenching as what we'd already heard.

The counselor told everyone to be as honest and vulnerable as possible, and Scott took the advice to heart.

"Mom, I love you more than anything," he began, "but I'm so mad at you for leaving Ken and ripping our family apart." What he said was already like a bucket of ice water, but he wasn't done. "He was the only father I really knew— and now *he* abandoned us, too." With that, my anger and denial were shattered. Scott started crying and Stephanie and Haley followed, and somehow, I knew they were tears of solidarity. They were crying because of decisions I had made.

"I am so sorry, Scott," I said. "You're right. You all deserved so much better." I couldn't hold back my own tears either as I heard echoes of my own mother's voice: *mea culpa, mea culpa...*

When the session was over, we all hugged each other, feeling closer than we had in years.

"I'm so proud of you for being so vulnerable," I told him quietly. "We're going to get through this together." *I guess our family is fated to be in therapy for the rest of our lives*, I thought to myself.

After continuing through the rest of the rest of treatment

and our group family therapy sessions, Scott's spirit seemed slightly renewed, and he forged ahead with as much clarity as he could muster. He and Brandy had divorced and sold their house, though thankfully he was able to keep his job. After the separation proceedings were over, he found an old buddy from Salina who had recently moved to Salt Lake to move in with and prepared to settle into his new life in recovery. Meanwhile, I was finding it difficult to return to the life I'd had before Scott had gone to rehab.

The entire experience had been a wake-up call. I had plenty of things to be angry about, but I had underestimated how much responsibility I had for the other people in my life. I didn't only need to get better for my own happiness; I might actually need to get better for my kids as well.

I tried to continue my new course of healing, but my depression kept creeping in, undermining my thin façade of progress. I tried anti-depressants and sleeping pills to regulate my moods, but all they did was make me numb. I continued to work at the care center, but despite how much I loved my co-workers and the elderly residents, the constant reminders of how I had ended up there were getting to be too much to bear.

Utah County suddenly felt way too small and suffocating. Memories of Conner and my failure lingered everywhere, and I knew I needed to be closer to my kids. I started applying for jobs in Salt Lake as a practicing physical therapist and landed a job with the clinic I had worked for prior to meeting Conner. I thought this victory would solve everything, as I had loved working there before I met Conner, but I was still so depressed that I could barely function. Returning to the same clinic I'd left four years prior only reinforced the fact that I had just lost four years of my life and was starting all over again. I only lasted there for a month or two, then put in my notice before bawling in the fetal position for three days.

I didn't feel like myself anymore. Before Conner (*BC*, I thought ironically), I had not been a bitter, vengeful and depressed person—so why was I now? How had I ended up divorced three times with a trio of emotionally damaged kids? Through everything I'd endured and even lost in my life, I had always been able to stay positive and optimistic. Now, it felt like I might even lose that version of myself entirely—and I couldn't let that happen.

Rather than spending my entire Saturday cleaning house, which had been my routine for years as a working woman, I decided to try to break out of my slump by doing something for myself. After furiously cleaning until noon, I drove to a Barnes & Noble in Midvale. Feeling very self-indulgent, I ordered a latte and made my way to the self-help section, not knowing what else to do. I skimmed endless titles from *How to Make Your Marriage Work* (*too late for that*, I thought) to *Tantric Sex* before running my fingers over the spine of a book titled *The Secret*. The title caught my eye, and I studied the cover: written by Rhonda Byrne. Nothing else I'd seen all day had jumped out at me, and suddenly the book felt hot in my hands.

I found a soft chair nearby and settled in to read a little. Before I knew it, I realized I was halfway through the book and hadn't even taken a sip of my coffee. One of the under-lying rules of reality, the author wrote, was the Law of Attraction—the principle that one's thoughts had the power to change the world directly. I found this thought astounding, especially since my world seemed like it was in the toilet. *If I change the way I think,* I thought, *could I really change the outcome of anything around me?* I wasn't sure, but I intended to find out.

I left Barnes & Noble with the book in tow and had it finished it by night's end. After finishing, I couldn't help but be a little skeptical of the book's claims. All the concepts were completely foreign to me, and they seemed almost too good to be true. I decided to test out the book's theories immediately in a practical way by keeping a daily journal, focusing on gratitude, forgiveness and the power of positive thinking. First, I would make a running list of all the things I had to be thankful for in my life, no matter how much negative resistance I felt. I started off as simple as I could:

I'm most grateful for my children and grandchildren. They are the one accomplishment I am most proud of. Stephanie, Aidan and Baylee, Scott and Haley—you have my whole heart.

I took a step back and looked at what I'd written, noticing that my kids were rightfully at the top of my list— and they had been my entire life. *You haven't acted like it,* my brain piped up almost immediately. After quieting my mind again, I let the truth sink in. It was true: I had been wrapped up in my own selfishness and drama for longer than I cared to admit. I had been going through difficult times, but so had they. By letting my pain get the better of me, I had neglected to be present for them, and it had caused some serious problems. Even if they were adults now, they were still my children, and they still needed their mother. I kept writing, and my list grew longer and longer until I had an entire page full of positivity. It felt truly monumental—where were all those overwhelming negative thoughts that had been eating up everything just hours before?

As I studied what I'd written, something suddenly became clear. It may have been true that I was a 51-year-old, thrice-divorced woman, but I could still be grateful for the good things I had and the loved ones in my life. If this little gratitude practice worked this well, then maybe I could use it as a tool. It could be a pickaxe I used to chip away at the mountain of problems in my life—and best of all was that it was a tool nobody could take away from me.

I booked an appointment with Dr. Graham to talk about everything that had happened recently with Scott, but before we could go into that, I had to share my discovery of *The Secret* and of gratitude journaling. To my surprise, he told me he'd read it, too.

"I had to read it," he said, laughing. "Most of my patients won't stop talking about it." Though I still had other things to talk about, our session remained focused on a discussion of Rhonda Byrne's concept of the Law of Attraction.

"I liked the book a lot at first, but the more I think about it, it makes me mad," I said. "I didn't ask for all these bad things to happen. I love my kids, and I've only ever tried to do what's the best for them!" I slumped in my chair, feeling deflated. I sighed, nervously twisting my bracelet. "But the fallout is still showing up. I have screwed up so badly. I can't deny it anymore."

"The book takes some creative liberties," Dr. Graham said carefully, "but one thing that does seem true is that your damaged self has been choosing certain people and putting you in certain situations that were harmful, even if it was beyond your conscious control at the time."

"Scott only had to go to rehab because of me," I blurted. "And what if his treatment doesn't work? What if he relapses?" I started sobbing again (it seemed like the only thing I could reliably do anymore) and Dr. Graham handed me a box of tissues.

"You're making progress, Diana," he said. "Right now, you just need to have compassion for yourself." With that, the timer chimed, signaling the end of our session.

In light of everything he'd revealed in rehab, I had no idea how to navigate my new relationship with Scott—how could I help him and take responsibility for my part of the problem while also not taking so much responsibility that I couldn't still live my life and be there for my other children who also needed me? On Dr. Graham's recommendation, I started going to Alanon meetings to at least get some support, if not concrete answers.

After going to a few meetings, I met a woman named Linda, who had dyed her hair flaming red to cover up her gray and who was about 10 years older than me. As we got to know each other, she explained that her daughter was a drug addict who had relapsed several times over the course of 20 years. Even so, she was still trying her best to stay sober—and Linda was still doing her best to support her.

"Even if she might still slip up or I might make a mistake as a mom," Linda said, "Being there for each other is helping our relationship. And it's making us both happier."

After our initial conversations, I decided to take Linda's advice to try to keep the channel open with Scott. Maybe forcing myself to take a longer-term view and embracing the fact that everything wasn't going to get solved at once was the only way forward. In the meantime, I would keep going to Alanon meetings, as talking to Linda was helping me feel less alone. The more we got to know each other, the more I liked spending time with Linda and hearing her thoughts. Eventually, we talked less about my kids and more about me —about my own relationships with my parents but also about the stories of past failed marriages, which were starting to sound funnier the more I talked about them.

"So, are you ready to get back out there?" Linda asked me over coffee one night, taking me a little aback.

"I dunno," I stuttered. "I wouldn't mind going on a date every now and then, but I'm scared shitless I'll find another sociopath."

Linda laughed but kept talking about a local dating service she had just signed up for in Salt Lake, specifically for professionals.

"I'm sick of dating guys that live with their mothers and can't afford to buy me dinner," she said, gnawing on a bagel.

"Is that really all that's out there?" I asked, slightly horrified.

"Pretty much," she replied. "Trust me, you want to sign up for this service."

I liked the idea of becoming a sexually free and open woman (someone like Samantha on *Sex and the City*, I imagined), but my track record proved that might not be possible. I tended to fall in love far too easy. I intended to ignore Linda's advice and toss the notion of dating aside and continued with my mindless television, family dinners and exercising for a few weeks before getting bored one weekend and pulling out the card Linda had given me once again.

Finally, I made an appointment with the dating service's office in South Salt Lake.

At the appointment, I nervously filled out an extensive questionnaire and went through a series of interviews with people who thought I was a perfectly eligible bachelorette for their service. The final selling points for me was that everyone in their system had to provide references and pass a background check, and that nobody's profile had any photos. This way, the focus was on real connections—plus what was the point of including photos anyway? People always posted pictures that made themselves look 20 years younger or 20 pounds lighter. I still wasn't ready to jump into anything too serious, but I was pleased with myself for trying something new, and the idea of potentially meeting other people was undeniably exciting.

Calls rarely came in for matches, which was fine with me —I was working 50 hours a week and spending most weekends with my kids. During a blizzard in February, I was midway through a plate of enchiladas when I got a call from an unknown number. I let it go to voicemail and then checked it when I got home:

"Hi, my name is Kelly. I'm calling from the dating program. I would really like to meet you if you're up for that. Call me!" He sounded friendly enough on the phone, so I called him back. To my surprise, we talked on the phone until very late. He seemed relaxed the entire time, and he made me laugh. When I hung up, I knew I wanted to meet him.

My personal rule for entering the dating scene again was to meet up for a quick coffee date first as a safety precaution.

It felt like a minimal, safer investment to see if there was any connection in the first 10 or 15 minutes.

Kelly and I had scheduled a coffee date for the upcoming Saturday, but he still called me the next morning to talk— and every other morning leading up to our date. I was really looking forward to meeting him and I tried to picture him from his voice, hoping he looked as nice as he sounded on the phone. On Thursday, he called me at 10 am like clockwork.

"Good morning," he said sleepily.

"Hi," I replied a little too chipper. I had already ingested several cups of coffee, so I was a bit jittery—plus I'd already been to the gym and seen two patients.

"Whatcha doing?" he asked.

"Driving to Tooele to see a patient," I replied. "And you?"

"Well, I'm laying here in bed, looking over the Swaner Preserve. It's a beautiful morning, and I'm just waking up and thought I'd call you." *Jesus, you're just waking up?* I thought.

"Are you kidding me? I've seen two patients and have five to go. I like your view better so scootch over because I'm coming up!" There was silence on the other end.

"Just kidding!" I laughed, worried I had freaked him out.

"Come up," he said. "Seriously, you should come up! I'll take you to lunch."

Even though it was one day early, I called to reschedule my patients, went home to shower and change out of my scrubs and found myself driving to Park City.

When I knocked on the door, a tall, dark and handsome man answered—he wasn't a model type, but I was pleasantly surprised! He invited me in, offered me a glass of water and we sat on the couch, staring at the exact view he had woken up to. Just like he said, it was breathtaking.

"Where are we going for lunch?' I asked brightly. He seemed a little nervous, so I was eager to keep things moving along. I smiled slyly.

"You'll see," he replied. "It's a surprise." We drove about 10 minutes up a windy road and through a gate to a magnificent community. I had never seen anything like it.

"Holy shit, who lives here?" I asked, astonished.

"Well, Michael Jordan, for one," he replied.

"Yeah, right," I said with a laugh—but apparently, he was serious.

As we pulled up to a circular driveway, a valet stood there smiling and greeted us warmly. I followed Kelly into a private and grandiose dining area with only a couple of other people where we had a fabulous sauvignon blanc–infused lunch. My mind was reeling.

"Where are we exactly?" I asked. As Kelly explained, he and his ex-wife had started construction on a house in the gated community we had just driven to, and we were now dining at the clubhouse. After our lunch, he gave me a tour of his house under construction, and then we started the drive back down the winding road to Park City. *He'll be a fun guy to hang out with,* I thought, *but we live in two different worlds.*

When we arrived back at his condo, he invited me in for a drink. I had been up since 4:30 am, but I still accepted—I would normally be in bed doing charting and going to sleep early, but I was having such a good time with him.

Kelly made one of the best damn margaritas I'd ever had, and one drink turned into two as we danced around the house playing Beyoncé as loud as the volume would go. I was in no shape to drive back down Parleys Canyon to Salt Lake, so he invited me to stay. Though I hesitated for a moment, the warmth in his deep brown eyes told me that I was safe, and I agreed to stay. *Maybe I'm cut out for the* Sex and the City *life after all*, I thought.

What I thought would be my first-ever one-night stand turned into anything but. Two weeks later, Kelly invited me to go to Mexico with him—and to my kids' horror, I accepted. I didn't blame them for mistrusting a stranger or questioning my decision, given my track record. Still, I assured them that Kelly was no serial killer.

Our vacation together was just as blissful as I thought it would be, and we were growing closer in less time than I thought possible. Still, we were jarred back to reality by my sister Beth's panicked voice over the phone when we returned.

"Dad's gone," she gasped in a message left on my voice-mail. "I'm worried we will never see him again."

On April 28, 2009, while Kelly and I were gone in Mexico, Dad had endured the long flight to the Philippines and moved in with Minnie and a couple of her brothers to live like a king for the rest of whatever life he had left. When I started hearing mutterings about it from Beth and Messer, I didn't freak out. Though in the past, I had always gotten caught up in the drama, this time, I ran a warm bath, lit a candle and listened to Peter Gabriel. *If this is Dad's reality and what he wants*, I thought, *who am I to stand in his way?* Messer was keeping in touch with Dad and Minnie via email and was giving us all frequent updates anyway. *I have my own life to focus on*, I reassured myself as "Don't Give Up" played gently in the background. More accurately, my focus at that moment was on what was developing with Kelly.

It was clear that Kelly and I enjoyed traveling together, so six weeks after we started dating, he took me out on his boat, a custom-built Danish trimaran that he had named Lykke, the Norwegian word for happiness. As we sailed through the San Juan Islands off the Strait of Juan de Fuca, we spent our days island hopping, setting crab traps and getting to know the locals. I wasn't much of a first mate since I had not been on a sailboat before, but I loved watching him and was eager to learn.

I had always been a sucker for adventure, but never dreamed I would sail through cresting waves and live aboard a 36-foot trimaran. Everything felt unfamiliar and exhilarating. Toward the end of the trip, he got down on one knee and proposed over champagne, buttered asparagus and crab. The moment seemed perfect, but rather than saying "yes" as I had been prone to, I resisted.

"We've only known each other for two months," I countered. "You've been married twice, and I have three under my belt. Neither of us has a great track record. It's just too soon." Though he was a little confused, he didn't push me, and I was adamant that I wanted to take things slower this time around.

"I'm on a good path and want to keep working on myself a little longer," I continued. "Plus, you need to know everything about me before we jump into anything." At this, he smiled and held my hand.

"I love you," he said warmly, "so I'll wait until you're ready."

We talked about living together and simply being

companions for the rest of our lives, but it became clear that Kelly was old-fashioned. He wanted a traditional marriage, and as we kept dating, he brought it up again and again over the intervening months. I was smitten with his kindness, gentle calm and love for travel and adventure. Finally, after four months, I caved.

"Okay, I'll accept your proposal," I told him finally, "But we have to wait one year to marry." He agreed, and with that, we moved in together.

My father's "vacation" didn't last long, as Minnie emailed Messer in late May that Dad was very sick and had been bedridden for several days. Thankfully, and only God knows why, she and her family were taking care of him. All the same, he ended up dying on their couch on June 1, 2009. He and Minnie had never gotten around to getting married because he had been too sick, though it would have guaranteed her his social security benefits if they had. The only thing poor Minnie inherited was his beat-up porn-filled laptop. I had read a few articles about old rich white men being enticed by young girls abroad and scammed out of every penny they had, and I wondered if Minnie and her family had seen Dad as their financial savior. *Maybe he didn't die of natural causes*, I thought grimly. *Maybe they ran out of patience and rolled him into a river somewhere.*

I only lived one block from Messer, so I walked over to her house as soon as she called me about Dad's death. Together, we phoned the US embassy in Manila. We agreed to have Dad cremated in the Philippines and have the urn shipped home. A month later, we received a pretty wooden box. I set it on Messer's fireplace mantle as she instructed, wondering how a human life could be reduced to this. It didn't really seem possible that our eccentric crazy Dad was inside it.

On July 18, 2009, we held a brief memorial service for Dad in the Salt Lake Cemetery, where the rest of his family was buried. We chose this date because it was his birthday. I brought Kelly with me, who looked handsome in his off-white linen suit and tie. Since he didn't wear his curly brown hair in the typical Mormon missionary haircut, Kelly stood out. He looked stylish and worldly compared to the other dark-suited, short-haired men around him, and I was proud to hold on to his arm as I introduced him to my family.

Like a lot of other people in Salt Lake, he was curious about the Cannon family. He had seen my dad in the spotlight for so many years on TV and considered him somewhat of a celebrity. I appreciated that he was trying to be supportive, even if I hadn't had time to delve into the stories of my father and our complicated history yet.

I'm sure he wondered how I could be so detached at the service. I opted for no part in the memorial other than to read the obituary. My sisters wrote very emotional and lovely poems and speeches, and a bagpiper played "Amazing Grace" at the end. My brother Linc didn't attend, declaring that from his perspective, Dad had died a long time ago. Tom, his long hair now gray, kept his head hung low while Anna wept. Dan, Carol, Uncle Garn, Aunt MaryAnn and their kids Sammie and Linda all showed up, along with most of the grandchildren. We all stood among the sinking headstones of the old cemetery and watched his small wooden box of ashes lowered into a hole, where it would reside. A few of Dad's friends offered their condolences and most spoke in admiration of his intelligence and accomplishments.

But look where it got him, I thought. *Dead on a couch in the Philippines with complete strangers. Maybe he wasn't so smart after all.*

It was a memorial service, and he was gone, so there was no need to focus on the past—the delusions, the beatings, the jail time and suicide attempts. Deep inside, I felt relieved. I was finally free of him.

Making good on our one-year promise, Kelly and I married in September 2010 in the beautiful mountain resort at Deer Valley. While the family photos were being taken, I leaned over to Kelly.

"I'm so glad Dad's *not* here," I said, "but I think he would have really liked you."

"I wish I had met him," he replied.

"No, you don't—trust me." I left it at that and turned to smile for the photographer.

After our wild and festive reception, I surveyed the room full of empty champagne glasses, rose petals strewn across the floor and half-eaten plates of cake. *Oh shit, I've done it again,* I thought. *Better not screw this one up.* Still, shedding any pretense of my former Mormon restrictions in such a large and public way felt pretty damn good.

Chapter Thirty-Two
2010–2012

After Kelly and I honeymooned in Tahiti, the dreamiest place I had ever been, my thoughts turned to Mom. Dad was gone now, and it happened almost faster than I could register. Unlike Dad, Mom had been working hard toward getting healthier over the years and was now heavily engaged in writing poetry and even publishing a CD. Also unlike Dad, our relationship had been getting better over the years, bit by bit. Still, I had just learned that a random fall had left her with a fractured left hip that required major surgery and had prevented her from coming to my wedding.

Mom was now 77 and Norma was 80, and neither of them were traveling anymore. Upon returning from Tahiti, I knew I had to visit as soon as I could. After all, I didn't know how much time we had left. In October, I joined Anna, Beth and Messer on a trip to go see Mom with my skin still bronzed from the South Pacific, most of which we spent sitting in a circle, looking through volumes of Mom's and

Norma's scrapbooks, learning more about their love story and life they had built together for over a decade and a half. Mom dragged out boxes of pictures none of us had ever seen of our childhood, including a photo of the six of us from our Second Avenue house, taken just weeks after she had left us.

"Grandpa Ross sent this to me along with a letter scorning me for my decision to leave," Mom said. "It sat on my nightstand for years." I studied the six of us, all smiling as if we didn't have a care in the world.

"Look how happy you look," she said. *Of course we do*, I thought grimly. *Even if you just abandoned us, when Dad said smile for the camera, we grinned on command. If he said jump, we jumped.* Just then, we heard a knock at the door.

Mom got up to see who was at the door and brought her neighbors into the kitchen to meet us a few moments later. They were a good-looking couple with two adorable teen daughters. We all got up and tried to straighten the mess of photos.

"It's so nice to finally meet you all," the mystery mom said, extending a warm hand. "I'm Kate, and this is Don, Louise and Sarah. We've heard so much about you over the years!" Mom was beaming.

"Girls, this is our surrogate family," Mom said. "We've just loved having them as neighbors. Louise and Sarah are accomplished musicians! Sometimes they bring over their violin and flute and play for us." Louise and Sarah blushed politely and said thanks.

"Come in and have a seat," Mom said, pushing pillows off the couches to make room. After congregating in the living room, Don and Louise told us that they were from Germany and that they still traveled there often, so much so that the teens now spoke fluent German. As everyone got to know each other, I realized that this was the first time I was getting a glimpse of what my mom's life with Norma was actually like. They were part of a charming little community here, even if it felt a bit strange that Mom would need a surrogate family when she had a real one right in front of her.

After the neighbors left, I kept my commentary to myself and my sisters, and I sat and listened to Mom tell stories about the past for so long that we never got out of our pajamas, drinking coffee all day (Diet Coke for my sisters) and eating peanut M&M's. I fought the urge to ask the nagging question I had really wanted to ask: *Why didn't you at least take Messer and I with you, knowing we weren't Dad's kids?* Still, it seemed insensitive to ask in front of Anna and Beth, so I bit my tongue.

After a while, Mom stood up from the couch holding her book of poems.

"I have a good one here," she said. "Can I read it to you out loud?" We told her that we'd love to hear it, so she cleared her throat and began:

ADVENTURING

It took a mighty smack from life
to impel me to go grubbing around
in my personal compost heap
of childhood pains,
of sins and shameful memories.
Layer after layer
I dig deeper

with desperate yearning
that if I stir it up enough,
let in some air,
then maybe, just maybe,
way at the bottom
in the world of slime and mold
I'll uncover a tiny glimmer,
a whisper of hope
that somewhere in the turmoil
of my tempestuous life
is that one small spark of divinity
that will have made the journey
worth the pain of surviving.

Mom smiled from ear to ear, and we all gave her a standing ovation. We all gave her a group hug, which Norma joined in on.

"Your mother is a brave woman," she said warmly. I didn't particularly fancy poetry, and I also didn't see what was so brave about what we had all just witnessed, but I was surprised to feel so proud of my mom. She had clearly been doing so much work to heal from her own shame and guilt— even if a major cause of it was abandoning us. Mom's words made it clear that she had suffered for years over what she'd been through. Whatever sour feelings I had, I still had warm feelings for the strong, creative person in front of me, in spite of myself. Thinking back to my conversations with Dr. Miller, I knew my relationship with my mom might never be normal—but I also knew I wanted her and Norma in my life. I had lost my father, but it wasn't too late to create some type of relationship with my mother.

After the trip was over, we all said our goodbyes and I flew back to my new home with Kelly in Park City. With Mom's poetry still fresh in my head, I went upstairs to our loft and pulled the dusty book she had given me in 2008 off the shelf, deciding to read it in earnest this time. As I flipped through it, my eyes lingered on the shocking second entry:

LITTLE GIRL ON A WHITE RUG

See that girl
on the fluffy white rug
watching through slitted eyes
her small hand
under Daddy's large one
wrapped around his thing.
Up and down.
Up and down.

His other fingers
touch the girl down there.
She feels all tingly.

Like an exploding bomb
the door crashes open.
Mommy is huge
her eyes bug out
when she yells,
"Ross, what are you doing to that baby?"
That baby. That baby.
She's not a baby.
She's three years old.

Old enough to know it's the end of the world.

I hadn't even sat down to read yet before finishing the poem and realizing I had been holding my breath and now couldn't breathe. I flung the book as far from me as I could and watched it skid across the coffee table, holding my head in my hands and gasping for air. I couldn't believe the book had been on my shelf in my house for years and I'd never opened it. I had been so naïve to think I understood what my mom was feeling—or where her shame and guilt came from.

I heard Kelly rushing upstairs to check on me as I took more seizing breaths, trying to get control of my body again. My anger had never wanted to understand my mom's side of the story. Now, all I wished I had come to some of these realizations sooner—or that we could still reset the clock on our relationship for more time.

Chapter Thirty-Three
2010–2012

In 1979 when Kelly was 27, he had acquired his father in-law's automatic swimming pool cover company with a partner. Though they had started off manufacturing and selling their products domestically, over the course of five years, the two of them took the product international. Kelly became well-known in the industry for his emphasis on pool safety standards and drowning prevention, growing the company for 30 years. Finally, in 2010, Kelly sold his company, I quit my job and we started our retirement together—and since he had already traveled globally for work, we picked up our leisure travel right where work had left off.

We found ourselves going on incredible journeys together, sailing on Kelly's boat to revisit the San Juan Islands off the coast of Washington and Oregon. Now full of wanderlust, we took up exploring his Norwegian ancestry in the fjords of Norway and visiting friends in Oslo. We kept a sailor's log, and I journaled about our adventures, at least partially inspired by my mom's writing.

I also signed up for evening creative writing classes at the University of Utah. Though my science and medical background had taught me to be quite proficient at technical writing, but as I scribbled notes and worked on character development exercises, I was becoming pretty convinced that I hadn't inherited my mother's gift for creative writing. Still, I felt some comfort in having unearthed some new points of connection with her, since she'd always been such a mystery to me. Meanwhile, I could hear my ex-husbands' voices echoing in my head: *You're gonna end up just like your mother...*

Aside from our own journeys together, retirement also meant Kelly and I had more time to spend with our families —and even though I tried to warn him, there was no way he could've known what it meant to be enmeshed with the Cannon clan.

During the year leading up to breaking her hip, Mom had suffered a few diabetic comas, had chronic urinary tract infections and was diagnosed with lupus, which was attacking her skin. With all the recent hospital admissions, she had contracted C. diff, a nasty bacterial bowel infection that was known to be highly contagious, necessitating Hazmat suits for anyone entering her room. In early spring 2010, Beth and I flew to Reno after learning that Mom had been hospitalized.

She absolutely hated hospitals and threw childish temper tantrums, swearing at anyone who came into her room. When we arrived, it was no different. A foreboding sign and stainless-steel cart outside of her hospital room warned us that she was under quarantine, and all visitors had to protect themselves by putting on what looked like a Hazmat suit. Beth and I donned the yellow gowns, masks, booties, caps and bright blue gloves and entered the room cautiously, as the doctors had not given us good news about her prognosis.

"Get me the fuck out of this hospital," she hollered as soon as she saw us. Her face distorted as she pulled desperately at her bedsheets, throwing an empty plastic juice cup onto the floor at our feet. "I'm going to die in here. Help me get the fuck outta here, today!"

Beth, who detested the f-word, went to the bedside shaking her head and tisking while I slipped back out the door in search of a nurse.

"Is my mom getting any medication for anxiety?" I asked the nurses. "She's freaking out in there and is trying to get out of bed. I'm afraid she's going to take off!"

"We can give her something to help her relax," the tattooed male nurse calmly replied, "but it may take a while. I'll have to get an order from the doctor." Luckily, the nurse came in an hour later with a dose of Xanax, and within 10 minutes, she had calmed down significantly.

Mom looked gaunt and defeated, and Beth and I realized that something was different this time. The room became uncomfortably stuffy and stifling.

"How long can you two stay?" Mom asked, breaking the silence. "I need to ask for a favor. Our living will is locked up in a cabinet in my bedroom. I need you two to go to the house and read through it. It's in a big blue binder in my bedroom desk, clearly labeled on the front."

"Oh, let's not talk about that right now," Beth said, trying to be cheerful.

We left the hospital that evening and drove into the foothills of Sparks, Nevada, where Mom and Norma had made their home for 18 years. I turned on my phone's flashlight when we arrived and fumbled with the key. The house was in disarray, as we had recently moved most of the furniture into the assisted living center. Mom and Norma's African artwork still hung on the walls in every room, and the metal zebra sculpture and tribal masks seemed to glow in the dark, lending an eerie feeling to the house. Beth grabbed my hand as the animals and tribesman seemed to come alive. Turning lights on along the way, we went directly into Mom's bedroom in the back of the house. For years, Mom and Norma slept in separate bedrooms. Naturally, Mom had the coveted master, which was decorated in a more feminine version of their preferred African style.

Norma's bedroom across the hall resembled a cramped dorm room. She had lined her walls with maps, geology posters and a couple of framed pictures of her family and mom. One picture was boldly displayed: a shot of the two of them skinny-dipping at some lake. I tipped it over, a ritual I had been doing every single time I came to stay with them. *No child needs to see a parent and their lover naked, no matter the circumstances,* I thought.

When we turned on the lights in Mom's room, I headed straight for the desk and quickly found her files.

"Ta-da!" I sang, holding them up in the air. I thought Beth was right behind me, but when I turned, I found her snooping in Mom's headboard storage compartment. The dated king-sized bed had one of those wooden sliding doors, like the old rolltop desks, that spanned the entire width of the bed.

"Jackpot," Beth said, splaying herself onto the carpeted floor. Before I knew it, she was flipping through the pages of one of about 30 of Mom's journals. "I knew she had a bunch of journals, and here they all are!" I quickly flipped through the binder to be sure it was what we were looking for.

"Oh my heck, here's something I never knew about," Beth said, still reading.

"Stop Beth, it's not right to read her journals without her permission," I scolded. Beth closed the notebook.

"Okay, geez." She placed it carefully back into its spot, sliding the cabinet door shut. As we left, I made a mental note to keep the journals from being discovered and taken by anyone else. I was sure there was a gold mine of untold stories in those books.

Mom was eventually released to hospice care, but her condition quickly deteriorated. She had become too weak to eat and her body was swollen with water, so she kept slipping in and out of consciousness. I found myself at her bedside, cupping her hand.

"It's okay to go, Mom," I said quietly. "I love you. Thank you for being my mom. I am so happy we reconnected. I promise that us kids will protect each other, and we will stay close to Norma. It's okay to let go. Go to your property in the Sierras that you loved so much." The mountains were her favorite escape, where she and Norma had camped over the years.

Her cloudy dark gray eyes opened abruptly and just for an instant, I swear she saw me. She inhaled a long deep breath and that was it. I wanted to climb onto her bed and lay by her side, but didn't. I placed the back of my hand on her waxy cheek. "I love you, Mom."

A month later, Kelly and I were the only ones with the flexibility in our schedules to attend a memorial for Mom held by Norma and her family and friends. They had a casual, simple picnic at the park, and then those who were able hiked to the lake to spread half of Mom's ashes; the other half were buried at the Salt Lake Cemetery with Mom's other deceased family. Once we got to the lake, we pulled a bottle of white wine from a backpack and toasted Mom, telling stories of her skinny-dipping days in the freezing cold glacial waters, memorialized by the framed picture in Norma's room. I chuckled as I envisioned these middle-aged women stripping down and jumping to the freezing water and wondered what other crazy shenanigans had taken place.

Back in Salt Lake, the first thing I did was go to the post office to retrieve the boxes we had packed that held Mom's belongings, the journals spanning from 1983 to 2012 the most prized possessions among them. I began dissecting every word and page, learning the real and often sordid story of my mother's life—the source material for the poem that had given me a panic attack.

Writing had helped my mom become more herself, so as I received new free writing prompts in my own class at the University of Utah, I tried to channel her voice. I imagined what I would sound like out of time, if I could weave my own story in and out of the broken pages in the journals I was reading. I floated all the way back to the earliest years, where our sad little branch of the family had all started:

It was a sizzling-hot day in Farmington, New Mexico,

August 20, 1958 as the man who would be my father helped maneuver my mother's wide frame into their '55 green Chevy, beads of sweat dripping from his brow. Mom, whose pregnant basketball belly was protruding from her white cotton shirt, mumbled that she'd bake and die before they ever made it to the hospital. Her ruddy-faced husband of nine years shut the door, hurried around to his side and floored it down the deserted road without bothering to reply, the tension in the car as thick as the gathering smoke from their Lucky Strike cigarettes.

Dad was supposed to have had a vasectomy after the twins were born two-and-a-half years earlier, so I was either the latest immaculate conception or Dad flat-out refused the knife. I'm wagering it was probably the latter. Now, years later, I can reconstruct that day—and the unbalanced mix of miserable to happy days that followed—through many interviews and readings of my mom's extensive journals.

"I just can't believe you didn't follow through with getting snipped!" My mom complained through the smoke bursting from her mouth and nose. It was the 1950s, so doctors were recommending cigarettes to pregnant mothers as a way of controlling weight gain and settling nerves. "We can't have another baby," she continued. "I don't know how I'll manage!"

My father white-knuckled the wheel with his hands locked at ten and two and kept his eyes on the road, ignoring Mom as she doubled over from painful contractions.

I came into the world later that night—red, angry, and after nine months in my mother's womb, likely needing a smoke of my own. I was an eight-pound, 10-ounce, mostly bald baby girl full of promise and potential. I was also the first blonde in the Cannon family, which in retrospect was something of a bad omen.

"What on Earth? Look at those ears," my dad declared after joining us in the hospital room and doing a perfunctory job of holding his newborn. There I was; the unplanned, big-eared, largely unwanted new mouth to feed in a family that needed fewer problems rather than more.

Two days later, we pulled up in front of our tiny one-bedroom house, which was actually an out-building behind a much bigger and nicer home that towered over ours. Our little box had running water, heat, plumbing and cheap rent at $45 per month, and had been the Cannon family residence for the past year. Inside, my four siblings Linc, Tip and the twins anxiously awaited my arrival, all piled up on the couch and peeking out the window.

As soon as we walked through the door, Dad handed a few coins to our 15-year-old babysitter Jean, who ran out to the backyard and hopped the chain-link fence—conveniently for Jean, she lived in a pretty house directly behind our dilapidated one.

Mom took a seat in the living room on the tattered beige fold-out couch, where all us kids slept like a litter of puppies at night. As my siblings vied for position, Grandpa Ted and Grandma Dot walked through the front door. Grandma had a bouquet of limp garden flowers and a lemon cake in hand, no doubt standing there smiling and looking perfectly groomed in her pastel dress and signature pearls, unfazed by the 100-degree heat. Grandpa Ted was quite handsome, lean and fit for 50 and standing over six feet tall. With open arms, he invited Tip and Linc to climb into his arms, which they did like eager little monkeys, hoping to find candy and coins in his pockets.

Without a warm hello or kiss to my mother, Grandma Dot pulled me up to her nose to inhale a whiff of fresh baby smell. Finding the nearby rocking chair, she laid me on her lap, loosened the blanket and took in my big ears and few fuzzy blonde wisps of hair. She shot an incredulous look at Grandpa Ted while the twins wriggled and squealed for Mom's attention, but she just stared off into space.

Dad returned to the cluttered living room, where pinned-up sheets posed as curtains and water stains bled across the graying wallpaper. He offered his parents iced tea from a cracked plastic pitcher and Grandma Dot settled back into her chair, nervously rattling the cubes in her drink while eyeing Mom suspiciously. The two had never shared much affection for one another, as no one was good enough for Theodore Cannon Jr., in Grandma Dot's eyes. The long drive from the moral high ground of Salt Lake City to unruly New Mexico probably didn't help, either.

"What is her name?" Grandma asked my mom with an air of formality, like the Queen Mother inquiring after the latest branch on her royal family tree.

"Her name will be Diana, Goddess of the Hunt!" my father blurted out before Mom could answer. "She's a strong, athletic baby—our biggest yet!"

My dad's enthusiasm came from the fact that the twins had been born prematurely and my brother Tip had almost died from frailty.

My mother stayed silent and returned her tired eyes to me. There was no point in arguing; Dad had determined I was to be called Diana, and that was that. I can only imagine my mother taking in the reality of the situation: five kids, 500 square feet, a mother-in-law's scrutiny, no money and nowhere to go.

In 1960, it only took two days to pack up seven people and it was good riddance to the wild weekends, swinging house parties, free love and couple swapping. For my mom, it was goodbye to affairs with Rob who shared the backyard gate and the memories of Dick with all his whispered (and phony) tales of love and devotion. All the chaos and hedonism were wearing thin on my parents, and a fresh start at the University of Utah in Salt Lake City was just the ticket.

The four-door Chevy wasn't big enough for five children and all our belongings, so Dad's solution was to send the boys on the bus. They were unceremoniously dropped off at the station on our way out of town. Linc and Tip each received a little plastic box that held 3x5 index cards filled out with their name, Grandma Dot's address and some silver dollars glued on as spending money.

During the 416-mile ride to Salt Lake City, the boys had to navigate a few transfers on their own. Throughout the entire 15-hour trip, Tip and Linc lived on peanuts and saltine crackers and arrived at their destination dehydrated, ravenous and coated in dirt. Meanwhile, our Chevy rolled in with an overflowing ashtray and a backseat full of fast food bags and candy wrappers.

Grandma Dot and Grandpa Ted were waiting for us and had gotten Linc and Tip washed and fed before our arrival. With their solo trip behind them and clutching a bag full of Oreos between them, the boys were beaming, happy to be reunited at last.

Grandma and Grandpa lived only a few blocks away and

were thrilled that their only son had returned home. After all, the Cannons were among the original settlers of Salt Lake City and boasted a long history with the Mormon Church. George Q. Cannon, my great-great-grandfather, was Brigham Young's First Counselor, a prestigious position in the church's hierarchy.

All throughout my childhood, Grandma Dot would tug at her pearls, overcome with emotion as she told us how important our family was to the beginning of the Church of Jesus Christ of the Latter-Day Saints (LDS) in Salt Lake City, otherwise known as the Mormon Church. Our religion began informally in 1820 when a 14-year-old boy named Joseph Smith prayed to God and asked what church he should join. While standing in a grove of trees in Palmyra, New York, he claimed God and his son, Jesus Christ, appeared and told him not to join any of them but to be an agent for God and restore the "true" church of God. He deemed himself president and began converting members. A few years later, he was visited by the angel Moroni who told him that he should dig up and translate a holy book that was written on golden plates containing an ancient history of America and its people. This took another several years, and all through God's guidance, Joseph was able to publish the Book of Mormon and formally establish the Mormon Church on April 6, 1830.

According to Grandma Dot and various impassioned Sunday school teachers of my youth, the founding of the Mormon Church angered many Christians in the state of New York, and Joseph Smith and his followers were eventually driven west in 1844. During their trek to safety, Joseph was imprisoned, shot and killed by an angry mob in Carthage, Illinois. Smith's devoted follower Brigham Young became the succeeding prophet and led the faithful LDS congregation to Salt Lake City, Utah.

Tired, battered and half-starved, the Mormon pioneers arrived in the Salt Lake Valley on July 24, 1847—and who'd have thought the most recent group of Cannons would show up in more or less the same condition two centuries later?

Upon arrival, our family piled into a tiny brick house on D Street and 4th Avenue in the respected and pleasant neighborhood called "The Avenues," a middle and upper-middle class trolley suburb where most residents were members of the LDS Church. The neighborhood started off whitewashed and homogenous, dotted with Victorian-era architecture, brick bungalows, charming boutiques, churches and corner cafes. Over time, a mix of university professors, merchants, families and other non-Mormons moved in, transforming and modernizing the area. It was just the place to turn over a new leaf as the wayward descendants of Mormon royalty: we had traveled across the desert and back to the Promised Land.

While most of the neighborhood homes were freshly painted with picket fences and blooming gardens, ours was in utter disrepair. Still, none of us saw it that way at the time; as kids, we were used to living in shambles and squalor.

Aunt MaryAnn and Uncle Garn, my dad's sister and her husband, came to see us a couple days after we had settled in. A tall and youthful blonde, my Aunt MaryAnn was calm, sweet and devoted to the church, and my Uncle Garn, a stout and always-cheerful man, adored her. Though quite the opposite of my mercurial father, I never heard my father raise his voice or even argue with her. Somehow, they understood each other and got along beautifully.

While searching for her two nephews in our ramshackle

house, my aunt made it halfway down the basement stairs when the foul odor of feces and rodents filled her nose. With only a dim, red light illuminating the path, she gasped—the ground was moving! Our basement was alive with cockroaches and mice, illuminated red in a way that must have seemed straight out of a horror movie. Aunt MaryAnn abandoned her mission to find the boys she raced back upstairs, visibly shaken and choking back her own vomit. After that, she quickly made up an excuse and left with Uncle Garn in tow.

This became a pattern throughout my early childhood: an adult would be confronted with some horrible truth about our living situation and would be concerned but too polite or afraid to intervene, and we kids would continue to pay the price.

They say it takes a village to raise a child, but it also takes a village to allow children to suffer—and it could happen even when that village was just a stone's throw from a temple.

Chapter Thirty-Four
2016

In the two years since Mom died, I had read most of her journals and been fascinated and hurt by what I'd learned. Beth and Anna never wanted to hear all the juicy stories Mom had written and were unsettled by her very descriptive love life, so I constantly bothered Messer, reading passages out loud over the phone.

"I just cannot imagine Mom doing this," I said. "She's talking about having rug burns on her elbows, for God's sake! Why the hell would she document it?" Messer was always right there to listen to me or talk about my findings. She had fewer memories than I, since she was so young when Mom left. Now an adult, she was eager to hear the tales, and we giggled at Mom's sexual escapades.

As I considered Mom's life in its entirety, I remembered Jean Hoesley. It had been 18 years since she had sent me a postcard inviting me to San Diego. I hadn't pursued the lead before, but something inside me was suddenly curious again. I felt an urgent need to see her for myself to decide if there was any chance we were really related; since she was 15 years older than me, I wasn't even sure she was still alive. Even though Mom and Dad were convinced Rob Hoesley was my and Messer's father, I was beginning to have doubts. Based on Mom's steamy journal entries about orgies and swinging, my father could have been any number of men. The only thing I knew for certain was that Ted Cannon was *not* my father—at least not biologically.

I booked a flight to San Diego in the spring of 2016. Jean requested that we meet somewhere neutral for lunch, so I booked a room at a lake resort near her home in San Marcos. I planned on staying a couple of days so if things went well, we could spend more time together. We met for lunch the day I arrived at a funky little bar in downtown San Marcos, which made me like her immediately. Somehow, I imagined we would meet at an Olive Garden or Denny's. Instead, we had fish tacos and goblets of sauvignon blanc. By the end of our three-hour lunch, we were planning an outing to Temecula for the following day. The more time I spent with her, the more I could see some resemblances, though they were not obvious. I wondered if I was simply imagining them.

Initially, she was quite guarded with any personal information. I was dying to know about "my father" Rob, but also didn't want to seem pushy. When the time felt right, I asked a few questions.

"What do you remember about our family and my parents from when we were neighbors in Farmington?" I asked.

"I just remember that there were a bunch of loud kids," she replied. "I didn't really like babysitting because there were too many of you, but my father insisted." I noticed she had the same scratchy, gruff voice as me and Messer—but then again, so did our mom.

"Did you know that your parents and mine were big partiers? Did you know they were into orgies and couples swapping?" I prodded, wishing I had been less direct. Jean sat back and her posture stiffened.

"I remember a lot of parties, but I refuse to believe my mother was involved in that," she said. "She would have never done that. Mom and I knew Dad was up to no good and that he drank and smoked too much." I told her how I had come to learn of my family secrets and tumultuous times while in Farmington, and how the dysfunction had continued during our childhood in Salt Lake. She sat quietly across the table from me, her wine glass empty in front of her. As soon as I finished telling my side of the story, she flagged down the young server and asked for another glass— and when I glimpsed her left ear, I about fell off my chair. She had been fussing with her hair trying to cover up her enormous ears our entire visit!

Holy shit, I thought. *We're related for sure!* I was about to say something about our giant matching ears, but instead, I simply tucked my hair behind my right ear to see if she would react. She stared incredulously at me for a moment and then mimicked my action. Her ears were even larger than mine. There was no denying it.

A few months later, we jumped on the technological bandwagon and joined the millions of other people who had just started getting their DNA tested. The results confirmed that Jean and I were indeed half-siblings who shared the same father. It also verified that Messer and I were full sisters, and I was surprised at how much more love I felt for her and even Jean at that moment. Tears flooded my eyes as I wondered what it might have been like for Messer and me to have known her sooner.

I called Messer first, knowing she was freaking out about it.

"I'm so happy to have proof," she said, sighing in relief. "I couldn't have handled any other news. It would have killed me. Thanks for being so brave and taking this on."

"Can you imagine how Jean must feel?" I asked her. "She has lived her entire life thinking she was an only child, and now she has two sisters. I'm not sure how she'll react to that, but I hope we can get to know her better now."

Jean and I corresponded through email, as she was too hard of hearing to talk on the phone, which was supremely ironic. I sat at my computer to send her the news, attaching a copy of the report. She emailed back right away: *Well, look at that. I have two half-sisters, and I'm very happy about that.*

I never needed a DNA test to know Messer was my sister—our bond was greater than even genetics. But knowing who my father was once and for all? That was a hole that felt good to fill.

After Carol turned 82, her health started declining more quickly and Dan and I provided more care, which meant getting her to doctor appointments and helping her go grocery shopping. She was genuinely intrigued by my discovery of Jean and started inviting me for weekly lunch dates. On our visits, Carol would sit in her recliner, and I would sit on the couch next to her, sharing Chinese food and talking for hours. When she learned that I was writing more about my life, she agreed to tell me everything she could remember (which wasn't much because of her drug-addled mind), and I jotted down notes on napkins and recorded her memories on my iPhone.

Even though Carol was still very active in the church and understood that I had no interest, the time we spent together was bringing us closer. I had brought lunch for the two of us one afternoon and sat next to her on a love seat perpendicular to her La-Z-Boy. She settled in with a TV tray in her lap, bib covering her chest and dug into her salad. Always the avid reader, she said she was anxious to read some of the chapters I was working on.

I took a breath, preparing myself for a topic of conversation we hadn't mentioned since it took place in 1970, four decades prior. If she was going to read my writing, I needed to prepare her for some of the stories that would be difficult for her to read, as they were so difficult to recount.

"Carol, there's something I have wanted to bring up for a long time, and just haven't had the courage," I said. "But I think it's time. I don't want you to read my writing before we have a chance to talk about one difficult memory from my childhood." She genuinely seemed to not have a clue as to what I was talking about. Was it the pain pills? Dementia? It was crushing, but I was certain that once I reminded her, she would remember.

"I'm referring to the time when you and Dad beat me with the belt," I continued. She swallowed hard and put her fork down, looking me in the eyes nervously.

"Oh, honey," she said. I waited a moment but that was all she said.

"Will you tell me what you remember about that night?" I asked. Her eyes darted around, straining with effort.

"I remember that when you came home that night and lied about where you were, your dad beat you with his belt," she said finally. "I'm so sorry honey. That must have been awful for you." *Of course she's not going to accept any responsibility for this*, I thought, struggling I had to control my disbelief and anger.

"Do you remember that *you* told Dad to go get the belt and sat and watched the whole time?"

"Oh, honey! I would have never done that," she said quickly. "You have that wrong. But I am so sorry for my part in it. We should have handled that differently."

I wasn't going to let her off the hook that easy. "Well, it's not just my memory," I said. "You might not have known this, but the other kids that were home that night witnessed and heard the whole thing, and they all remember it how I do." I was proud of myself for being so direct and finally talking to her about it. She just shook her head.

"I would never do such a thing," she insisted.

She wanted to blame the whole thing on my dad, saying it was his idea to get the belt. She apologized profusely, but I got the idea that it was all a blur to her and she had blocked it from her memory.

Our lunch ended with a long hug and her kissing me on the cheek, telling me how proud she was of me. I seethed for a day or two before realizing she was doing what everyone in my family had been doing for years: living in denial for self-preservation. With that thought, something inside me unclenched a little. It still felt good to have that one last unspoken trauma out on the table. Even if I couldn't control Carol's reaction to it, I needed her to know how hurtful it had been for me before she passed. I never got the chance to talk to Dad about it, but I also honestly knew I would never muster up the courage to do so. Eventually, I returned to visit Carol with some printed pages I'd been working on, which she dove into like she was reading the newest Agatha Christie.

That Christmas, Carol handed me a packet containing an updated version of our family tree, looking worn out and frail. Debi had sadly passed away at 53 from breast cancer, leaving behind a husband and seven children to mourn her untimely death. Pam was estranged from the entire family by choice, and Mark had literally disappeared. Luckily, Dan lived nearby and together, they worked on her yearly Christmas project. It surprised me how well Carol handled having a gay non-Mormon son. I was proud of her for that, and I loved that the two of them were very close.

Even though Carol had known all along that Messer and I were not the offspring of Mom and Dad, she still filled our names in on the family tree.

Though Carol's tree looked neat, in my mind, I conjured up a very different vision of a giant tumbleweed. What had once started as shallow-rooted sagebrush eventually uprooted itself and had been blowing in every direction ever since. To me, tumbleweeds were beautiful: a complex, lacey network of thorny branches with no plan but to blow with the wind. Like so many in our family, they sometimes got stuck on the grille of a car or a chain-link fence. Even so, they always eventually broke free, ready to roam again.

Epilogue

Though much of my early childhood remains hidden in the shadows and in the deep recesses of my mind, thankfully, my mother found the time and courage to record her thoughts. Not yet 30, depressed and raising five children with an unstable husband, she had already abandoned all attempts at being a doting parent by the time I came around —and barely even acknowledged my existence. Even privately, in her own personal reflections, she spent all of one sentence describing me in her otherwise long-winded and self-absorbed journals.

Over the years, I only came across a couple of photos of me. I would inspect them carefully for clues, tracing my fingers across the fading images on the black and white Polaroids whose edges had curled. On the back, there was always a date and my name, but I wanted more information to help me piece together my past. Why was I named Diana? Where was I born? Why did we leave Utah to live in New Mexico? In my childhood, there were no Saturday afternoon scrapbooking sessions, no bedtime stories or snuggly chats with Mom and Dad by the fire. I had to scavenge for details by asking relatives to weave together my past and place in our toxic family.

Despite being direct descendants of George Q. Cannon, an apostle to Brigham Young, we Cannons were not a typical white-picket-fence, church-going Mormon family—not with all the booze-soaked parties, burning cigarettes and swingers my parents encountered in their early years, nor with the ongoing visits from the police, spells of mental illness and bruised bodies and minds that filled our early home life. Our days and nights always had an element of survival that pressed heavily upon our souls. At the time, I didn't know anything else. Fortunately, I now have a wider perspective.

When I decided to write this memoir, I fully understood that telling the truth, *my truth* about family secrets and the Mormon Church, would be a slippery slope. Sharing my tale would inevitably stir up long-buried feelings and potential conflict between family members and myself. I have tried to be as respectful as I know how to be while revealing my version of the past. It was never my intent to hurt or offend anyone, but rather to share an honest, candid story of *my* life as I remember it. It is I who must embrace the most vulnerability and culpability by sharing my journey in finding my lost self, but I know if I don't, I will never be free of it.

I ultimately left the Mormon Church in 2016 because it hindered my journey of growth, discovery and contemplation. I choose to share my experiences in the church, for better or worse, because they shaped me in numerous ways. I do feel a moral obligation to speak of the confusing and troubling cult-like concepts and rituals, which can feel chauvinistic, oppressive, out-of-touch and even dangerous in today's world. I know others feel differently and have had other experiences than mine, but here, I write my truth with a desire to help those who might be having similar questions, or who are facing what feels like an insurmountable amount of fear, self-doubt, shame or guilt.

For many years, I believed that by having these negative thoughts, let alone committing them to a book to share with the world, I would be struck by lightning or go to Hell. I am now 63 years old and feel free to speak my mind. The church's threats would have come to fruition by now, if they were true—Lord knows I have put them to the test time after time. Today, I am alive and happier than ever. I am grateful to be free to believe in what I choose. My family may disagree with my beliefs, but we can love each other, regardless.

Am I completely sane or healed from all the years of anguish and torment? I'm not sure. I still struggle with certain memories and wounds from my past, but I feel more complete and content than I ever have. I now understand it will take a lifetime of work to process and unravel what I have gone through, make peace with my tumultuous past and live with the wounds of my childhood. I still haven't quite let go of worrying, waiting for the other shoe to drop or putting other people's problems first. Yet through counseling and taking control of what I can, I obsess about it less. Even if I am only able to make microscopic improvements in myself, it's a part of a larger journey. I hope that as I heal and continue the fight for my sanity, my family and future generations will be healthier for it.

Writing this book has made me realize there is hope for

families born into chaos, mental illness and severe dysfunction, especially if that family chooses to hold onto each other no matter what. I now feel an even stronger affinity to my mythological name, Diana. I am a strong huntress, mother, grandmother and lover of nature. Mother Nature herself has become my higher power and feeds my soul. I have told my unvarnished truth from a place of love, not hate, and hope readers receive it the same way.

I have learned to love and appreciate my family tumbleweed, accepting our imperfections and embracing our differences. I still love and feel very connected to everyone in the bush, and through every mile our weed has tumbled, most of us have remained close. We may have lost a couple of clumps —Debi, Mom, Dad, and since writing this book, Carol and Pamela—and some of the branches are a bit thornier than others, but mostly and surprisingly, our tumbleweed remains intact. We all may remain a bunch of loose cannons, some aligned and others swinging wildly in different directions, but we're Cannons nonetheless. In the end, that means something, too.

Acknowledgments

I am grateful beyond measure to so many people who have believed in this book enough to love and support me every step of the way. Thanks to Mom and Dad who unknowingly helped shape this book. I'm grateful they documented so much of their lives and hope they would be proud of my words and decision to tell my story.

This book wouldn't have been possible without the love and support of my husband Kelly. Thank you for sticking by my side through my journey of self-discovery no matter how dark or intense the road.

To my children and step-children, my siblings (Linc, Tom, Anna, Beth and Melissa, Debi, Mark, Pamela and Dan), my Aunt/Mom Carol, aunts, uncles, and cousins and many friends: Thank you for your generous contributions of time and conversations, for reading multiple drafts for the past eight years and for revisiting both happy and painful memories. It's been a labor of love, and I marvel at the fact that I have the most amazing team behind me.

A million thanks to my ghostwriter (who has asked to remain anonymous). She has always seen the vision and brilliantly crafted and shaped this memoir. In the process, she quickly became a very close friend and confidant.

Thanks to the team at Legacy Launch Pad, especially

Kaitlin Anthony, Anna David and my editor Ryan Aliapoulios, for their support and enthusiasm in helping me tell and launch my story. Ryan had the challenging task of weaving together my writings with my parents' journals and helped craft the story beautifully.

A big thanks to my dear friend Pamela Quigley for your time, energy and artistic contributions. And thanks to Platte Clark, a witty writer and seasoned editor who helped structure the earlier drafts.

Finally, thank you from the bottom of my heart to all of my friends for the countless conversations and the time you spent reading chapter after chapter to help create this memoir. I am especially grateful to those who believed in me from the start and gave me the courage to share this intimate look at my colorful and chaotic family so I could finally free myself and speak my truth.

About the Author

Diana Cannon-Ragsdale is an author, retired physical therapist and mental health advocate for survivors of abusive and dysfunctional families. Diana attended Utah State University on a dance scholarship, and later graduated from the University of Utah with a bachelor's degree in Health Sciences. In retirement, she has dedicated herself to travel and creativity. Today, she lives happily in Salt Lake City and is married and a mother of five and grandmother of eight. *Loose Cannons* is her first book.

Made in USA - North Chelmsford, MA
1318519_9781956955224
07.18.2022 1057